Islam

This series offers brief, accessible and lively accounts of key topics within theology and religion. Each volume presents both academic and general readers with a selected history of topics which have had a profound effect on religious and cultural life. The word "history" is, therefore, understood in its broadest cultural and social sense. The volumes are based on serious scholarship but they are written engagingly and in terms readily understood by general readers.

Other topics in the series

Published

Heaven	Alister E. McGrath
Heresy	G. R. Evans
Islam	Tamara Sonn
Death	Douglas J. Davies
Saints	Lawrence S. Cunningham
Christianity	Carter Lindberg
Dante	Peter S. Hawkins
Spirituality	Philip Sheldrake
Cults and New Religions	Douglas E. Cowan and David G. Bromley
Love	Carter Lindberg
Christian Mission	Dana L. Robert
Christian Ethics	Michael Banner
Jesus	W. Barnes Tatum
Shinto	John Breen and Mark Teeuwen
Apocalypse	Martha Himmelfarb
Paul	Robert Paul Seesengood
Islam 2nd Edition	Tamara Sonn

Forthcoming

The Reformation	Kenneth Appold
Monasticism	Dennis D. Martin
Sufism	Nile Green

Islam

A Brief History

Second Edition

Tamara Sonn

A John Wiley & Sons, Ltd., Publication

This second edition first published 2010
© 2010 Tamara Sonn

Edition history: Blackwell Publishing Ltd (1e, 2004)

Blackwell Publishing was acquired by John Wiley & Sons in February 2007. Blackwell's publishing program has been merged with Wiley's global Scientific, Technical, and Medical business to form Wiley-Blackwell.

Registered Office
John Wiley & Sons Ltd, The Atrium, Southern Gate, Chichester, West Sussex, PO19 8SQ, United Kingdom

Editorial Offices
350 Main Street, Malden, MA 02148-5020, USA
9600 Garsington Road, Oxford, OX4 2DQ, UK
The Atrium, Southern Gate, Chichester, West Sussex, PO19 8SQ, UK

For details of our global editorial offices, for customer services, and for information about how to apply for permission to reuse the copyright material in this book please see our website at www.wiley.com/wiley-blackwell.

Wiley also publishes its books in a variety of electronic formats. Some content that appears in print may not be available in electronic books.

Designations used by companies to distinguish their products are often claimed as trademarks. All brand names and product names used in this book are trade names, service marks, trademarks or registered trademarks of their respective owners. The publisher is not associated with any product or vendor mentioned in this book. This publication is designed to provide accurate and authoritative information in regard to the subject matter covered. It is sold on the understanding that the publisher is not engaged in rendering professional services. If professional advice or other expert assistance is required, the services of a competent professional should be sought.

Library of Congress Cataloging-in-Publication Data

Sonn, Tamara
    Islam : a brief history / Tamara Sonn. – 2nd ed.
      p.   cm. – (Blackwell brief histories of religion series)
    1st ed. published in 2004 under the title: A brief history of Islam.
    Includes bibliographical references and index.
    ISBN 978-1-4051-8094-8 (hardcover : alk. paper) – ISBN 978-1-4051-8093-1 (pbk. : alk. paper) 1. Islam–History. 2. Islam–Essence, genius, nature. I. Sonn, Tamara – Brief history of Islam. II. Title.
    BP50.S65 2010
    297.09–dc22

                                                                   2009030170

A catalogue record for this book is available from the British Library.

Set in 10/12.5 pt Meridien by SPi Publisher Services, Pondicherry, India
Printed in Singapore by Ho Printing Singapore Pte Ltd

1   2010

For John

Contents

Illustrations

Foreword

When Americans defeated Saddam Hussein and occupied Baghdad in early 2003 they confronted a society with a distinctly different way of looking at history. For Americans, history moves in a linear progression. The future beckons bright and promising. For Arabs, the history of the past still inspires and informs their present. That is why, when Americans were expecting Iraqis to talk of setting up democratic institutions, media networks, and commercial institutions influenced by the West, one of the first things the Iraqis did was to march to Karbala, the site where the grandson of the Prophet of Islam was martyred in the seventh century. About 2 million Iraqis made the pilgrimage to one of the holiest sites in Islam particularly revered by the Shia, the majority population of Iraq. The television images of this spectacle created further questions in the minds of Americans. It appeared that the Western world and the Islamic world not only looked at history differently but were doomed to stare at each other with incomprehension.

If it was so difficult to understand history, then how was the West to understand Islam itself? After September 11, 2001 the question assumed more than academic relevance. It was no longer the stuff of academic debate but involved policy and practical matters relating to what Americans called a global "war on terror" involving different Muslims living in different societies.

Scholars talked and wrote of an ongoing clash of civilizations between the Western world and the Islamic world. Outright prejudices and plain ignorance were seeping into discussions of Islam.

Few in America understood the religion. After September 11, Sikhs were killed as they were mistaken for Muslims. Yet here was a civilization with 1.3 billion people, and America was involved with Muslims at different levels in different countries. Indeed America's "war on terror" was primarily against members of this very population.

As a result of the intense interest around Islam, countless instant experts emerged to write books and commentaries. Many of these linked Islam to terrorism and violence and failed to provide valid explanations of either Islamic history or society. Most of these attempted to answer the basic question being asked by Americans and echoed by President George W. Bush himself: "Why do they hate us?"

The answers to this question came thick and fast but remained incomplete. Without an understanding of history it is difficult to explain Muslim behavior and impossible to understand Muslim politics.

Professor Tamara Sonn, in *Islam: A Brief History*, combines the skills of the historian with the insights of the scholar of Islam. Her history therefore is not simply about the rise and fall of dynasties but a clear and coherent picture of a dynamic, complex, and global religion.

In particular, she emphasizes the great clashes of ideas that have motivated Islamic history from the earliest times. History, then, is not a random series of unconnected acts; there is a clear pattern of cause and effect as Muslims attempt to live up to a notion of an ideal society inspired by their vision of God.

Professor Sonn sets the theological stage in the opening paragraph of Chapter 1. She places Islam squarely in the Abrahamic or monotheistic tradition. That opening itself indicates her sensitivity to both her subject and her audience: although Muslims will appreciate the reference, they will not be surprised; many Western readers will be, for not many know that Islam is closely related to the Abrahamic tradition.

Indeed the last paragraph of the book, so eloquently written, once again reflects this sensitivity. In the last lines Professor Sonn quotes Sura 2, verse 177. It is in essence the definition of a good human being in the light of Quranic advice. Once again it will reassure Muslims of how well Professor Sonn has understood their religion and will no doubt inform non-Muslims of the true nature of Islam. It will also challenge many of the stereotypes of Islam depicting it as a religion of extremism and violence. In her first chapter Professor Sonn creates the ideal model of Islam. She points out the importance of compassion and tolerance in this model. She does not avoid the more controversial aspects of Islam in the West such as polygamy. The second chapter is called "The Pursuit of Knowledge in the Service of God and Humanity: The Golden Age." This was the great age of Islamic civilization: "During the Middle Ages, Islam's unique system of religious freedom and administrative flexibility allowed for remarkable stability and growth. It also produced a period of peace and prosperity in which the sciences and arts were brought to new levels of perfection. The Islamic world from Spain to India – with its plurality of cultures, ethnicities, and religious communities – produced an unrivaled cultural efflorescence."

Chapter 3 discusses division and reorganization in Muslim society and sets the stage for Chapter 4, on colonialism and reform. There is an important discussion of *ijtihad*, which allows Islamic law openness and flexibility. The chapter ends with a discussion that connects the great Arab historian Ibn Khaldun, living in the fifteenth century, to Muhammad Iqbal, "the advocate of dynamic, adaptable, progressive Islam" who advocated Pakistan as a modern Muslim state, in the twentieth century.

Chapter 5 discusses and is called "Obstacles and Prospects for Islamic Reform." Towards the end there is a highly relevant discussion of the mid-twentieth-century figures Hasan al-Banna and Sayyid Qutb, the fathers of the radical Islamic movements, whose influence on men like Osama bin Laden is widely acknowledged. What emerges is an appreciation of history as an ongoing dialectic between the will of people to order society according to their comprehension of God's commands and the reality of changing times. That is why there can be no understanding of contemporary Islamic political behavior without an expert on hand to help us make sense of the history motivating and informing it.

This is a book Professor Sonn was born to write. She is the right person at the right time to write a brief history of Islam. She is presently the Kenan Professor of Humanities and Professor of

Religion at the College of William and Mary. Professor Sonn's Ph.D. is from the University of Chicago, where she sat at the feet of the late great Islamic scholar Fazlur Rahman. She has written well-received books on Islam but is no ivory tower scholar. Until recently she was the active president of the American Council for the Study of Islamic Societies.

In the charged atmosphere around the understanding of Islam after September 11 there is perhaps no greater service a scholar of Islam can perform than helping to explain Islam in the context of its history. Most commentators have been overwhelmed by the task. That is why Professor Tamara Sonn deserves the gratitude of all those who wish to understand the post-September 11 world in which we find ourselves. In a masterly fashion and with admirable brevity she has presented us with an indispensable guide to understanding Islam in the twenty-first century.

Akbar S. Ahmed
American University, Washington

Preface

A great deal has changed since 2004, when the first edition of *Islam: A Brief History* was published. At that time there was a degree of optimism that the wars in Iraq and Afghanistan would end in a timely manner, allowing people to get on with the process of reconstruction. The progressive Mohamed Khatami was still president of Iran, and although there were signs of frustration with the slow pace of reform there were also indications across the Muslim world that recovery from decades of colonialism and bad governance was, if not imminent, at least possible. Today, the picture is slightly less optimistic. The war in Iraq is ongoing, although the administration that was inaugurated in the United States in January 2009 promises to end it. The war in Afghanistan continues, and has spread to Pakistan. Terrorist attacks have increased, some of them attributed to Muslims. The most recent as of this writing targeted tourists and Jews in Mumbai, killing over 150.

During 2007 I was asked by a private research institute to assess the viewpoints of "moderate" Muslims through a series of focus group "listening sessions" in Eurasia (Turkey, Iran, and Uzbekistan), South Asia (Pakistan, Bangladesh, and India), and Southeast Asia (Thailand, Malaysia, and the Philippines). The inspiration for the project was United States government officials' insistence that the "war on terror" was directed not against Islam but against radical Muslims. As President George W. Bush put it, "Our war is against evil, not against Islam."[1] "Moderate" Muslims had nothing to fear.

But who were these moderate Muslims? There was general consensus that a key characteristic distinguishing radical from moderate Muslims was the radicals' willingness to use violence to achieve their goals. But beyond that there was little specificity regarding the characteristics that identify "moderate" Islam. The goal of the research was to gain an understanding of the key concerns and attitudes of Asian Muslims who might be described as moderate.

The project found enormous diversity in Muslims' views across Eurasia, of course, but there was broad agreement on a number of issues. First, the phrase "moderate Islam" is misleading; it hints that moderate Islam is a subcategory of Islam overall – that Islam in general is somehow immoderate. Muslims interviewed for this project insisted overwhelmingly that mainstream Islam is quintessentially moderate. This has been ordained by the Quran, which addresses Muslims as the "median" or "moderate community" (2:143), exemplified by Prophet Muhammad, and evidenced throughout history. Second, Muslims are at least as concerned as anyone else about growing religious extremism. Yet they believe that the primary causes of extremism are beyond their control. Those causes include the lack of good governance – characterized by transparency, respect for human rights, and inclusiveness – and the failure of governments to provide basic services and economic opportunity.

Ongoing research has revealed as well that while mainstream Muslims reject violence as a means to achieve their goals, they share with radicals negative perceptions of the West – in particular, the United States and the United Kingdom. Those negative perceptions stem from specific foreign policies, including the military operations in Iraq, Afghanistan, and now Pakistan, support for non-democratic governments in Muslim countries, and support for Israel despite its violation of United Nations Security Council resolutions 242 and 338 (calling for withdrawal from occupied Palestinian and Syrian territory). Moderate and radical Muslims also share the impression that the West has little regard for Islam and in many cases is hostile to it, an impression informed by memories of colonialism and intensified by current policies. Indeed, mainstream Muslims believe these policies undermine their own efforts, and strengthen the positions of radicals.

As dark as this description appears, it does provide a ray of hope. Not only does it reflect shared values and concerns across the globe – a basis of collaboration among "moderates" everywhere, but it indicates a direction for that collaborative effort. If radicalism is fueled by specific policies, then change in those policies would seem to be in order.

This edition of *Islam: A Brief History* incorporates recent developments and presents an overview of mainstream Muslim viewpoints on issues of global concern (in Chapter 5). In response to readers' requests, it also includes an expanded description of the Quran (in Chapter 1), of Sufism (in Chapter 2), and of Muslim views on human rights (in Chapter 5).

As always, my gratitude goes to my mentor, Professor Fazlur Rahman (d. 1988), whose brilliance and wisdom continue to inspire me, and to my students, who ensure that I continue to learn. There is no treasure so great as the student who teaches the teacher.

TS
Williamsburg, Virginia
November 2008

Preface to the First Edition

A Brief History of Islam was written as an introduction to the religion of nearly one-fifth of the world's population, the dominant religion in over 50 countries, and the fastest-growing religious minority in Europe and the United States. It was written as a history because nothing helps explain the current state of affairs in any community better than a description of how those affairs developed. And perhaps no community senses a greater need for understanding today than Muslims. A glance at some of the recent titles about Islam is revealing: *Islam Under Siege*; *What Went Wrong?*; *Unholy Terror* (by Akbar Ahmed, Bernard Lewis, and John Esposito, respectively). These are books that have come out only within the past year – after the infamous events of September 11. Although the atrocities committed that day constitute a tragic aberration from Islamic values and have been condemned by Muslims worldwide, they continue to color many people's perceptions of Islam. Even before September 11, Muslims felt terribly misrepresented in Western media. As early as 1989, according to Reeva Simon's *The Middle East in Crime Fiction*, Arabs and Muslims had become the most common villains in movies and crime fiction. By the mid-1990s, discussions of an emerging "clash of civilizations" between Islam and the West were inescapable in American universities, thanks to the work of historian Samuel Huntington.

How did one of the world's major religions, a tradition that inspired some of the greatest cultural achievements in the pre-modern era, come to be associated almost exclusively with terrorism and tyranny?

How did a religious tradition that shares its history, beliefs, and values with Jews and Christians become so isolated? The answer indeed lies in a clash of civilizations, but not the one Huntington writes about. The critical clash between Christendom and the Muslim world took place over the past two to three centuries. On one side were the European powers who believed that taking control of Africa and Asia was their destiny. It was the "white man's burden," part of their "civilizing mission." On the other were the people whose land, resources, and power were usurped. For them, Europe's actions were nothing but crass imperialism, and they profoundly changed the course of Islamic history (along with the history of other parts of the colonized world).

Muslims had built the most advanced civilization in the Western world by the Middle Ages. They had preserved, consolidated, and advanced the learning of the ancients, developing the world's highest levels of mathematics, science, philosophy, arts, and technology. By the time Europe began its colonial incursions, the Muslim world was undergoing change. Reformers were calling attention to the need for reorganization and modernization. But these efforts were interrupted by Europe's economic and political expansion. The combined weight of European imperialism and domestic efforts to repel imperialism was sufficient to derail reform and modernization efforts in the Islamic world. Economic development was forestalled by Europe's desire for natural resources and raw materials, rather than the products of an industrialized economy. Political development was curtailed by Europe's desire to work through local leaders willing to advance Europe's interests. And even religious and social reform efforts were interrupted, as clinging to tradition became a symbol of resistance to the imperialists.

The countries that make up the Muslim world today achieved their independence only within the past century and, as in the rest of the formerly colonized world, only with a great deal of struggle. Typically, polite requests for independence, petitions, and demands were ignored. As efforts to achieve independence intensified, so did the intransigence of the colonial powers. Activists and resistance leaders were viewed as criminals and treated accordingly. Arrests, deportations, and executions generally eliminated civilian leadership, resulting in the militarization of independence movements. This is not to say that all problems in the Muslim world are the fault of the West; many of the problems recognized by early reformers have nothing to do with foreign intervention and many of them remain, compounded by the results of colonialism. However, the pattern just sketched does account for the prevalence of military and non-democratic rule throughout the formerly colonized world. It also accounts for high levels of hostility toward the West.

Fortunately, however, conflict with the West is neither inherent in Islamic sources nor inevitable, as we will see in the following chapters. Tracing the development of Islam from its origins in seventh-century Arabia to the present, we will see that in fact Islam is an integral part of the monotheistic tradition. Like Judaism and Christianity, its adherents worship one God, believed to be the creator and merciful judge of all humanity. Muslims revere Abraham, Moses, and Jesus, along with other figures familiar to readers of Jewish and Christian scripture. Perhaps most importantly, Muslims value human dignity and social justice as highly as any other community on earth. Islam's troubled modern history has resulted in enormous diversity of opinion about how to address the challenges of development and modernization. In some cases, political setbacks have produced desperation, radicalization, and even mutation of Islamic values. Nevertheless, commitment to human dignity and justice remains a value shared among both the victors and victims of the colonial clash. Those values constitute a common ground, a basis for communication concerning shared goals and cooperation to achieve them. Facilitating that communication and cooperation is the goal of this work.

I would like to thank my colleagues – especially John Esposito, John Voll, and Akbar Ahmed, for their insightful critiques of my work, and my students at the College of William and Mary for inspiring me to finish it. As always, my deepest appreciation goes to John and Jordan.

TS
Williamsburg, 2003

Map 1 Expansion of the Muslim world 632–750
© Richard C. Martin. Reprinted with permission of the author.

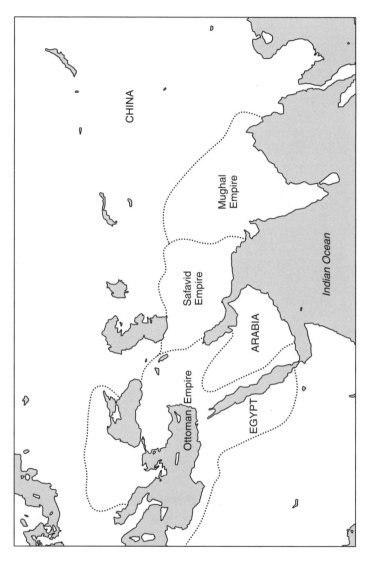

Map 2 The Muslim world in the sixteenth century

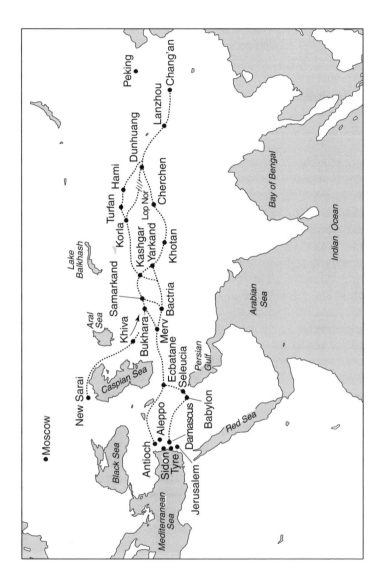

Map 3 The Silk Road

Chapter 1

Many Paths to One God
Establishing the Ideals

When Jews speak of their religion, they call it Judaism or the Judaic tradition. When Christians speak of their religious traditions, they often refer to Judeo-Christianity, since Christianity was an organic outgrowth of Judaism. In the same way, Muslims refer to their religion as part of the Abrahamic or monotheistic tradition, since Islam shares the history, basic beliefs, and values of Judaism and Christianity. Muslims consider Jews and Christians to be their spiritual siblings. They are among the *ahl al-kitab*, the "People of the Book" or "People of Scripture." This is the family of monotheists, those who believe in one supreme God, the creator, the sustainer, the benevolent and merciful judge of all humanity. "The Book" is revelation contained in scripture; Muslims believe all revelation came from the only God, who revealed His will to humanity repeatedly, in various times and places to different groups.

The Quran

The Quran ("Koran" is the archaic spelling) is Islamic scripture, the book containing Islamic revelation. It is in Arabic, the language of the prophet through whom it was revealed, Muhammad (d. 632 CE). The term *qur'an* means "recitation," reflecting the belief that the Quran is the word of God (Allah, from the Arabic *al-ilah*: the [one] god), not the word of the prophet who delivered it. Although the Quran was revealed (or "sent down" – *munzal*, in Arabic) in the seventh century CE, Muslims believe that it is actually timeless. As the word of God, it is co-eternal with God. Like God, it has always existed. It therefore was not created, but was revealed word for word in the Arabic language at a particular time, through God's final messenger, Muhammad. The Quran says that its specific words reflect a divine archetype of revelation, which it calls "the preserved tablet" (*al-lawh al-mahfuz*, 85:22). Although anthropomorphic language (using human traits to describe God) is recognized as only symbolic in Islam, still it is not uncommon to hear the Quran described as reflecting the eternal "will" or "mind" of God. However it is described, the Quran is considered eternal.

The term *qur'an* is sometimes interpreted as "reading," even though Prophet Muhammad is described by the Quran as unlettered or illiterate (7:157, 62:2). Rather than "reading" a message, Prophet Muhammad is described as delivering (or "reciting") a message that God had imprinted upon his heart (26:195, e.g.). At one point the Quran refers to Gabriel (Jibril) as the one "who has brought it [revelation] down upon your heart" (2:97). As a result, traditional interpreters claim that the angel Gabriel was the medium through whom Muhammad received God's revelation.

The Quran uses the term *qur'an* seventy times, sometimes generically referring to "recitation" but usually referring to revelation. The Quran commonly refers to itself as simply "the Book" (*al-kitab*), a term used hundreds of times to refer to scripture, including the Torah and the Gospels. Muslims therefore frequently refer to the Quran as The Book. They usually use adjectives like "holy," "noble," or "glorious" to show their respect for the Quran. They commemorate annually the beginning of its revelation on the Night of Power (or Destiny, *laylat al-qadr*), during the last ten days of Ramadan, the month during which observant Muslims fast from sunrise until sunset.

The Quran consists of 114 chapters, called suras (in Arabic, *surah*; plural: *suwar*). The verses of the chapters are called *ayat* (singular: *ayah*). The chapters range in length from 7 to 287 verses. The first sura is very short, but the remaining suras are arranged from longest to shortest (i.e., in descending order of length), rather than in chronological order.

Chapters of the Quran may be referred to by number, but each also has a name, such as "The Opening" (Sura 1), "Women" (Sura 4), and "Repentance" (Sura 9). These names were ascribed after the Quran was canonized (established in its authoritative form) and typically derive from major references in the chapters. All but one sura (Sura 9) begins with the phrase "In the name of God the Merciful and Compassionate." Twenty-nine suras are also preceded by a letter or brief series of Arabic letters, whose meaning is unclear. Some scholars believe they refer to elements within the sura itself, some believe they refer to early organizational components of the suras or served as mnemonic devices, and some believe these letters have mystical or spiritual meanings. Whatever their significance, these letters are considered to be part of the revelation itself.

People reading the Quran for the first time will notice that it often speaks in the first person ("I" or "We," used interchangeably), and may assume that this usage indicates the voice of Muhammad. But Muslims believe the Quran is revealed in the voice of God. For example, in the verse about the first night of revelation (*laylat al-qadr*), the Quran says, "Surely We sent it [revelation] down on the Night of Power" (97:2). In this voice, the Quran frequently addresses Muhammad, instructing him to "say" or "tell" people certain things, sometimes in response to specific issues. For example, when people doubted Muhammad's role as prophet, the Quran instructs him: "Say, 'O People, indeed I am a clear warner to you. Those who believe and do good works, for them is forgiveness and generous blessing'" (55:49–50). The Quran also offers advice to Muhammad. When people accused him of being a mere poet or even a fortune-teller, the Quran says, "Do they say that you have forged [the Quran]? Say, 'If I have forged it, my crimes are my own; but I am innocent of what you do'" (11:36). The Quran also offers encouragement to Muhammad when his efforts seem futile: "Have we not opened your heart and relieved you of the burden that was breaking your back?" (94:1–2). At other times, the Quran speaks directly to the people about Muhammad. Concerning the issue of the authenticity of his message, the Quran addresses the community, saying, "The heart [of the Prophet] was not deceived. Will you then dispute with him about what he saw?" (53:12–13). Many of the Quran's verses seem to be in the voice of Muhammad, addressing the community with the word of God and referring to God in the third person. For instance, we are told, "There is no compulsion in religion. Right has been distinguished from wrong. Whoever rejects idols and believes in God has surely grasped the strongest, unbreakable bond. And God hears and knows" (2:257). But such verses are generally embedded in longer passages that begin with the divine command to "tell them" the information thus revealed.

To whom was the Quran addressed? Although its message is meant for all times and places, the Quran's immediate audience was the community of seventh-century Arabia, where Prophet Muhammad lived. That is why the Quran explains that it is purposely revealed in the Arabic language. Interestingly, and uniquely among monotheistic scriptures, the Quran assumes both males and females among its audience, and frequently addresses the concerns of both. For example, it tells us that God is prepared to forgive and richly reward all good people, both male and female:

Men who submit [to God] and women who submit [to God],
Men who believe and women who believe,
Men who obey and women who obey,
Men who are honest and women who are honest,
Men who are steadfast and women who are steadfast,
Men who are humble and women who are humble,
Men who give charity and women who give charity,
Men who fast and women who fast,
Men who are modest and women who are modest,
Men and women who remember God often.

(33:36)

Still, the overall audience for the scripture is humanity as a whole. The Quran refers to itself as "guidance for humanity" (*hudan li'l-nas*).

The Quran was revealed through Prophet Muhammad to the community in seventh-century Arabia over a period of twenty-two to twenty-three years, but it was recorded and canonized soon after Muhammad's death. During his lifetime, Muhammad's followers sometimes recorded his pronouncements; some even memorized and transmitted them orally. After his death, and upon the deaths of some of those who memorized the Quran (*huffaz*), the Prophet's companions decided to establish a written version of the Quran so that it could be preserved and transmitted accurately to future generations. This process was begun by a close companion of Muhammad, Zayd ibn Thabit (d. 655 CE), who collected written records of Quranic verses soon after the death of the Prophet. The third successor to the Prophet (caliph), Uthman ibn Affan (d. 656 CE), is credited with commissioning Zayd and other respected scholars to establish the authoritative written version of the Quran based upon the written and oral records. This was accomplished within twenty years of Muhammad's death. That text became the model from which copies were made and promulgated among various Muslim communities, and other versions are believed to have been destroyed. Because of the existence of various dialects and the lack of vowel markers in early Arabic, slight variations in the reading of the authoritative text were possible. In order to avoid confusion, markers indicating specific vowel sounds were introduced into the language by the end of ninth century, but seven slightly variant readings (*qira'at*), or methods of recitation, are acceptable.

Copies of the Quran were produced by hand until the modern era. The first printed version was produced in Rome in 1530; a second printed version was produced in Hamburg in 1694. The first critical edition produced in Europe was done by Gustav Flügel in 1834. The numbering of the verses varies slightly between the standard 1925 Egyptian edition favored by many Muslim scholars and the 1834 edition established by Flügel, used by many Western scholars. (Editions from Pakistan and India often follow the Egyptian standard edition, with the exception that they count the opening phrase, "In the name of God, the Merciful, the Compassionate," of each sura as the first verse.) The variations in verse numbering comprise only a few verses and reflect differing interpretations of where certain verses end.

The Quran is considered to be authentic only in Arabic. Even non-Arabic speakers – the vast majority of Muslims – pray in Arabic. Although Arabs comprise less than one-third of the world's Muslim population, the Arabic language still serves as a symbol of unity throughout the Muslim world. Nevertheless, numerous translations of the Quran have been produced. The first Latin translation was done in the twelfth century, commissioned by Peter the Venerable, abbot of the monastery of Cluny in France. It was published in Switzerland in the sixteenth century. Translations (or, more accurately, "interpretations" of the Quran) are now readily available in virtually all written languages and on the internet. Still, Quranic calligraphy remains not only the highest form of visual art, but a spiritual exercise. Beautifully hand-wrought copies of Quranic verses adorn many Muslim homes – in ink on paper, stitched into fabric, or carved into wood, metal or stone. It is also very common for Muslims to wear verses of the Quran in lockets or on necklaces. And each year during the pilgrimage season a special cloth embroidered in gold with Quranic verses is created to drape the Kaaba (the sanctuary in Mecca which is the object of the annual Islamic pilgrimage, the *hajj*).

Many pious Muslims maintain belief in the miraculous power of the words of the Quran itself. Carrying a small replica of Quranic verses is popularly believed to offer protection against illness or accident. Yet by far the most popular way to experience the Quran is by listening to it. The art of Quranic recitation (*tajwid*) is highly developed and extremely demanding. A student must memorize the Quran, in any of the seven pronunciation and intonation patterns (*qira'at*) mentioned above, understand its meaning (even if one is not an Arabic speaker), and observe a number of rules dealing with spiritual attitudes (such as humility), purity, and posture (such as facing the direction of Mecca, if possible). So important is the experience of hearing the Quran properly and reverently recited that learning Quran recitation is traditionally considered a communal obligation (meaning that not everyone in a given community is required to learn Quran recitation, but enough people must do so to ensure that there are sufficient Quran reciters to serve the community).

Gifted Quran reciters are highly respected throughout the Muslim world. In recent years, a number of women have joined the ranks of popular Quran reciters. But even Muslims who are not able to recite the Quran demonstrate their respect for the Book by making sure they are in a state of spiritual purity when they handle it. As in Orthodox Judaism, blood and other bodily fluids are believed to be agents of impurity in Islam. Therefore, the passing of any bodily fluids requires that Muslims wash before touching a copy of the Quran. Thus, for example, women who are menstruating are traditionally not allowed to touch a copy of the Quran. Most importantly, the Quran is the focal point of all Islamic belief and practice. It is the miracle of Islam. Unlike Jesus, who according to the Quran performed many miracles, Prophet Muhammad brought no other miracle besides the Quran. And although Muslims are utterly devoted to Prophet Muhammad, frequently express their love for him, and consider him eminently worthy of emulation, Muhammad does not occupy the position in Islam that Jesus occupies in Christianity. The Quran does. The Quran tells us that when people asked Muhammad to demonstrate the authenticity of his prophecy by performing miracles as other prophets had done, he simply and reverently referred to the Quran. The exquisite beauty of its language and wisdom of its sublime message are considered beyond compare and impossible to imitate. This belief is conveyed in the doctrine of the "inimitability" of the Quran (i'jaz). Thus, while Christians consider Jesus' life as miraculous and the basis of their religion, Muslims consider the Quran to be the cornerstone of Islam. Muslims are required to pray five times daily: at sunrise, midday, afternoon, sunset, evening. At each of these times, verses of the Quran are recited in a specified order and number of repetitions (ranging from twice at morning prayer to four times at evening prayer). Extra prayers may be added individually but, again, they are based on the Quran. The weekly congregational prayer (at midday on Fridays) follows the same pattern, although it includes a sermon (khutbah), often based upon a Quranic theme. As well, devout Muslims read the entire Quran during the holy month of fasting, Ramadan. The book is divided into thirty sections for this purpose.

The Quran and Other Scriptures

The Quran contains numerous references to earlier monotheistic scriptures, which it identifies as the Torah, the Psalms, and the Gospels. Muslims believe that the Quran reiterates, confirms, and completes these earlier scriptures, calling upon all people to remember and respect the truths carried in them. Indeed, it assumes people are familiar with those texts. It therefore does not recount their historic narratives. Instead, it uses characters and events familiar to Jews and Christians in order to make specific moral or theological points. As a result, while references to Adam, Noah, Abraham, Isaac, Ishmael, Jacob, Moses, and Jesus, for example, appear frequently, they are not arranged in chronological order.

The Quran refers to its religion as *al-din*, the monotheistic tradition that began with the covenant between God and humanity marked by the obedience of Abraham. (Interestingly, the term *din*, often translated as "religion," actually means "judgment"; the Quran calls the Last Day, for example, the *yom al-din*, "day of judgment." The term is related to "obligation," "debt," and "law," as it is in Hebrew.) Adam is actually considered the first prophet, because through the story of Adam and his wife in the garden – the same story revealed to Jews and Christians – humanity began to learn that God created us with a purpose. Fulfilling that purpose requires obedience to the divine will, and disobedience will bring suffering and punishment. But Abraham is the first major prophet, given the profound impact of his message.

The story of Abraham is familiar to all monotheists. He was an aged Iraqi shepherd who had longed for a child for years. God chose to favor Abraham with a child, but then asked him to demonstrate his obedience by killing his beloved son. At the last minute, God spared the child, but Abraham's willingness to sacrifice his son rather than disobey the command of God sealed the agreement between God and humanity. God promises eternal reward to all who submit to the will of God; "one who submits" to the will of God is a *muslim*. Likewise, God promised punishment for willful disobedience. One of the disagreements between Muslims and Jews concerns the identity of the son Abraham was willing to sacrifice. Although the Quran does not state it explicitly, Muslims believe that Abraham intended to sacrifice his son Ishmael (Ismail), rather than Isaac (Ishaq), and that Muslims are thus spiritual descendants of Abraham through Ishmael and his mother Hagar (Hajar).

As well, according to Islamic teaching, Abraham's act was personal; its reward was not bequeathed to successive generations. The patriarch serves as a model for others to follow, but each individual must earn his or her own reward from God by likewise submitting to the divine will:

> Those to whom We gave the Book
> and who follow it accurately,
> they believe in it; and whoever disbelieves in it,
>   they are the losers.
> Children of Israel, remember My blessing
> with which I blessed you, and that I
> have preferred you above all others;
> and fear a day when no soul shall substitute
> for another, and no ransom
> will be accepted from it, nor any
> intercession will help it,
>   and they will not be assisted.
> And when his Lord tested Abraham
> with certain words, and he fulfilled them.
> He said, "I make you a leader
> for the people." He said, "And what of my progeny?"
> He said, "My covenant does not extend to oppressors."
>   (2:221–4)

In other words, it is not the group one belongs to that determines salvation; the Quran says that it is demonstrating submission (*islam*) to the will of God through good works that brings reward. Nevertheless, Muslims agree that Abraham's willingness to sacrifice his son was of utmost importance; in thus demonstrating his commitment to the will of God he established the foundational covenant between God and those who believe in Him. Jews and Muslims are both descendants of Abraham and heirs to that covenant.

Through another great messenger of God, Moses (Musa), the Torah was revealed. Mentioning the Torah eighteen times, the Quran reminds believers that its guidance continues to be valid. The Quran actually describes itself as "confirming the truth of the Torah that is before me" (3:50) and calls upon believers to "bring the Torah now, and recite it" (3:93). Believers are expected to be honest, charitable, care for the needy, fast, obey dietary regulations, and overall to honor God and respect His creation, just as the Torah instructed.

The last great messenger before Muhammad was Jesus ('Issa). Mentioned twenty-five times in the Quran, Jesus is called the Messiah (although the meaning of that term is not made clear), the son of a virgin, and one who brought great signs from God. His message, the Gospel, is confirmed and described as consistent with the messages of all prophets. Speaking through Muhammad, the Quran says that God is sending the same religion (*din*) that He sent through Noah, Abraham, Moses, and Jesus, saying: "Establish [true] religion [*din*] and do not be divided about it" (42:13). But the Quran does assert that those who believe that Jesus is divine, the son of God, and part of a divine trinity, are mistaken:

> O People of Scripture, do not exaggerate your religion or say anything about God but the truth. The Messiah, Jesus son of Mary, was only a messenger of God, and His word which He sent to Mary, and a spirit from Him. So believe in God and His messenger and do not say "Three" ... God is only one. (4:171)

Still, like the messages of the other prophets, Jesus' message is true, according to the Quran, and the Jews were mistaken to reject it.

Muhammad is presented as the last in the succession of prophets sent by God to reveal the divine will: "And when Moses said to his people, 'O my people, why do you hurt me, though you know I am the messenger of God to you?' ... And when Jesus, son of Mary, said, 'Children of Israel, I am indeed the messenger of God to you, confirming the Torah that is before me, and giving good tidings of a messenger who shall come after me, whose name shall be Ahmad'; then when he brought them clear signs, they said, 'This is sheer sorcery'" (61:6–7). ("Amhad" is a variation on the name Muhammad, and refers to Prophet Muhammad in this passage. Muslims believe that the prediction of the coming of Muhammad was deleted from Christian scriptures.)

Thus, although this monotheistic religion had been accurately revealed before the time of Muhammad, the Quran says that the communities that received those scriptures had become confused about it (42:13). Whether through ignorance or by deliberately distorting the message, many Jews and Christians had fallen into disagreement, each claiming to have the truth. Indeed, the Quran chastises both Jews and Christians for their mutual rejection. "The Jews say the Christians have nothing to stand on, and the Christians say the Jews have nothing to stand on, while they both recite the same Scripture" (Quran 2:113). It is God who will decide on all people's fate, on the Day of Judgment, when all deeds will be weighed in the scale of justice. Those who have demonstrated their true belief through good deeds "have nothing to fear, nor shall they grieve" (2:112).

The Quran advises that if Jews and Christians understood their scriptures properly, there would be no dispute and, what is more, they would recognize that the Quran truly confirms what had been revealed before. "This is a blessed Scripture We have revealed, confirming that which was before it ..." (6:93). "This Quran narrates to the children of Israel most of what they disagree about. It is a guide and a merciful gift for believers" (27:77–8).

Again, the continuity of the monotheistic tradition is asserted. The Quran also refers to prophets unknown to Jews and Christians. For example, there is a sura named for an Arab messenger, Hud (Sura 11), who warned his community to follow God, but they rejected him. The same community then rejected another messenger, Salih, and they were punished with tragedy. Similarly, the Quran relates the story of the Midianites, who were done away with when they rejected their messenger Shuaib. The point of these stories, like that of the people of Lot, is that people reject the message of God at their own peril. The Quran mentions over twenty prophets or messengers between Adam and Muhammad, and notes that "there is no distinction among prophets" (2:136; 3:84), referring to consistent truth of all their messages.

In fact, the Quran states that every nation has been sent a messenger from God. ("Every nation has its Messenger" [10:47]; see also 16:36: "We sent forth among every nation a Messenger," and cf. 16:63 and 35:24.) The Quran does note that some prophets excel others (2:253), generally assumed to refer to those who left laws or texts, or whose historical impact was greater than that of others. But the message is always essentially the same: God rewards those who do His will and punishes those who do not. The Quran informs its audience that Muhammad's revelation is an integral part of the same tradition:

> He has laid down for you as religion
> what He charged Noah with, and what
> We have revealed to you, and what We
> charged Abraham with, Moses and Jesus:
> "Practice the religion, and do not separate
> over it."
>
> (42:14)

The Quran calls upon believers to recognize the religion of Abraham, clearly positioning itself as revelation in the same tradition:

> And they say, "Be Jews or Christians and
> you shall be guided." Say: "No, rather
> the creed of Abraham, a true believer;
> he was no idolater."
> Say: "We believe in God, and
> in what has been revealed to us
> and revealed to Abraham, Ishmael,
> Isaac and Jacob, and the Tribes,
> and what was given to Moses and Jesus
> and the Prophets from their Lord; we
> make no division between any of them, and
> to Him we surrender."
>
> (2:136–7; cf. 26:193–8)

The Quran then confirms that it is the final clarification of the message. Those who accept the message brought by Muhammad are called "the best community brought forth to people, enjoining good and forbidding evil, and believing in God" (3:111). The "People of the Book" – those who have received the earlier scriptures – will suffer for rejecting true prophets. "Some of them are believers," the Quran claims, "but most of them are sinful" (3:112–13). The Quran is the perfect expression of the divine will; no other is necessary. As the Quran puts it in a verse delivered toward the end of Muhammad's career: "Today I have perfected your religion for you, and I have completed my blessing upon you and approved submission [*al-islam*] as your religion. Whoever is forced by hunger to sin ... God is forgiving, merciful" (5:4). Therefore, the succession of prophets ends with Muhammad. The Quran calls him the "seal of the prophets" (33:41). Thus, the Quran reiterates, confirms, and completes Jewish and Christian scriptures. It does not try to establish a new religion, but rather to inspire people to new commitment to the one true religion of monotheism. The term *islam* is used only eight times in the Quran, and is referred to as the true religion. But in the Quran the term means the act of submitting to the divine will, rather than an organized religious group separate from other monotheistic traditions. By contrast, the term *din*, meaning the true religion revealed by the one God at various times throughout human history, is used over ninety times. Muslims believe that although the Quran corrects some misinterpretations of previous scriptures, overall it focuses on inspiring Jews, Christians, and Muslims to work together toward their shared goal of justice and, in so doing, to achieve eternal reward: "People of the Book, come together in agreement on a word, that we worship only God" (3:65).

Themes of the Quran

Because the Quran teaches that God has sent revelation to all communities, and that revelation includes specific rituals and laws, Muslims do not find it surprising that communities differ in their perceptions and practices. The Quran also says that if God had wanted all people to be the same, He would have made them that way. "For each of you We have established a law and a way. And if God had willed it, He would have made you one people. But [you were made as you are] to test you by what He has given you ...." The differences among religions are therefore believed to be part of the divine plan. The Quran invites all people to participate with Muslims in the struggle to do the will of God. In its words, "So compete with one another in good deeds" (5:48).

Solidarity among individuals and communities in doing the will of God is therefore among the themes of the Quran. And the Quran does provide specific regulations for its own community, the Muslims, including purity, prayer, charity, fasting and dietary regulations, and pilgrimage. But the majority of Quranic verses deal with overarching themes and moral guidance, rather than specific regulations. As noted above, the Quran refers to itself, as well as to the Torah and the Gospels, as "guidance for humanity" (3:4, e.g.). That guidance is expressed through a number of inter-related themes.

The fundamental theme of the Quran is monotheism: *tawhid*. Derived from the Arabic term for "one," *tawhid* does not appear as such in the Quran (although other forms of the term do), but it conveys the rich complexity of the Quran's insistence on the oneness of God. It entails first of all that there is only one God, the god (*al-ilah*), Allah. None of the deities worshiped by the Meccans is actually divine, the Quran asserts. They can be of little help to human beings. God has no partners. Placing others in his stead or "associating" (*shirk*) partners with God is bound to lead to failure in the human quest for happiness. Further, God is uni-tary: without parts. The Quran insists, as noted above, that God is not part of a Trinity, as the Christians believe (see 4:172, 5:74). The notion of *tawhid* goes beyond simple monotheism, however, particularly in the view of modern Islamic thinkers. Just as there is only one God, there is only one creator of all human beings, one provider, protector, guide, and judge of all human beings. All human beings are equal in their utter dependence upon God, and their wellbeing depends upon their acknowledging that fact and living accordingly. This acknowledgment is both the will and the law of God. Modern Islamic commentators such as the Egyptian Muhammad Abduh (d. 1905), Muslim Brotherhood ideologue Sayyid Qutb (d. 1966), and revolutionary Iranian leader Ayatollah Khomeini (d. 1989) stress, therefore, that *tawhid* implies that we must order society in accordance with the will of God. A *tawhid*-based society is one in which people devote themselves to serving God by contributing to a society that reflects and safeguards the dignity and equality in which all were created. Submission (*islam*) to that will is the route to our happiness, both in this life and the hereafter.

The Quran presents detailed discussions of the major character-istics of a *tawhid*-based society, and chief among them is mercy, another major theme. Although the Quran frequently warns of punishment for those who violate the will of God and describes vividly the scourges of hell, its overriding emphasis is on divine mercy. "The Merciful" (*al-rahman*) is one of the most frequently invoked names of God, equivalent to Allah. As noted above, all but one sura of the Quran begins by invoking the name of God "the merciful and compassionate." Divine mercy is often paired with divine forgiveness. "God is forgiving and merciful" is a common refrain. At times, especially in the early suras, the Quran sternly warns people that they ignore its message at their own risk: "Woe to the slanderer and backbiter, who collects wealth and counts it continually. He thinks his wealth will bring him eternal life, but no, he will certainly be thrown into hell" (104:2–5). "Have you seen the one who makes a mockery of faith? He is the one who neglects the orphan, and does not encourage feeding the poor. Woe to those who pray but do so only to impress others. They like to be seen [praying] but [then] do not give charity" (107:2–8).

The Quran balances these warnings with sympathy for the weaknesses of human nature: "Indeed, the human being is born impatient. When evil touches him he is anxiety-ridden, and when good things happen to him, grudging" (70:20–2). In this context it offers advice and encouragement: "As for the human being, when God tests him and honors him and blesses him, he says, 'My Lord has favored me.' But when God tests him and restricts his livelihood, he says, 'My Lord has forsaken me.' No; you do not honor orphans or work for the wellbeing of the poor, you take over [others'] inheritance and are overly attached to wealth" (89:16–21).

> [W]hen you are aboard ships and they sail with a fair breeze and [those on board] are happy about it, then a violent wind overtakes them and the waves come from every side and they think they are drowning, then call upon God, practicing religion properly [and saying that] if you spare us from this we will be indeed grateful. But when He has rescued them, indeed they begin oppression on earth. O People, your oppression will only hurt yourselves! (10:22–3)

Given this understanding of human nature, the Quran repeatedly reassures people that God is merciful and compassionate. "My mercy encompasses everything" (7:157). "On the day when every soul is confronted with what it has done, good and evil, they will desire a great distance from [evil]. God asks you to beware; God is full of pity for servants. Say: If you love God, follow me; God will love you and forgive you your sins. God is forgiving, merciful" (3:29–31). Thus Quran thus sets an example for people to emulate in their efforts to establish a just society. Variations on the term "be compassionate" or "show mercy" (*rahima*) occur hundreds of times in the Quran. People are told to be kind and cherish their parents (19:14; 19:32), and even to ask forgiveness from God for them if they make mistakes (60:4). Even though the people of Mecca initially rejected Prophet Muhammad and his followers, and persecuted and evicted them from their homes, the believers are told that they should show kindness and justice toward those Meccans who did not participate in the aggression. But the Quran places particular emphasis on compassion for the most vulnerable members of society. It mentions orphans often, calling for their care and protection. Their wellbeing is routinely mentioned as the measure of the piety of both individuals and society. For example, the Quran instructs Muhammad to tell people when they ask about orphans: "Promotion of their welfare is great goodness" (2:21).

> True piety is this:
> to believe in God and the Last Day,
> the angels, the Book, and the prophets,
> to give of one's substance, however cherished,
>   to relatives and orphans,
> the needy, the traveler, beggars,
>   and to ransom the slave,
> to perform the prayer, to pay alms.
> And they who fulfill their promises,
>   and endure with fortitude
>   misfortune, hardship and peril,
> these are the ones who are true in their faith
> these are the truly God-fearing.
>   (2:177)

Interestingly, the Quran's permission for polygyny (multiple wives) is made in the context of concern for orphans. In a sura entitled "Women" (Sura 4), people are told to protect the rights of orphans for whom they are responsible – if necessary, by marrying them. In seventh-century Arabia, a society plagued by warfare and poverty, there were many orphans. Female orphans were particularly at risk, since this was not a society in which women had economic independence. Unless they inherited wealth women were entirely dependent upon men. Because of the brutality of that society toward women, female infanticide was common. People killed their baby girls, fearing they would not be able to provide for them and that they would be subjected to the whims of those who had no respect for women. Out of concern for the protection of women, the Quran forbids female infanticide. It also rebukes men who are ashamed when a daughter, rather than a son, is born. On a very practical level, it requires that females be given inheritance shares (4:4–12) and that the traditional dowry required at weddings be given as a gift to the bride (4:4), rather than to the bride's parents as a "bride price." The Quran also insists that men and women both are entitled to whatever wages they earn. With regard to the orphans in Medinan society, the Quran tells men to treat them fairly, and if they are afraid that orphans are not being treated fairly, that they may protect them by marrying up to four, but only if they can treat them all impartially. If they do not feel they can avoid slighting one of their wives, then they should only marry one (4:3). Although the focus of this verse is compassion for the weak and equity for women, traditional interpreters conclude that it simply allows men to marry four wives at a time. Modern interpreters tend to return to the focus of justice, and incorporate the Quran's high ideals for mutually satis-factory spousal relationships when discussing marriage. The Quran says that spouses were created by God to find comfort in one another and to be bound by "love and kindness" (30:21). As a result, many modern interpreters believe the Quran advocates monogamy except under extraordinary circumstances (for exam-ple, those in seventh-century Arabia). They believe that the Quran's emphasis on human equality implies that they should work to establish societies in which polygyny is not necessary to protect women.

Similarly, the Quran also acknowledges the institution of slav-ery but says that moral superiority lies in freeing slaves, as well as in feeding the hungry and orphans (90:5–17). Freeing slaves and feeding the hungry are enjoined as ways of making up for sins (5:90).

Another group for whom the Quran shows special concern is debtors. Charity is to be used to help debtors, and people are supposed to pardon debts owed to them as an act of charity. The Quran is particularly concerned with abolishing usury, which was common in seventh-century Arabia. Pre-Islamic records indicate that interest rates were exorbitant. The Quran therefore forbids usury, stating that usurers "will not rise again" (2:275).

So important is concern for the poor that the Quran warns those who pray but then "are neglectful of their prayer," and those who pray but then "mistreat orphans and scarcely work toward feeding the poor." These people, says the Quran, make a mockery of their faith (107:1–7). Praying and performing other rituals, according to the Quran, are obligatory not because they please God in themselves; they are meant to keep people focused on their reason for existing in the first place, and motivated to work toward the fulfillment of God's will in all spheres of life. The Quran says, for example, that the meat that people sacrifice does not reach God; it is for the benefit of believers that rituals are performed: "Their flesh does not reach God nor their blood, but your righteousness reaches God" (22:8). Similarly, sin does not hurt God; it hurts the sinners and their communities: "Muhammad is only a messenger, like those who have passed away before him. When he dies or is killed, will you reject [his message]? Those who do so do not hurt God; God will reward the grateful" (3:144). What is important is not the ritual of prayer or sacrifice itself, but the virtuous life and good deeds it encourages:

> A kind word with forgiveness is better than almsgiving followed by injury. God is absolute and forgiving. O believers, do not make your charity worthless through insult and injury, like the person who gives of his wealth only for show but does not believe in God and the Last Day. (2:263–4)

In the same context, charity is also extremely important in the Quranic perspective. "Surely God recompenses the charitable," we are told when the story of Joseph is being recounted (12:88). Charity is often described as a means of making up for offenses. The Quran maintains the biblical ethic of retaliation, a standard means of maintaining order in societies lacking legal enforcement institutions. But it says that forgoing retaliation as an act of charity will help make up for sins (5:45). Charity is also prescribed as a means of self-purification (9:103). All Muslims are required to give charity according to Islamic law. The term used for this kind of charity (*zakah* or *zakat*) actually means "purification." The idea is that wealth is a good thing, as long as it is used for good purposes like helping the needy and "those whose hearts are to be reconciled," and freeing slaves and debtors (9:60).

Overall, the society envisioned by the Quran is characterized by justice: "O Believers, be steadfast [for] God, giving testimony in justice, and do not let a people's hatred cause you to act without justice. Be just, that is nearer to righteousness" (5:9). "Believers, establish justice, being witnesses for God, even if it [works] against yourselves or against your parents or relatives; regardless of whether [those involved are] rich or poor, God has priority for you" (4:135). Thus the profile of a *muslim* (or *muslima*, the feminine form), "one who submits to the will of God," is integrally linked to the theme of justice. Indeed, the Quran says repeatedly that God has not only called for justice (7:29, e.g.) but that "God loves the just" (5:42, 49:9, 60:8).

A society characterized by justice, wherein the wellbeing of the entire group is measured in terms of the wellbeing of its most vulnerable members, is the external manifestation of *islam*. The internal manifestation may be found in a set of virtues that form the Islamic conscience. Muslims are expected to be guided by the will of God in every encounter, every decision, every action. They are called to live their lives guided by *taqwa*, a term whose common English translation as "fear of God" or "righteousness" does not do it justice. It is a more comprehensive term, indicating the characteristics of a well-formed conscience, an internalized morality, or simply "God-consciousness." The Quran gives guidance on some specific matters, often describing a particular choice as "closer to *taqwa*" or "approximating *taqwa*." For example, in response to questions about divorce before consummation of a marriage, men are told that they should provide support for the divorced bride fairly, in accordance with their means, even if it is not required by the marriage agreement. That is called "closer to *taqwa*" (2:237). Likewise, believers are told that they must never let hatred for a people lead to unjust behavior. "Act justly, that is nearer to *taqwa*" (5:8). In general, people are told to help one another in the effort to achieve *taqwa* (5:2) and to "conspire for virtue and *taqwa*" (58:9; see Chapter 2, "Spirituality," for further discussion of *taqwa*). Thus, along with *iman* (belief in God) and *islam* (submission to the will of God), *taqwa* is one of Islam's quintessential virtues. Belief in God is considered essential for human beings to be able to overcome their innate insecurities and selfishness. It is also considered natural, an inborn instinct to recognize the existence and supremacy of God. Submission to the will of God is believed to be the proper response to recognition of God, indeed the only possible response. True recognition of God inevitably results in *taqwa*, a conscience guided by God and the best interests of humanity.

Similarly, Muslims are called upon to be a "median" or "moderate community" (*ummat al-wasit*), a balance between extremes, "so that you may be witnesses to the people" (2:143). In yet another refrain of the Quran, believers are told that they are the best of communities in that they "enjoin honorable actions and forbid the objectionable" (*amr bi'l-ma'ruf wa nahiy 'an al-munkar*, 3:110; see also 3:104, 3:114, 7:157, 9:67, 9:71, 9:112, 22:41, 31:17).

Through these themes and some specific legislation, the Quran guides humanity. But it does not regulate all human activity. In many cases, it takes the realities of its historic context into consideration, establishes goals, and challenges humanity to achieve them. For example, as indicated above, the Quran provides a significant amount of legislation concerning the treatment of slaves. It allows the common practice of concubinage, but demands that slave women not be forced into sexual relations (24:33). The Quran acknowledges that slaves do not have the same legal standing as free people; instead, they are treated as minors for whom the owners are responsible. But it recommends that unmarried Muslims marry their slaves (24:32), indicating that it considers slaves and free people morally equal. It also instructs Muslims to allow their slaves to buy their freedom, and even to help them pay for it if possible (24:33). The Quran clearly recognizes that slavery is a source of inequity in society, since it frequently recommends freeing slaves, along with feeding and clothing the poor, as part of living a moral life (90:12–18) and a way to make up for offenses (5:90, 58:3). Yet despite its overall emphasis on human dignity and equality, the Quran does not abolish the institution of slavery. As in the days of the Hebrew Bible, slavery was an integral part of the economic system at the time the Quran was revealed; abolition of slavery would have required an overhaul of the entire socioeconomic system. Therefore, instead of abolishing slavery outright, virtually all interpreters agree that the Quran established an ideal toward which society should work: a society in which no one person would be enslaved to another. Therefore, although slavery is permitted in the Quran, it is now banned in Muslim countries.

The principle demonstrated in this example is that there is a distinction between the reality of legal slavery in the Quran, and the moral recommendations concerning slavery. The former is considered a contingent circumstance, able to be changed. The latter reflects the eternal model of human dignity. At the time of the early Muslim community, the immediate emancipation of all slaves would have caused economic chaos – which obviously would not have been conducive to Islamic goals of wellbeing for all people. But the ideals toward which the community should strive were clearly set forth in this case. Applying the ideals in the modern world requires the abolition of slavery, a goal that has largely been achieved in the Muslim world.

But there is disagreement among Muslims about some other issues in the Quran. For example, in the context of concern for debtors, the Quran allows people to lend money but not to charge usurious interest rates, and when they lend money they must record the amount so that no disagreements will arise. The Quran says that the parties involved in the transaction should get someone to write it down fairly. It specifies that the debtor (or the debtor's guardian, in case the debtor is incapable) is to dictate to the scribe and that he must disclose the full amount of the debt. The Quran then specifies that the transaction must also be witnessed by two men, or by one man and two women in case two men are not available (2:282). All this care is taken to avoid inequity in lending practices. But another question arises concerning the specification that two women's evidence is required to substitute for one man's testimony. Does this verse imply that women should always be unfamiliar with the details of finance and that therefore their testimony on financial issues is always in need of verification? Or does it mean that women's testimony on any issue in general would always need verification? Or does it mean that the testimony of anyone who is uneducated needs corroboration, and that the verse is simply using women as an example, so that the testimony of educated women should actually be considered reliable? Traditional interpreters derive from this verse that women's testimony in court is worth only half that of men. Modern thinkers believe the requirement for two women in place of one man pertains only to circumstances, like those of seventh-century Arabia, in which most women were uneducated and unfamiliar with business transactions. They believe the Quran's essential egalitarianism indicates that the economic skill of women in the Quran's discussion of lending practices is simply an example, not an eternal ideal.

As these examples demonstrate, there is no single formula for achieving justice, but the Quran establishes the standard of human dignity and provides guidance in the struggle to uphold that dignity in ever-changing circumstances. And it informs human beings that the effort to establish justice is the basis on which they will be judged. Those who "believe and do good works," the Quran states repeatedly, will have nothing to fear in the afterlife; they will be richly rewarded. "Believers, bow down and prostrate yourselves in prayer and worship your Lord and do good deeds, and you will prosper. And struggle for God as you should struggle" (22:78–9). This struggle "on the path of God" (*fi sabil Allah*), as the Quran often puts it, is the root meaning of the term *jihad*. Indeed, the Quran presents a challenge to humanity. Using Prophet Muhammad as the model and remembering the forgiveness and mercy of God, people must strive to create a just society. As in the case of earlier societies described by the Quran, communities as a whole will be judged in history; God does not allow oppressive societies to flourish indefinitely. But individuals will be judged in the afterlife, based upon whether or not they have attempted to contribute to this effort:

> To God belongs whatever is in the heavens and earth. He forgives whom He will and punishes whom He will. God is forgiving, merciful.
> Believers, do not consume usury, doubling and redoubling [the amount]. Do your duty to God and you will be successful.
> Protect yourselves from the fire prepared for disbelievers.
> And obey God and the messenger, and you will find mercy.
> And compete with one another for forgiveness from your Lord, and for paradise as great as the heavens and earth, prepared for the righteous.
> Those who [are generous] in [times of] prosperity and adversity, and those who control their anger and who pardon others; God loves those who do good;
> and those who, when they commit an offense or wrong themselves, remember God and beg forgiveness for their sins – and who can forgive sins except God? – and who do not repeat knowingly what they have done;
> these are the ones whose reward from their Lord is forgiveness and gardens with rivers flowing beneath, where they will abide, a great reward for those who work.
> Indeed there have been ages before you, so travel the earth and see what was the end of those who disbelieve.
> This is a clear sign for people and guidance and a warning to the righteous.
> Do not give up or grieve, and you will certainly prosper if you are believers …
> And God will make clear those who believe and blot out the disbelievers.
> Do you think that you will enter heaven without God recognizing those of you who struggle and those who are steadfast?
> (3:129–42)

The Exemplary Life of Muhammad, Prophet of Islam: The Sunna

The Quran thus presents human beings with a formidable challenge. It requires not simply following laws concerning prayer, charity, fasting, pilgrimage, proper diet, and cleanliness. Those rules have been clearly established in revelation and are not subject to change. But the struggle to put the Quran's comprehensive guidance into practice – to be steadfast in faith, honest, sincere, just, merciful, and charitable – requires ongoing effort in diverse and dynamic circumstances. Muslims look to the life of Prophet Muhammad as an inspiring example of how to follow Quranic guidance in all circumstances, no matter how conditions change.

Muhammad was born in poverty in sixth-century Mecca, (modern-day Saudi) Arabia. Most people, including Muhammad's father, worked in the caravan trade for the ruling family of Mecca, the Quraysh. Muhammad's father died before Muhammad was born, and his mother died when he was around 6 years old. He was taken in by family members, first his grandfather and then his uncle, and entered the caravan trade business as a young man. Even before his call to prophecy, at around age 40, Muhammad achieved success in business and a widespread reputation for honesty and fairness. Upon accepting the call to prophecy, he devoted himself entirely to the service of God.

At the beginning of his career as a prophet Muhammad had only a small group of followers. They were persecuted by the wealthy rulers of Mecca, who felt threatened by his call for worship of the only God and an end to social injustice. Muhammad and his small community were driven from their homes, forced to live in separate quarters on the outskirts of town, and boycotted. Yet they persevered in their commitment to follow the guidance of God. They were instructed to suffer injustice with dignity. "Call them to the way of your Lord with wisdom and good arguments and reason with them [offering] a better way ... If you punish them, do so in the same measure as you were punished. But if you endure patiently, it is better for you" (16:125–6).

Despite persecution, Muhammad continued to warn people of the dire consequences of ignoring God's will. He reminded people that God's will is for a just society, one that reflects the equality all people share in the eyes of their Creator. His message was extremely attractive, and he quickly gained a significant following in Mecca and beyond. Muhammad's reputation as a wise and just arbitrator reached Yathrib (some 200 miles north of Mecca), a town that had been suffering under inter-tribal warfare for years. Delegates from Yathrib invited Muhammad to move to their town, promising to abide by his guidance in return for his settling their disputes.

After some hesitation Muhammad accepted the invitation and, with his followers, moved to Yathrib in the year 622 CE. This event begins the Islamic calendar (called the Hijra calendar, to commemorate the "emigration" from Mecca to Yathrib) because it marks a profound shift in the fate of the Muslim community. In Medina, the new name of Yathrib (its full name became "City of the Prophet," *madinat al-nabi*, anglicized as Medina), the Muslims became an autonomous community, able to establish the religious practice and social vision revealed by God through Prophet Muhammad. They were able to create a community guided by the Quran's view of human dignity and compassion for the weak.

As the new community of the Prophet grew and its strength increased, so did the Meccans' hostility toward it. When the Meccans tried to destroy the Muslims in Medina by confiscating their properties and attacking their families back in Mecca, the Quran guided the Muslims to fight back rather than suffer patiently:

And fight in the way of God with those who fight you, but do not be aggressors; God does not love the aggressors. And slay them wherever you find them, and expel them from where they expelled you; persecution is more grievous than slaying ... But if they [cease hostilities], surely God is all forgiving, all compassionate. Fight them until there is no persecution and religion is God's. Then if they [cease hostilities], there shall be no hatred except for evildoers. (2:190)

This is an example of the kind of guidance given by the Quran that is geared toward specific circumstances. In the first instance of oppression, the community is advised to endure with patience; in the second, it is given permission to fight in self-defense. Scholars of Quranic interpretation (*tafsir*) study the circumstances of revelation in order to determine the applicability of verses such as these. There are several approaches to determining appropriate applications of Quranic verses. The majority of traditional *mufassirun* (scholars of *tafsir*) believe that later verses abrogate earlier verses, so that the verses revealed in Medina, after the Hijra, become the standard guidance. (This is called the theory of abrogation, *naskh*.) According to this approach, then, Muslims must fight when they are attacked or have been evicted from their homes, rather than suffer in patience as they were told to do in Mecca. Other scholars, however, believe that the advice given in Quranic verses is geared toward the circumstances in which it was revealed. According to this approach, if Muslims are weak and outnumbered, as they were in Mecca, they should not attempt to fight, but if they are strong and able, as they were in Medina, retaliation against attacks is required. In either case, it is necessary to know the "circumstances of revelation" (*asbab al-nuzul*), as they are known in Quranic studies. For those who believe that later verses abrogate earlier verses, the circumstances of revelation provide the data necessary to determine the historic order of revelation of the verses since, as noted above, Quranic verses are not arranged in chronological order. For those who believe that Quranic guidance is geared to specific circumstances, the *asbab al-nuzul* provide data that allow believers to identify the historic conditions that were being addressed in various verses.

Not all Quranic guidance is dependent upon circumstances, of course. The verses that give specific legislation such as the requirement for prayer, charity, fasting, pilgrimage, and dietary laws, as well as prohibitions on murder, theft, usury, prostitution, gambling, and the like, are considered eternal; there are no foreseeable circumstances in which requirements for worship will be abrogated or violations of human dignity be sanctioned. However, as we have seen, the majority of Quranic verses are more general, presenting a consistent and coherent vision for a just society, based on divine providence and mercy, and encouraging people to struggle to establish such a society. The task of fully submitting to the will of God is thus all-consuming. It requires constant effort, but not because any single individual is expected to take more responsibility than she or he can manage. The Quran often counsels that God does not require from people anything beyond their strength (2:286, 6:152, 7:42, 23:62). People will be judged on their intentions: "God ... will hold you responsible for what your hearts have earned" (2:226). Nor is any one group expected to be successful in the struggle to establish a just society in a given time or place. But believers are expected to work toward that goal, by following the guidance given in the Quran and the model established by Prophet Muhammad in Medina as a guide. Thus, Muhammad's role extends beyond the task of delivering revelation. His life is also a model for humanity of how to live every moment, and make every choice, in accordance with God's will. The way he lived his life is described by the Quran as the best example of Islam: "Indeed in the messenger of God is a good example for those who look to God and the Last Day and remember God often" (33:22). Together, the Quran and the example (called the Sunna) set by Prophet Muhammad comprise the guidance Muslims need in their collective responsibility to establish justice.

The Early Muslim Community and the Pillars of Islam

The community established by Prophet Muhammad in the seventh century was resoundingly successful in its effort to create a society characterized by justice, peace, and harmony. The decades of internal strife that had plagued Medina ceased. Upon his arrival in Medina, the Prophet struck an agreement among the various tribes there and his community of Meccans. This agreement is recorded in history as the Constitution of Medina. According to the provisions of the agreement, all religious communities in Medina form a single community, "separate from other people."[1] They are to be mutually supportive, particularly in case of attack. Reflecting the Quran's teaching, Jews and Muslims are expected to maintain their own religious practices; disputes are to be referred to Prophet Muhammad and God. There were no Christian tribes in Medina, but later on Christians and other religious groups were accorded religious freedom, based on the Quran's prohibition of compulsion in matters of religion (2:256) and on the precedent established in the Constitution of Medina. Prior to the establishment of the Islamic community in Medina, tribes had been the dominant form of social organization. Tribes were extended families, under the leadership of dominant males, and each was an autonomous unit. Although occasionally alliances would be formed through marriage, there was no effective precedent in the region for a social organization that included peoples of varying families and religious traditions cooperating in the pursuit of shared ideals.

The peace and prosperity of this community comprised of various tribes with differing religions living in harmony quickly attracted the attention of its neighbors. There had been some internal dissent. On three occasions local tribes were believed to have violated the constitution by conspiring with outsiders against the Medinan community. They were therefore expelled (in the first two cases), or executed (in the third case). Because all three of these tribes were Jewish, some people think that the community in Medina turned against Jews. In fact, some verses from the Quran referring to incidents such as these caution the Muslims against trusting Jews and Christians. (For example, "O you who believe, do not take Jews and Christians for friends. They are friends of one another," 5:52.) However, other Jewish tribes continued to live in peace in Medina. Furthermore, the majority of verses of the Quran, as noted above, endorse pluralism. The following verse is typical of the Quran's acceptance of Jews and Christians (among others): "Surely, those who have believed, and the Jews and the Sabians and the Christians, whoever believes in God and the last day and does good deeds need have no fear nor shall they grieve" (5:71). Most commentators therefore agree that the verses criticizing other religions are directed at specific beliefs or actions, not against the groups as a whole.

Indeed, the model of inter-tribal harmony established at Medina seems to have been attractive to the surrounding communities.

During the lifetime of the Prophet, most tribes of the Arabian peninsula accepted Islam and pledged their allegiance to the Prophet, making Muhammad the most powerful leader in the region. Within eight years of the Hijra, and after several battles, the Meccans also recognized the authority of the Prophet. The event was dramatic. In 628 it was revealed to Muhammad that he would pray in Mecca (48:27). He therefore set out with about one thousand unarmed pilgrims who also wanted to pray in Mecca. They were stopped outside the city at Hudaybiyyah by the Meccans. In order to preserve peace, the Prophet negotiated a ten-year truce, agreeing to postpone the pilgrimage for a year. But two years later the truce was violated and Muhammad marched on Mecca. He was met by the leader of Mecca's leading tribe, the Quraysh, who accepted Islam and negotiated peace. Granting amnesty to the city that had persecuted his community, Muhammad entered the city peacefully, and rededicated the Kaaba, the ancient shrine at the center of Mecca. According to the Quran, the Kaaba was originally built by Abraham and his son Ishmael to honor the one God, but it had since been taken over by local tribes, who had filled it with symbols and relics of their polytheistic religions. Local tribes made annual pilgrimages to Mecca, in combination with the city's annual trade fair and cultural events. When Prophet Muhammad returned to the Kaaba, he cleared the idols from it and made it the focus of pilgrimage for Muslims.

The pilgrimage (*hajj*) is known as the fifth pillar or basic practice of Islam. The first pillar is the *shahadah*, the pledging of commitment to God and the teachings of His prophet, Muhammad. "I bear witness that there is no god (*ilah*) but the God (*al-ilah/* Allah) and Muhammad is the messenger of God." Anyone who sincerely commits to live according to this pledge is considered a Muslim.

The second pillar is prayer (*salat*). Muslims pray five times daily (at sunrise, midday, sunset, evening, and nighttime). The prayers consist of recitations of verses of the Quran performed in a series of submissive postures (including bowing low from a kneeling position, so that the forehead touches the ground), and are meant to keep Muslims focused on the will of God in all aspects of life. Many people perform their prayers in mosques (*masajid*, "places of prostration"), although prayers may be performed anywhere that has been swept clean (symbolizing entering a state of purity). The prayer rug, a small carpet usually with a directional indicator to be pointed toward Mecca (the proper direction of prayer), is often used for this purpose. Some people substitute a piece of cloth or cardboard if they have no rug. Believers are instructed simply to precede prayer by washing (or symbolically washing, if no water is available), to prepare themselves spiritually to focus entirely on God. On Fridays the midday prayer should be performed communally in the mosque. At that time, the prayer leader (*imam*) often offers a sermon (*khutbah*) on the topic of his choice.

The third pillar is *zakah* (also spelled *zakat*), or charity. As noted above, all Muslims are required to be charitable; *zakah* requires all adult Muslims to give a share of their wealth annually for the support of the poor and to further the cause of Islam.

The fourth pillar is fasting (*sawm* or *siyyam*). All healthy Muslims (i.e., neither the very young nor the very old, nor those who are sick, pregnant, or nursing) are expected to fast from sunrise until sunset during the ninth month of the Islamic calendar (Ramadan). This is a very spiritual time, during which Muslims pray regularly and read the Quran, and focus on the equality of all people in their utter dependence on God. At the end of the month of fasting comes one of Islam's two major holidays, the one that celebrates the breaking of the fast (Eid al-Fitr). Families and communities celebrate this feast for three days, sharing joyous meals and giving gifts to the children.

As noted, the *hajj* is the fifth pillar. Muslims are obligated to make the pilgrimage at least once in their lifetime if they are physically and financially able, during the month designated as "the month of pilgrimage" (*dhu al-hijja*). During that time pilgrims dress in simple clothes, removing any indicators of social rank, and together perform ceremonies designed to remind them of the founding of the Kaaba and their utter reliance on (submission to) God. The pilgrimage culminates in the feast of the sacrifice (Eid al-Adha), the other major holiday. Sheep are slaughtered, symbolizing Abraham's sacrifice; the meat is then consumed and any excess is given to the poor.

The five pillars (*arkan*) are the basic practices of Islam. They structured Islamic life in Medina, as they continue to do today. The pillars are simple practices designed to remind believers constantly of their commitment to the divine will. They also focus attention on the core values of Islam: the equality of all human beings in the eyes of God and the responsibility of all believers to contribute to the wellbeing of society. Around these practices and core values, the early Muslim community was built and prospered. Following the rededication of the Kaaba in 630, Prophet Muhammad received overtures from tribes throughout the Arabian peninsula, accepting Islam and becoming part of the community, or pledging alliance with the Prophet. The Christian tribes among the bedouin (desert-dwelling nomadic herders) and Jewish tribes, many from the desert oases, generally kept their religious identities, as in Medina, while the polytheistic tribes generally became Muslim. By the time of the Prophet's death, the Islamic community based in Medina was the most vibrant moral, social, and political force in the Arabian peninsula.

The Successors ("Caliphs")

When Prophet Muhammad died after a brief illness in 632 his followers were distraught. Abu Bakr, one of his closest companions, declared to them, "If anyone worships Muhammad, [know that] Muhammad is dead. But if anyone worships God, [know that] God is alive and does not die." His goal was to refocus attention on the message, rather than on the Messenger. Muslims maintain the deepest respect for Muhammad and continue to be inspired by his example. But he was a man, a servant of God, as Abu Bakr reminded the community on this sad occasion when he repeated the Quranic verse, "Muhammad is only a messenger; messengers have died before him. When he dies will you turn your back on him? Whoever turns back does no harm to God but God will reward the grateful" (3:144). The believers were comforted and inspired by this; they were to maintain their commitment to the will of God, taking individual responsibility for their actions. But what about the community as a whole? Who would lead them?

A number of possibilities were suggested. Some of the nomadic tribes around Medina felt that their allegiance had been to Prophet Muhammad. For them his death meant the end of their affiliation; they indicated their withdrawal from the alliance by ending their *zakah* payments to Medina. Some believed that in the absence of Muhammad's central leadership, the tribes and communities – including Mecca – should revert to local leadership. Others believed that the Prophet had designated his cousin and son-in-law, Ali, as his political heir and that leadership of the community should remain within the Prophet's family. These would be called the "partisans of Ali, *shi'at* Ali, or simply Shia or Shii. (The development of Shii thought will be discussed further in Chapter 3.) But the majority believed that the Prophet had not discussed political systems or specified a successor to take over after his death. Abu Bakr was among these. He and other close companions of the Prophet were convinced that leadership should be chosen by tribal representatives, as was common in Arabia. They would be called the Sunnis. They believed, further, that Muslims had to remain a single community – not just morally unified through commitment to monotheism and the message of Prophet Muhammad, but politically unified as well. Their opinion prevailed. The companions of the Prophet pledged allegiance to Abu Bakr as leader of the community, referring to him as the Prophet's representative (*khalifah* or "caliph"). (He preferred the title "leader of the believers," *amir al-mu'minin*.) He was first among equals, leading through consultation (*shura*) with other elders in the community, just as the Prophet had done, and in accordance with the Quranic directive: "So pardon them and ask forgiveness for them and consult with them on the conduct of affairs" (3:159).

Abu Bakr then led the community in a momentous decision: to bring the tribes that had seceded back into the community by force, if necessary. The Quran stipulates that "there is no compulsion in religion" (2:256). It reinforces that position elsewhere. For example, when discussing preaching to the People of the Book, Muhammad is instructed:

> If they argue with you, say my followers and I have surrendered ourselves to God. And say to those who have received Scripture

and to the illiterate: "Have you surrendered [to God]?" If they surrender [to God], then they are rightly guided, and if they turn away, then it is your duty only to preach. (3:20)

This verse, in fact, guides Muslim attitudes toward proselytizing. Nevertheless, the decision was made to enforce the political unity of the believers militarily. The seceders were declared apostates, and the campaigns against them are still known as the wars of apostasy (*riddah*). The decision to enforce unity among believers had a significant effect on the development of Islam. It established a policy that resulted in one of the most extraordinary political expansions in history. By the time Abu Bakr died in 634, almost all the tribes of the Arabian peninsula had been brought into the Islamic political orbit. Under Abu Bakr's successors, Umar and Uthman, the Islamic army set out to rid Syria and Mesopotamia (Iraq) of the hated Byzantine and Sasanian empires. (Further implications of the decision to enforce political unity will be discussed in Chapter 4.)

At that time the Middle East was in the final throes of devastating competition between the eastern Roman empire (the Christian Byzantines) and the Sasanian Persian empire (Zoroastrian). The Byzantines had occupied coastal Syria, which at that time included parts of the present states of Syria, Lebanon, Jordan, Israel, and the Palestinian territories, and Egypt. The Sasanians of Persia (called Iran since the 1930s), controlled most of present-day Iraq. After decades of debilitating wars, both empires were weakened internally. Arab tribes on the frontiers of the empires readily accepted the leadership of the Muslims. The formerly great Roman and Persian armies were defeated with little trouble.

The Byzantines had long persecuted their Jewish subjects, as well as those Christians who rejected Orthodoxy. For these groups Muslim rule was especially welcome. Those who accepted Islam were taught the basics of the religion by Quran reciters. But Christians and Jews were free to retain their religious identity. In addition, the taxes imposed by the Muslims were generally lighter than those of the older empires and, unlike many conquering armies, the Arab Muslims were not allowed to take control of the conquered lands for personal use. Thus, Jerusalem was liberated from Roman rule in 636, Mosul was taken from the Persians in 641, and the Romans were defeated in Alexandria by 646. The last Sasanian ruler was killed in 651, the Roman fleet was destroyed by Muslim sea power in 655, and the Muslim state headquartered in Medina became the most powerful in the region.

Early Communal Disputes

The phenomenal expansion of Islamic sovereignty was a result of the early decision by the Prophet's successors that Islamic unity must be assured through political unity. But political unity proved virtually impossible to maintain as Islamic sovereignty continued to spread. Efforts to enforce that unity engendered conflicts that called into question the very nature of the Islamic community. A recurring theme in the early conflicts was the tribal nature of Arab culture. In pre-Islamic times, tribes were the basic unit of social organization, and each tribe had its own values, sources of authority, organization, rituals, and beliefs – all of which would later be identified as aspects of religion. This is the context for understanding the gravity with which the question of apostasy was treated in early Islam. To change one's religion was not simply a matter of spiritual persuasion as we see it today. Since religious loyalty and political loyalty were often linked, to change one's religion was tantamount to changing one's political loyalty, a potentially treasonous act. Christianity had attempted to supersede this religio-political identity. Jesus' command "to render unto Caesar the things that are Caesar's, and unto God the things that are God's" (Matt. 22:21) could allow people to follow their religious conscience without it calling into question their political loyalty. People could be Christian in the Roman empire without being considered subversives. But the equation of religious and political loyalty was reimposed when Christianity was declared the official religion of the Roman empire. The Quran's teaching of religious freedom was a return to the ideal espoused by Jesus. It was a reassertion of the independence of religious and ethnic identity. This ethic was institutionalized in the Constitution of Medina, when Prophet Muhammad included Jews and Muslims in the same political community. Again stressing the struggle against tribalism, the Prophet said in his final speech that Arabs have no superiority over non-Arabs. Nevertheless, the tribal tendency to equate religious and ethnic national identity was so well entrenched that it re-emerged soon after the Prophet's death. Umar, the second caliph, determined that only Islam would be allowed in the Arabian peninsula, the Quran's teaching and the Prophet's example of religious tolerance notwithstanding. Under his administration, Jews and Christians were expelled, so that all Arabs (meaning those who lived in the Arabian peninsula; later on, the term "Arab" would apply to all Arabic speakers) were Muslim; thus, religious and ethnic identity were rejoined. Umar's successor, Uthman, reasserted a tribal tendency that challenged even other Arab Muslims. He headed an administration staffed almost exclusively by members of his own Meccan clan, the Umayyads, resulting in numerous protests. Umar's policy concerning land taxation also resulted in protests. It stipulated that revenues from conquered land would be sent to Medina for the benefit of the central administration, the conquering Arab soldiers and their families. Non-Muslim Arabs felt that their land taxes should be used locally. Policies such as these seemed to violate Islamic norms of justice and equality, and resentment mounted. Umar was murdered by a Christian Persian slave in 644. Uthman continued Umar's policies, resulting in more discontent. Minor rebellions broke out in towns established solely for Arab Muslim conquerors in Egypt (al-Fustat) and Iraq (Kufah). In 656 rebellious Muslims from Egypt marched to Medina and assassinated Uthman.

Those participating in the growing discontent found a champion in Ali, the Prophet's companion, cousin, and son-in-law. Following Uthman's death, Ali was chosen by majority opinion within the community to be the next "leader of the believers." He was well respected and, as noted above, had been a contender for the office since the death of Prophet Muhammad, but he was not as senior as Abu Bakr, Umar, and Uthman. His Shii supporters believed that he should have succeeded Prophet Muhammad as leader of the Muslim community, and that the first three successors (Abu Bakr,

Umar, and Uthman) were actually usurpers. But not all Ali's supporters believed that his legitimacy rested on the Prophet's designation. Many supported him because of his piety, wisdom, and courage, particularly in this time of civil strife. These included a group later identified as the Kharijis (or Kharijites, "the Seceders"), who believed that Uthman's nepotism (staffing his administration with members of his own family) was such a serious violation of Islamic principles that he was no longer eligible even to be called a Muslim, let alone a caliph. But Ali also had enemies. Chief among them were Aishah, widow of the Prophet and daughter of the first caliph Abu Bakr; and Muawiyah, the governor of Damascus appointed by Uthman. Aishah, who held personal grudges against Ali, led a rebellion against him near Basra (in Iraq, near Kufah, where Ali had established his headquarters) in 656. Ali's troops easily defeated her troops (which she personally led). Muawiyah challenged Ali to find and punish the assassins of his kinsman Caliph Uthman. When he did not, Muawiyah led an army against him (657). On the verge of defeat, Muawiyah's troops asked for arbitration, which Ali granted. The arbitration allowed Muawiyah to maintain his post in Damascus. Unfortunately, this effort at reconciliation cost Ali the support of the Kharijis. In 661 Ali was assassinated by one of them, leaving the caliphate to the Umayyad family in Damascus. (For further discussion of the Kharijis, see Chapter 5.)

Conclusion

The violent end of three of the first four caliphs reflects the turmoil that gripped the Muslim community after the death of Prophet Muhammad. The community had the Quran and his example (the Sunna) to guide them, but still they were left with an enormous challenge. As noted above, the Quran is not a law book but a guide and source of moral inspiration. It reaffirms the covenant accepted by Abraham, the "trust" that human beings accepted at creation, the agreement that God offers eternal reward to those who take up the struggle to re-create in society the equality all human beings share in the eyes of God. But there are no formulae for ensuring that justice is always done. That is the part human beings have to figure out, each community and every generation, in an endless variety of circumstances. They must evaluate the circumstances in light of moral guidance, and then determine what actions and institutions are most conducive to justice in those specific circumstances. And they must do it in cooperation with others, since no one can create justice alone. The Quran describes its guidance as very clear, and it is; there is no doubt about what the goals of a just society are. But it is very difficult to figure out how to achieve those goals "on the ground" – as anyone who is engaged in social activism knows.

Early Muslims were faced with the enormous challenge not only of institutionalizing justice in their own communities, but also sharing those ideals and institutions with others who had suffered injustice just as they had. It is certainly to their credit that they relieved the region of the heavy burden of Roman and Persian imperialism. That conflicts would arise over the practical matters of governance is not surprising. It is natural that, among tribal people, some would believe leadership should stay within their own community, while people outside that community would reject that model of leadership. It is just as natural that, among moralizing people, many would believe that leadership should be based on piety, and many would rebel against rulers deemed unjust. In reality, the early years of Islam reflect both the benefits and the difficulties encountered in the transition from a community whose security is based on tribal bonds of mutual and unquestioned loyalty to a community committed to justice on a global scale. This is a struggle that continues to this day. Like people of many other faiths, Muslims continue to explore the implications of working for justice in a pluralist society. Is salvation reserved only for Baptists, or Catholics, or Jews, or Muslims? Must we separate religious beliefs from political convictions in order to be able to live peacefully with people of other faiths? Indeed, can we separate the two? Does accepting the legitimacy of other faiths require abandoning one's own, or a "willing suspension of disbelief"? These are questions that confront all religions today. They are the same kinds of questions that the early Muslims struggled with.

The fact that there was conflict reflects the complexity of the problems faced and the depth of commitment on the part of the participants. In the context of Islamic history, it does not detract from the valiance of their efforts. Although Shii Muslims continue to believe Ali was the first legitimate successor to the Prophet, the majority of Muslims, the Sunnis, believe the first four caliphs were "rightly guided" (al-rashidun). They look to this period as one in which the Quran's moral challenge dominated Islamic life. The Muslim community, with all its conflicts and failings, extended every effort "in the way of God" (fi sabil Allah). Even today, traditionalist Muslims look to this community as an example of truly Islamic life, and accept some of the precedents established during this period (such as the death penalty for apostasy). Reform-minded Muslims, on the other hand, respect the efforts of this early community, while rejecting some of its precedents, and look to the Quran and Sunna for guidance in facing the challenges of modern life.

Whether Sunni or Shii, traditionalist or reformist, all Muslims consider this period the time during which Islamic ideals were established. Although the Shiis do not accept Abu Bakr, Umar, and Uthman as legitimate leaders of the community, and modern-day reformers reject some of their specific judgments, all Muslims believe this community took up the challenge of the khalifah. This term, appropriated in the political sphere to mean "successor" of the Prophet, actually has a much broader meaning in the Quran, where it is used twice. In a famous passage that encapsulates much of Islamic teaching, the Quran says that God created humanity to be His khalifah (2:30). Clearly the meaning here is "steward" or "deputy". Human beings were put here to be responsible for maintaining the equality in which all were created. Elsewhere, the Quran describes God addressing King David as his khalifah who, as such, must judge in all things with honor and justice (38:26). Despite its weaknesses and conflicts, the early Muslim community accepted the challenge of stewardship and struggled to enjoin good and prevent evil. It is that legacy that has continued to inspire Muslims throughout the ages.

Chapter 2

The Pursuit of Knowledge in the Service of God and Humanity
The Golden Age

The conflicts that gripped the Muslim community during the caliphate of Ali interrupted the spread of Islamic sovereignty. But following his death and the establishment of the seat of Islamic government in Damascus in 661, expansion resumed, with continued success. After replacing Roman rule in Egypt, Muslim forces pushed across North Africa. Joined by Berber (indigenous North African) converts, the Arabs crossed the straits from Africa to Andalusia (in modern-day Spain), ascending the mountain to which their leader Tariq gave his name ("Gibraltar" comes from the Arabic *jabal tariq*, Tariq's Mountain or Mount Tariq). Within just one century of Prophet Muhammad's death, Muslims had established Islamic sovereignty throughout much of Spain, which remained Islamic until the Reconquista in 1492. The Muslims' advance into Europe was stopped in Gaul (France) by Charles Martel at the battle of Tours in 732.

In the east, Islamic rule was established throughout former Sasanian lands, all the way to the Indus river and the border of China by the early eighth century. Islam continued its eastward spread through the fourteenth century, when traders and itinerant preachers traveled to China, South Asia, and Southeast Asia, establishing roots for the current Islamic countries of Indonesia and Malaysia. The Indian subcontinent was ruled by Muslims from the thirteenth century until the British took control in 1857. It was, indeed, a phenomenal expansion. And with it came the development of a highly sophisticated culture. Marked by openness and creativity, it was inspired by the

Quran and Prophet Muhammad's example, and still serves as a model of what many believe a truly Islamic society can achieve.

Institutions

As noted in the previous chapter, many subjects of the Byzantine (eastern Roman) and the Sasanian Persian empires generally welcomed Muslim rule since it allowed respite from religious persecution and resulted in overall lower taxes. This reflected the rationale for the expansion of Islamic rule; Muslims sincerely believed that Islam was divinely ordained to bring peace and relief from oppression for all humanity. Thus, when Muslims approached a new community, they offered the protection of Islam. Those who chose not to accept Islam as their religion were offered treaties; they could pay a tribute in return for the right to retain religious freedom and internal autonomy. Those who refused either to accept Islam or to live in peace with Muslims through treaty agreements were forced to submit by means of military action.

This method of conquest resulted in a division of the world into three parts: *dar al-Islam, dar al-'ahd* (or *sulh*), and *dar al-harb. Dar al-Islam* refers to those territories in which Islamic law prevails. *Dar al-'ahd* (region of covenant) and *dar al-sulh* (region of truce) were both regions whose leaders had agreed to pay the Muslim leaders a tribute and to protect the rights of any Muslims or Muslim allies who lived there, but who otherwise maintained their autonomy, including their own legal systems. *Dar al-harb* was a region whose leaders had made no such agreement and where, therefore, Muslims and their allies were neither guaranteed the right to live by Islamic law nor were protected by it. For this reason it was called "region of warfare." This does not mean that such regions were automatically subject to attack by Muslims, since *harb* is not legitimate warfare in Islam. When warfare is sanctioned in Islam, it is called *jihad*, struggle "in the way of God" that is carried out through military means and according to strict rules of engagement. This is the only kind of warfare allowed under Islamic law. Referring to a region as *dar al-harb* reflects the perception that the region itself was warlike and Muslims were not safe there.

Through this system, the Muslim world – a region where Muslims made up the vast majority – was transformed into the Islamic world – a world dominated by Muslim institutions but including significant non-Muslim populations. Such an enormous and complex world required administration beyond the simple model established by the Prophet and his earliest successors. That model had been relatively informal, and based on direct interaction of community members and leaders. In the expanded Islamic empire, more sophisticated administrative systems became necessary.

A system of taxation was the first order of business. In general, the Muslim conquerors allowed local authorities to collect taxes according to their established customs. Since some of the newly acquired territories had been variously administered according to Roman law, Persian law, and other regional systems, the system of taxation under Muslim rule became quite complex. Iraq, for example, was conquered through military victory over the drained Sasanian forces, with the help of local Arab tribes. The native Arabs were left in control of taxation and followed the Sasanian tradition, which included both a land tax and a poll tax (a tax based on the number of people living there). But the poll tax varied according to the degree of wealth among the populace, except for the aristocracy, who were exempt from the poll tax. In Syria, where Islamic dominance was achieved largely by treaty, tax collection was left to the discretion of the native administrators. They followed in basic outline the fiscal system of the previous Roman overlords, which was even more complex than the Persian system.[1] The central treasury therefore had to be very sophisticated to keep track of all these differing systems of taxation.

Law

Of far greater importance than taxation, however, was the institutionalization of law, since it regulated Islamic practice overall. In this area, too, the Muslim practice of leaving in place systems that had dominated a region prior to the coming of Islam was evident. In accordance with Islamic principles and the Prophet's practice, religious freedom was the norm throughout Islamic realms. The right accorded to Jews in the Constitution of Medina to maintain their religious and legal systems was extended to Christians, and later to Zoroastrians, Hindus, and Buddhists. But what about those who chose to become Muslim? The inclusion of vast new populations in the community of Muslims meant that an expanded legal system had to be developed. According to tradition, Prophet Muhammad stipulated that local customs were to be tolerated as long as they did not interfere with Islamic principles. But someone had to determine what was or was not in accordance with Islamic principles. Muslims had to develop a legal system that would be flexible enough to function effectively throughout Islam's expansive and diverse realms, but rigorous enough to maintain a distinctive Islamic identity.

In the days of the first caliphs, when the system was still relatively informal and modeled on the practice of the Prophet, Muslims were simply expected to follow Islamic practice, including regular prayer, charity, fasting, and pilgrimage. Regarding other issues of governance and in matters of conflict, the Quran had stipulated that Muslims were to "obey God and the Messenger and those among you in authority" (4:62). But beyond that, the Quran had specified no particular form of government. Muhammad's early successors, therefore – as his "representatives" (caliphs) and "leaders of the believers" – attempted to follow the Prophet's example by living lives of piety and arbitrating disputes when they arose. But with the expansion of Islamic sovereignty this informal practice proved insufficient, and was gradually transformed into a legal system that could function independent of the head of state.

The first major transition in Islamic governance came with the assumption of power by the Umayyads, descendants of a powerful Meccan family. Although some people had argued that Ali should be appointed successor to the Prophet because of his family relationship with him, hereditary leadership was not a pattern common in Arab society. But after the Umayyad Muawiyah was recognized as caliph, his family kept control of that office until a revolution ousted them in 750. During the Umayyads' reign, a distinction between specifically religious and the coercive/executive levels of political authority developed. Damascus became the political or administrative capital of the empire while Mecca remained the religious/legislative center. But still there was no theory upon which the government was based. As noted, the caliphs left in place whatever systems had prevailed before the Muslim conquest. For other legal issues, the Umayyads introduced into their administration a new office, that of judges (sing. *qadi*). These were political appointees with varied administrative responsibilities, including police and treasury work, but generally charged with settling disputes in accordance with local custom and Islamic principles. They were allowed a great deal of latitude, exercising their own judgment about what was permissible in view of Islamic principles and administrative necessities.

However, it soon became apparent, to some people at least, that Umayyad leadership no longer was the model of wisdom and piety that Islamic leadership ideally symbolized. This recognition gave rise to opposition groups, including scholars who objected that Umayyad policies violated Islamic principles. In the process of discussing which actions and policies were Islamic and which were not, scholars actually developed the formal theories of Islamic law that became the core of Islamic life.[2] When Christianity became politically institutionalized in Rome in the fourth century, it devised a way to determine who was really a Christian by developing a "creed," a list of beliefs. Whoever accepted the beliefs of Christianity was a Christian and therefore a full citizen; those who rejected Christian beliefs were non-Christian and considered a threat to the Christian community. That is why the major discipline in Christianity is theology, a discussion of beliefs. In Islam, on the other hand, just as in Judaism, the emphasis is not so much on beliefs as on actions. Belief is important; correct behavior is assumed to be based on correct belief. But the critical point of religious identity is based on the discipline that deals with practice, and that is law. This does not mean that Islam became legalistic, however; like Judaic law, Islamic law is not simply a code of injunctions enforceable in a courtroom. As modern Islamic scholar Fazlur Rahman put it, Islamic law is "an endless discussion on the duties of a Muslim rather than a neatly formulated code or codes."[3] Law was therefore central to Islamic life in terms of daily life and religious practice, as well as state administration.

By the mid-eighth century there was a discernible body of scholars who were popularly regarded as having the authority to identify and interpret the sources of Islamic law. They fell into schools of thought that generally developed according to regional practice. In Medina, for example, a school of Islamic legal thought developed based on local practice and in view of the interpretations of scripture and reports (*ahadith*; sing. *hadith*) from the local people about what the Prophet said or did (his normative or exemplary practice or "Sunna"). This body of ideas about practice was expressed in the work of Malik ibn Anas (d. 796), and is known as the Maliki school of law. Another center, with different local customs and different *hadith* reports, grew up in Kufa (in Iraq): the school of Abu Hanifa (d. 767), largely developed by his students Abu Yusuf (d. 798) and al-Shaybani (d. 804), and known as the Hanafi school. The development of these schools was essentially democratic; decisions about what was proper practice, in accordance with the Quran and the Prophet's example, were based on local consensus (*ijma*). In cases where there were no apparently applicable precedents in the Quran or Sunna, legal scholars used their discretion to determine the implications of revelation for the question at hand. They practiced *ijtihad*, the name given to this interpretive work.

The Umayyads lost control of the caliphate when they were overthrown by the Abbasid family in 750 CE. As members of the opposition to the Umayyads, the legal scholars (*fuqaha'*) were naturally favored by the Abbasids. The new ruling family appointed these scholars as judges, rather than simply calling upon loyal functionaries, as the Umayyads had done. This represented a significant step in the formalization of Islamic law. As legal historian N. J. Coulson put it, "The legal scholars were publicly recognized as the architects of an Islamic scheme of state and society which the Abbasids had pledged themselves to build, and under this political sponsorship the schools of law developed rapidly."[4] The scholars began to identify weaknesses in the system and the need for greater rigor in legal thought. Thus, a third school of Islamic law developed around the idea that legal reasoning should be consistent throughout the Islamic world. This was not an argument for uniform practice or judgments, only for agreement upon the sources of Islamic law and the ways to achieve sound legal rulings in cases for which no precedent could be found. It was an argument for procedural continuity, reflecting a growing awareness that, regardless of the shifting political winds, the core of Islamic unity was law. The school that emerged from this movement was named for its energetic founder, Muhammad ibn Idris al-Shafii (d. 820). It is called the Shafii school of legal thought.

Al-Shafii had traveled to the major cities in the Muslim world, and noticed significant variations in legal reasoning. He set out to achieve consistency in legal procedures by articulating clearly the roots of Islamic law and their rank in terms of priority. For al-Shafii, as for all other Muslims, the first source is the Quran. In cases for which the Quran offers no specific judgment, the next source of guidance is the practice of Prophet Muhammad, the Sunna. But at the time of al-Shafii, the process by which the Sunna was communicated was still largely informal, based on the opinions of educated people about the Prophet's principles or ways of making decisions. Al-Shafii attempted to formalize the Sunna by equating it with credible *hadith* reports of what the Prophet said or did in specific circumstances. As a result, the concept of the Sunna was eventually restricted to specific examples of the Prophet's behavior. These could concern personal matters with no significant legal implications, such as how to clean one's teeth or whether or not to shave, as well as matters with important legal significance, such as how to conduct business or deal with poverty. In either case, these precedents became models to be imitated. And once they achieved such an important place in Islamic administration, the process of collecting, verifying, and codifying *hadith* reports began in earnest. By the ninth century, there were two collections of reports that were considered "sound" (*sahih*, meaning that the people who reported them had been scrutinized and found trustworthy, that the content of the report was in keeping with Quranic teaching, etc.) and therefore authoritative. Those were the collections of two individuals – Bukhari and Muslim. Four other collections were considered valuable sources of insight concerning the Prophet and/or the Quran, but not as authoritative as the collections of Bukhari and

Muslim. (The Shiis also have *hadith* collections, verified by virtue of transmission through Ali and his descendants.)

The third source of law for al-Shafii was the consensus of the community. The Prophet is reported to have asserted that his community would never agree on an error, and group consensus has therefore always been important in Islam. But al-Shafii concluded that only the consensus of the entire Islamic community should be considered authoritative, not just consensus within the various regions. And by the time he was working, given the extent the Islamic community had reached, full consensus was virtually impossible to attain. Therefore, al-Shafii believed it was preferable to follow precedent as much as possible. The third source of Islamic law, then, became judgments that had been reached by consensus of earlier generations about the meaning and application of the Quran. Independent reasoning (*ijtihad*), the fourth source of Islamic law, could be practiced only as a final resort, and it too was circumscribed. The intellectual effort to determine the implications of the Quran and Sunna was to be carried out through syllogistic reasoning, or reasoning by analogy (*qiyas*), rather than the more informal *ijtihad* based on personal opinion (*ra'y*).

Al-Shafii's school of jurisprudence remained only one of several within the Islamic system. A fourth school of thought was developed by one of his students, Ahmad ibn Hanbal (d. 855). Called the Hanbali school of legal thought, it places even greater emphasis on precedent than the Shafii school, although it also allows greater freedom in the use of *ijtihad*. Shii Muslims would develop a school of legal reasoning as well, known as the Jafari school. Nonetheless, al-Shafii came to be known as the "architect of Islamic law" because his work consolidated Islamic legal thought into a recognizable discipline at the core of Islamic life.[5] From his time on, a Muslim was officially defined as one who follows Islamic law.[6]

The systematization of legal administration gave the Islamic world a basic structure that has endured to this day. The Maliki, Hanafi, Shafii, Hanbali, and Jafari schools of legal thought still characterize the Islamic landscape worldwide. Each tends to predominate in a specific region: Maliki law in North and West

Africa; Hanafi in areas formerly under Ottoman control and India; Shafii in Indonesia, Malaysia, and the Philippines; Hanbali in Saudi Arabia and Qatar; and Jafari in Shii regions such as Iran. But the schools of thought differ relatively little and are, in fact, mutually acceptable. For example, all Muslims accept the five-part division of actions into those considered required (such as the five pillars), those recommended (such as giving charity above and beyond the required *zakah*), those considered neutral (such as smoking, according to most Muslims), those that are discouraged (such as divorce), and those that are forbidden (such as consuming intoxicants, eating pork, or gambling). Actions in the first category are believed to be rewarded, and willful failure to perform them is punishable. Actions that fall into the second category are rewarded, but failure to perform them will not bring punishment. Actions considered to be neutral bring neither reward nor punishment. Those who avoid discouraged actions will benefit from their abstinence, and those who perform forbidden (*haram*) actions will be punished.

The classic formulations of Islamic law, accepted by all schools of thought, reflect the Quranic ethic of punishment by retaliation (*qisas*) for physical offenses, from assault to homicide. The person who strikes a physical blow is subject to whatever offense he has committed. As the Quran says, "A life for a life, an eye for an eye, and a nose for a nose, and an ear for an ear, and a tooth for a tooth, and for [other] injuries, fair retaliation" (5:46). The victim or the victim's family may choose to accept compensation (*diyah*) instead, and this is encouraged by the Quran. (The foregoing verse continues: "And whoever waives the right to this in charity, it will be an atonement [for sins].") There is another class of crime for which Islamic law has established specified mandatory punishments (*hadd*; pl. *hudud*), provided the perpetrator acted in full control of his senses and with full knowledge of his offenses, and that strict rules of evidence can be met. These *hudud* punishments include capital punishment for apostasy, highway robbery, what we now call terrorism (i.e., crimes against random victims), and illicit sex between married people; amputation of the hand for theft; and whipping for illicit sex between unmarried people or legal minors, or for drinking. (See Chapter 5 for further discussion of terrorism.) The rules of evidence required for these crimes are indeed strict. For example, conviction of adultery requires substantiation by four adult male eyewitnesses. Although such punishments seem harsh, they are considered primarily deterrent and, in fact, have proven to be effective in that regard. Most Muslims also believe that the *hudud* punishments are applicable only in conditions where high social standards have been met. They are not applicable in conditions of widespread ignorance, poverty, or social instability. Throughout history there are very few reports of the punishments actually being administered.

In traditional Islamic law, the courts are used to decide any issues other than physical injury or death, and those requiring *hudud* punishments. These include detailed laws concerning transactions (sales, rentals, loans, gifts to non-profit organizations [*waqf*; pl. *awqaf*], etc.), family law (such as marriage, divorce, guardianship, custody), and laws of inheritance. In the traditional Islamic court, the judge (*qadi*) is given significant latitude. He may ask for an authoritative opinion (*fatwa*) from a professional legal scholar (*mufti*), but is not required to do so. Individuals may seek legal representation but in general are expected to state their case personally. The judge decides whether the plaintiff or the defendant bears the burden of proof, upon which the prosecutor must produce two witnesses (for most cases). If the evidence is unconvincing, the defendant is given the opportunity to swear innocence by a sacred oath. If the defendant refuses to offer such an oath, the case is decided in favor of the plaintiff.

In the modern era, traditional Islamic civil and criminal law was largely replaced by European legal codes during the period of colonization. Only matters considered private in European culture – those concerning family law – were left to Islamic courts. This has led to an interesting dynamic. Because of the centrality of law to Islamic society, there was a strong sense that the Europeans were stripping Islamic society of its identity. As a result, there was a tendency to safeguard traditional Islamic legal codes whenever possible. We will discuss in greater detail in Chapters 4 and 5 the tension this tendency has created in the modern era between reformers and traditionalists. Despite such tensions, however, Islamic law continues to represent the unifying element of diverse

Islamic societies. Throughout the numerous political upheavals that have marked Islamic history, Islamic law has provided a sense of unity and allowed the Muslim community to remain coherent. Scholars, far more than rulers, are considered the symbols of Islamic unity.

A good illustration of this phenomenon is found in the adventures of Ibn Battutah, the fourteenth-century legal scholar and world traveler, Islam's precursor to Marco Polo. From his home in Tangier, Ibn Battutah traveled throughout the Muslim world, including all of North Africa; the Arab, Turkish, and Persian Middle East, the Maldive Islands, Sri Lanka, Bengal, and as far as China. His diary, still available, records that as a legal scholar he was welcomed in town after town all along his route, and given fine hospitality and respectful audiences. In the modern era, instant communications have made such international travel and personal contact unnecessary. Yet it is still the religio-legal scholars who have the potential to appeal well beyond their ethnic, national, and sectarian origins. As we will see in Chapters 4 and 5, scholars, more than politicians, have influenced events in the Islamic world from North Africa to Southeast Asia.

Political Structure

There is no characteristic political system in Islam. A government is not marked as Islamic based on the nature of its executive authority. Throughout history Muslims have devised numerous political systems, from simple tribal groups led by elders (sheikhs); to empires ruled by caliphs, sultans, or shahs (kings); to constitutional democracies and military dictatorships. What is required for political legitimacy in Islam is that whatever executive or administrative system exists, the law of the land must be based on Islamic sources. This was explicitly articulated in the eleventh century by Shafii scholar al-Mawardi (d. 1058). In a work entitled *Al-Ahkam al-Sultaniyya* (The Rules of Government) he explains that the duties of political leaders fall into three categories: defense, treasury, and executive.[7] He is to defend the community from attack (article 3), maintain frontier defenses (article 5), and wage war against those who refuse to either become Muslim or enter into treaty with Muslims (article 6). Regarding fiduciary responsibility, he is to collect both the alms payments (*zakah*) required of all Muslims, and the legitimate spoils of wars (article 7). He must fairly determine and pay salaries from the treasury (article 8), and make sure those he appoints manage the treasury honestly (article 9). But most importantly, the ruler must make sure that the established principles of religion are safeguarded (article 1), and that legal judgments and penalties are enforced (articles 2 and 4). In other words, the ruler's authority is strictly executive/coercive. This position was reinforced by the great fourteenth-century Hanbali scholar Ibn Taymiyya (d. 1328), who said that the form of government can vary from time to time and place to place, depending upon custom and circumstance. But legal authority – articulating and adjudicating the law – does not only remain distinct from executive administration but is also of primary importance: the ruler can be any of a number of kinds, but as long as he makes sure an Islamic legal system is maintained, the government is legitimate.

In the medieval period, as the wealth of the Islamic empire grew, the office of the ruler became increasingly absolute in matters that concerned him. In fact, the Abbasids (who were called caliphs) adopted the pre-Islamic Persian model of kingship in which the monarch was considered "the shadow of God on earth." However, the matters that concerned the caliph were not generally those that concerned the population at large. It is ironic that, despite the caliph's absolute power, classical Islamic government allowed for unprecedented freedom among the populace. Other than collecting taxes, the government did not interfere in the daily affairs of society. People were born, educated, married; they made their living and bequeathed their wealth; they engaged in trade and other kinds of business – all without interference from the central government. Virtually all of daily life was under the purview of Islamic law, articulated and administered by legal scholars who operated for the most part independent of the central government.

It is often said that in Islam there is no distinction between politics and religion. This claim is misleading, however. It is true that Islam does not distinguish between political and religious values. The values that guide political or public life are the same as those that guide personal or private life. But in terms of administrative structure, Islamic law was quite separate from the executive branch. The executive branch had the authority to appoint judges, of course, but the judges were trained in institutions that were autonomous. In a system that bears striking similarities to our modern separation of powers, Muslim legal scholars maintained their autonomy through sources of income independent of government control. Their independence was maintained through a system of charitable foundations, called *awqaf* (singular: *waqf*) that have throughout history been at the core of Islamic civil society. A *waqf* is a kind of trust fund, a gift or bequest of property or the proceeds from a business to benefit society. People could give money or various business funds to establish something as small as a local fountain or as large as a hospital. Mosques are common beneficiaries of *waqf* trusts, and such endowments often include the education and support of legal scholars. These endowments had to be legally registered and were bound by the law of perpetuity; they could not revert to private use but had to continue to be used for charitable purposes as specified in their original charters. *Waqf* endowments were administered privately, by someone designated as the trustee at the time of endowment. There have been notorious cases of misuse of *waqf* funds, and government confiscation of *waqf* properties in order to control civil society. Theoretically, however, *waqf* endowments remain independent funds. As such, *waqf* funds allow for the independence of the institutions that trained legal scholars, the arbiters of political legitimacy in the classic Islamic model.

It should be noted, too, that ordinary citizens always had the right to appeal to the caliph if they felt that justice had not been served by the Shariah courts. Special courts were maintained for this purpose, called *mazalim* courts. Staffed by representatives of the central government, the officials of these courts had full discretionary power. People could come and appeal the decision of a local official or court, or lodge a criminal complaint, and the *mazalim* judge could make any decision he felt suitable, without being held accountable to standard Islamic law as established by the legal scholars.

Cultural Achievements

During the Middle Ages, Islam's unique system of religious freedom and administrative flexibility allowed for remarkable stability and growth. It also produced a period of peace and prosperity in which the sciences and arts were brought to new levels of perfection. The Islamic world from Spain to India – with its plurality of cultures, ethnicities, and religious communities – produced an unprecedented cultural efflorescence. At its root was an openness to diverse heritages and intellectual influences. The environment produced was one in which learning was both a cherished value and a collective pursuit. Muslim scholars who discovered long-forgotten Greek texts in Egyptian libraries worked with Christian scholars who could translate them into their native Syriac and then into Arabic. Combining them with the intellectual heritage of Persia and India, these scholars built a magnificent cultural edifice that included the most advanced science and arts of the age. As Dennis Overbye has characterized it:

> Commanded by the [Quran] to seek knowledge and read nature for signs of the Creator, and inspired by a treasure trove of ancient Greek learning, Muslims created a society that in the Middle Ages was the scientific center of the world. The Arabic language was synonymous with learning and science for 500 years, a golden age that can count among its credits the precursors to modern universities, algebra, the names of the stars and even the notion of science as an empirical inquiry.[8]

The Abbasid court of Harun al-Rashid (d. 809), immortalized in the stories of the *Thousand and One Nights*, is best known in the West for its splendor. The royal palace, surrounded by beautiful gardens, was so huge that its upkeep required hundreds of servants. It reputedly had thousands of finely woven carpets and curtains of spun gold. The queen's table was set only with dishes of gold and silver, inlaid with precious stones. The king's audience chamber was known as the Hall of the Tree, named after the decorative artificial tree that was its centerpiece; it was handmade of gold and silver and had mechanical golden birds chirping in its branches. Baghdad was undoubtedly the center of the civilized world. It received envoys from around the globe, including the court of Charlemagne, Harun al-Rashid's contemporary. (Harun also sent envoys to Charlemagne. In response to a request from Charlemagne, Harun sent as a gift to the court at Aachen a white elephant. Its name was Abu Abbas, meaning "Father of Abbas," in honor of the Abbasid caliphate. The elephant survived for eight years in the harsh European climate.) The wealth of Harun's court was based not only on taxes collected from the Abbasids' enormous holdings, but from trade in prized goods from Africa, India, China, central Asia, Russia, and beyond. Coins minted there have been found as far north as Germany, Sweden, and Finland. Medieval Islamic Spain was at least as sophisticated as Baghdad. In the tenth century Cordoba, the capital of Umayyad Spain, was known throughout Europe as a great city. Under Muslim rule, its population had nearly quadrupled to 100,000, roughly equivalent to the population of Constantinople at the time. Its streets were illuminated by thousands of state-maintained lanterns; it had hundreds of fountains and baths supplied by aqueducts. It enjoyed great prosperity based on an agricultural revolution that included the introduction of new irrigation techniques and crops. Oranges (the name comes from the Arabic *naranj*) and lemons (from the Arabic *laimon*), artichokes (from the Arabic *ardi shoki*), cotton (from the Arabic *qutun*), and sugar cane (from the Arabic *sukkar*) are among the many crops introduced to Europe at this time. The city also had public libraries. The court library alone had over 400,000 books. (The largest library in Europe at the time, in a Swiss monastery, held approximately 600 books.)

Indeed, although its political power would inevitably fade, intellectual achievements are the lasting legacy of the Islamic empire. Even before the time of Harun al-Rashid, translation of classical texts had begun. These were texts that had lain in oblivion in Egyptian libraries after the decline of classical Greece and Rome, and included the medical works of Galen and Hippocrates, and Ptolemy's and Euclid's work on mathematics and astronomy. The value of the texts was immediately recognized in the Islamic world, and the work of translation was considered so important that a family of Christian translators, Hunayn b. Ishaq (d. 873) and his son and nephew, achieved widespread fame for their work. They improved on earlier translations and expanded the works available in Arabic to include those of Aristotle and Plato. According to legend, Harun's successor al-Mamun placed so much value on learning that he paid Hunayn with the weight of the books he translated in gold.

Based on these translations, scholars in the Muslim world developed an intellectual culture unrivaled in the West since the days of classical Greece. Among the earliest areas to develop was the rational analysis of revealed truths. By adapting Greek rationalism to revelation, they developed Islamic philosophy. In doing so, their works became both sources for European knowledge of classical Greek learning, and models for developing Christian and Judaic philosophies. Al-Farabi (Alpharabius, in Latin; d. 950), for example, from Turkic central Asia, composed commentaries on Plato and Aristotle, as well as a highly original description of the ideal state. For him, that was "The Virtuous City" (al-madinat al-fadilah), headed by a morally and intellectually enlightened leader for the benefit of its inhabitants. The two most influential philosophers in the Muslim world were Ibn Sina (Avicenna, in Latin; d. 1037) and Ibn Rushd (Averroes, in Latin; d. 1198). Ibn Sina, from Bukhara (in modern Uzbekistan), was perhaps the most broad-ranging intellect of the medieval Islamic world. He wrote on art, astronomy, geometry, and medicine, among other topics. But his most lasting influence – even to the modern age – is in philosophy. His rational clarification of Islamic teaching was heavily influenced by his reading of Plato and Aristotle, and established the model for medieval philosophical theology. Ibn Rushd of Cordoba (Spain) interpreted Aristotelian thought more accurately than had Ibn Sina, and became early medieval Europe's most important source of knowledge of Aristotle.

The Muslim philosophers' work was controversial both in the Muslim world and beyond. Rational articulation of religious principles given in revelation, if kept within the limits of revelation, was acceptable to traditional scholars. That is what we call theology (called *kalam*, in Arabic; see Chapter 4 for a further discussion of Islamic theology). But philosophy had no theoretical limits to

Figure 1 Raphael's *School of Athens* showing Ibn Rushd with Aristotle. *Erich Lessing/akg-images*

its rational inquiry. In cases in which the results of rational inquiry seemed to conflict with revelation, philosophers generally concluded that revelation should be understood as metaphor for deeper truths inaccessible to the untrained mind. Such conclusions were unacceptable to religious scholars. This controversy prompted one of the most interesting philosophical exchanges of the medieval world: theologian al-Ghazali's critique of philosophers for "incoherence" (*Tahafut al-falasifa*, The Incoherence of the Philosophers), and philosopher Ibn Rushd's response (*Tahafut al-tahafut*, The Incoherence of Incoherence).

Al-Ghazali (d. 1111) was a Persian scholar of law, philosophy, and theology, but he experienced a spiritual crisis at the height of his intellectual career and turned to mysticism. There he found spiritual sustenance and became convinced that the practices of Sufism (see below) were the only source of the kind of certainty necessary to sustain a life of faith. That is what motivated him to write his diatribe against philosophers' attempts to find certainty through reason. He attempted to show that logical analysis was inherently incapable of dealing with religious truth and inevitably led to self-contradiction. Among his arguments was that if logic were capable of bringing certainty on metaphysical issues, then everyone would agree on them, just as everyone agrees on the conclusions of logic regarding mathematics, for example. But, in fact, philosophers disagree all the time about these issues. Al-Ghazali attacked a number of specific philosophical arguments, but was most concerned with proofs for the existence of God, since they entailed the claim that the universe is eternal, rather than created in time. Some philosophers had made use of Aristotle's argument about the need for a "prime mover" – a force to originate all motion, change, and causality in the universe – to prove that there must be a God, an "unmoved mover." The Prime Mover, as God, was eternal and perfect, and that means that the Prime Mover is also changeless, since change implies going from a state of incompleteness (or "potentiality," in philosophical language) to completeness ("actuality," in philosophical language). Therefore, the universe must also be eternal, or else one would have to claim that God changed (or moved) when He decided at some point to create the world. Because this conclusion contradicts the revealed truth of creation, al-Ghazali tried to demonstrate its fallacy. He said the problem was that the philosophers had failed to distinguish between the originator of the action and the action itself. He concluded that God willed from all eternity that the world and everything in it would eventually be created. But that does not mean that the created things themselves are eternal. In response, Ibn Rushd pointed out that al-Ghazali had failed to distinguish between willing something and actually doing it. One can decide to do something long before one does it, but it will not be done until the person who made the decision adds action to decision, bringing us right back to where we started: either the world is eternal or God is not perfect. Neither side was convinced by the other's arguments, and the theologians and philosophers parted ways.

In Europe Ibn Rushd inspired a school of thought known as Latin Averroism that vied with Thomas Aquinas' scholastic theology, which itself was based on the understanding of Aristotle that he had derived from the Muslim philosophers. This controversy prompted

Aquinas to pen one of his more famous works, *Summa contra Gentiles*, attempting to refute the beliefs of the "heathen" Muslims. It also landed Ibn Rushd/Averroes in Dante's lowest level of hell.

Jewish thinkers in the Muslim world also attempted to rationalize revealed religion by means of classical Hellenic philosophy. Working with texts that typically were translated from Greek into Syriac into Arabic and then into Hebrew, Jewish thinkers followed the same patterns as their Muslim compatriots. Ben Gabirol's (d. ca. 1058) *Yanbu' al-Hayah* (The Fount of Life) was an important source of Platonic thought in Islamic Spain as well as in Europe. The great Mosheh ben Maymon of Cordoba (d. 1204; Maimonides, in Latin; Musa ibn Maymon, in Arabic) was both a distinguished philosopher and physician, highly placed in the royal court. He was the personal physician to Salah al-Din (Saladdin, of Crusades fame; see Chapter 3).

Although highly respected in the Islamic world as in Europe, philosophy was relatively marginal to the daily life of medieval society. Of more obvious benefit were the practical sciences on which medieval Islam's advanced civilization was based. And of the practical sciences, the most prized was medicine. Al-Ghazali even counted the study of medicine as a communal religious duty, a kind of duty incumbent on a sufficient number of Muslims to meet the needs of the community. Medical expertise was so highly valued that, according to tradition, it was first revealed by God (through the prophet Idris/Enoch). Scholars in the Muslim world developed the most advanced medical research of the age. The Abbasids were particularly interested in supporting medical research. Harun al-Rashid established the first hospital in Baghdad under the guidance of Christian scholars trained at Gundaishapur Hospital, a research institute established in sixth-century Persia (Iran). By the end of the ninth century several other hospitals had been established in Cairo, Mecca, and Medina as well, and mobile medical units had been established for rural areas. These hospitals treated males and females, had outpatient facilities, and offered services for the poor. Many of the hospitals had mental wards, libraries, and classrooms. By the early tenth century, standard exams were needed in order to practice medicine in Baghdad, a city with nearly 900 registered physicians. The Mansuri hospital in Cairo, built in the thirteenth century, is still in use today for the treatment of the blind. It had a policy of turning away no one, regardless of gender, religion, or financial means, and was equipped with specialty wards, a pharmacy, lecture rooms, a library, and a chapel as well as a mosque. By the fourteenth century, a number of hospitals had been established in Islamic India as well. As in the Arab world, medical treatment was free, supported by *waqf* endowments and government patronage.

The famous Persian medical researcher al-Razi (d. 925) worked at an institute in Baghdad that had twenty-four doctors, each with a different specialization. His *Kitab al-Asrar* (Book of Secrets), translated into Latin in the twelfth century (*De spiritibus et corporibus*), was a foundational text on alchemy, the forerunner to modern chemistry. His compilations of medical knowledge were likewise translated into Latin and remained standard sources in Europe as late as the sixteenth century. Even more influential was the philosopher-physician Ibn Sina. Not only were his commentaries on Aristotle a primary source for Latin scholars, but his fourteen-volume compendium of Greek and Islamic medical knowledge – *al-Qanun fi'l-Tibb*, one of the first books to be printed in Arabic (1593) – was an authoritative text for European scholars. Completed in 1025, it was unsurpassed by Western scholars for 600 years.

Diseases of the eye were common in the Middle Eastern and North African climate of intense sun, sand, and dust. As a result, ophthalmology was among the medical specialties in which Islamic scholars made significant advances. The oldest existing systematic treatment of the subject is that of Ibn Masawayh from the ninth century. Trained as a mathematician, Ibn al-Haytham (b. 965) was inspired by Ptolemy's work on optics and made significant contributions to the understanding of vision. He developed a theory of vision incorporating Aristotelian ideas of matter and form with careful observations of anatomical experiments. In the process, he advanced the development of scientific method. His *Kitab al-Manzir* (Book of Optics) includes as well important descriptions of reflection and refraction.

Also associated with practical needs were technical developments, including those in the field of optics. Technicians produced magnifying and refracting lenses that aided in both microscopic and macroscopic viewing. Navigational instruments such as the astrolabe and sextant were perfected and produced in abundance. But perhaps the most universally useful technological development was the introduction of the use of paper, in the late 700s, replacing parchment (the skin of sheep or goats) as the preferred writing surface. The use of paper was introduced in the eastern Islamic empire from China. It spread quickly westward. In Islamic Spain writing paper was produced locally. It was via Spain that the use of paper was introduced to Europe, although its use was limited until the Europeans developed movable type.

Mathematics was a basic field in the medieval Muslim world and another area in which Muslim scholars excelled, again for very practical purposes. Accurate calculations were essential for efficient navigation, and the numerical system dominant in the ancient world simply did not allow the kind of accuracy these calculations demanded. Perhaps the most important contribution made in this area was Arabic numerals, replacing the letters used in the Greek and Roman letter-based systems. These numbers – which in Arabic are called *hindi*, since they were originally Indian – were adapted for use, along with the zero (*sifr*, in Arabic; in English, cipher), in advanced calculations by al-Khwarizmi (d. ca. 850) in the ninth century. Translated into Latin in the twelfth century, al-Khwarizmi's work was the source of the West's knowledge of algebra (*al-jabr*, which he developed in his book *Hisab al-Jabr wa'l-Muqabalah* [Calculation of Integration and Equation]). Al-Khwarizmi's work was also the source of the term algorithm, a Latin transliteration of al-Khawarizmi's name. Around the same time, al-Battani (d. 929) developed trigonometry. Like other mathematicians in the Islamic world, al-Battani studied the classical texts, verifying and refining their work. In al-Battani's case, he corrected some of Ptolemy's calculations of the lunar and planetary orbits.

Al-Biruni (d. 1050) was a prolific scholar and scientist, working in the eastern cultural center of Ghaznah (in modern Afghanistan). Knowledgeable in Persian, Arabic, Hebrew, Turkish, Syriac, and Sanskrit, al-Biruni wrote treatises on mathematics, astronomy, and ancient calendars, among other things. He supported the theory of the rotation of earth, conceived to be a sphere, against those who argued that the world was flat. He also accurately calculated the longitudes and latitudes of the earth. At the other end of the Islamic empire, the Spanish mathematician and astronomer al-Zarqali (d. ca. 1087) made numerous profound discoveries concerning the movement of the stars, and perfected the astrolabe in the process. Both al-Battani and al-Zarqali were quoted by Copernicus in *De revolutionibus orbium coelestium*. The science of astronomy was so highly developed in the Islamic world that permanent observatories were established. The ruins of what is probably the oldest observatory in the world are still visible in Maragheh, in northwestern Iran. Built in 1259, it attracted scholars from as far away as China, and included an extensive library. The contributions of astronomers from medieval Islam were also immortalized in the names they gave to various stars, such as Altair (*al-tair*, the flyer) and Betelgeuse (*bayt al-Jawzi*, the home of Jawzi, the Arabic name for Orion), as well as technical terms like zenith (*as-samt*) and nadir (*nadhir*).

The translations of classical Hellenic, Persian, and Indian texts, in the intellectually charged atmosphere of medieval Islam, became the basis of the Muslim world's great cultural flowering in the Middle Ages. They were the basis of Europe's, as well, and were transmitted there via Syria, Sicily, and, especially, Spain. A school was established in eleventh-century Toledo specifically for translating Arabic texts into Latin, the language of learning throughout Europe. There scholars came from as far away as England and Scotland to discover the learning of the Islamic empire and transmit it to Europe. The first translation of the Quran was produced at this school by Robert of Chester and Herman the Dalmatian at the request of Peter the Venerable, the abbot of Cluny in France. It was also in Toledo that the classics of Hellenic learning were translated from Arabic into Latin. The debt of Europe to the medieval Islamic scholars is impossible to measure. As historian Philip Hitti put it, "Had the researches of Aristotle, Galen and Ptolemy been lost to posterity the world would have been as poor as if they had never been produced."[9]

Preserving, developing, and passing on classical studies was not the only contribution of the medieval Muslim world to global culture. Islamic scholars also produced wholly original works, laying the foundations for academic disciplines that were not developed in the Western world until the modern era. The work of Ibn Khaldun (d. 1406) is a case in point. His *Muqaddimah* (Introduction [to the History of the Arabs, Persians, and Berbers]) is often cited as the first work of historiography and forerunner to the modern disciplines of anthropology, sociology, economics, and political science. In the *Muqaddimah*, Ibn Khaldun outlines patterns of social and political development, observing along the way patterns in history and economics. That is why historian Arnold Toynbee declared the *Muqaddimah* to be "the greatest work of its kind that has ever yet been created by any mind."[10] Ibn Khaldun was quoted more than once by US President Ronald Reagan, in fact, on the relationship between tax cuts and inflation.[11] He clearly predicted the observations of Marx concerning the impact of historical conditions on the development of ideologies. In order to understand social, political, and historical developments, he said, we must understand how the people in question make their living, their level of education, their religious beliefs and customs, whether they live in rural or urban conditions, and how they govern themselves. His insistence that individual events be understood in terms of their causes, since nothing occurs in a vacuum, became an essential principle of modern historiography. Ibn Khaldun was also an advocate of critical thinking. He rebuked scholars who simply transmit received wisdom without examining it in light of new information, and those who write with political bias, "smearing the reputation of others" for the sake of "selfish interests and rivalries, or swayed by vendors of tyranny and dishonesty."[12] Ibn Khaldun was fond of quoting Prophet Muhammad's assertion that "scholars are the heirs of the prophets," and perhaps no individual scholar or sentiment better captures the vibrant intellectual spirit of the medieval Muslim world than this brilliant and multifaceted scholar.

Spirituality and the Mystical Tradition: Sufism

There was another side to medieval Islam, besides the sophisticated bureaucracies and highly public, creative scholarship. The inward, personal side of Islam was also developing into a deeply spiritual tradition known as Sufism. For all the great achievements of Islamic rulers and scholars, Islam remains essentially a personal commitment. Law deals with the external manifestation of believers' personal commitment. But *islam* – submitting to the divine will – is more than a matter of mere obedience. Muslims believe that sincere belief will be manifested outwardly in righteous actions. But the core motivation for those actions is still internal. Pious actions reflect a kind of turning of the will that is at once passive and active. It is a giving of oneself to the divine will, but in so doing, it is also undertaking a commitment to do the things necessary to fulfill the divine will. This unique combination of acceptance and commitment – this *islam* – is expressed in the Quran as the virtue *taqwa*. The Quran calls for faith, hope, and charity (*iman, amal, sadaqa*) – the virtues most commonly discussed in Christianity – in terms that are directly parallel to their English meanings. But *taqwa* is not easy to translate. As discussed in Chapter 1, its common translation, "fear of God," is misleading. The term comes from a root that has to do with protection, preservation, or security. The Quran never defines the term, in the sense of limiting it to some specific action or actions. Instead, it gives examples of the kinds of actions that stem from a well-formed conscience. For example, the Quran tells people not to allow other people's unjust actions to lead them to unfair behavior. "So long as [the polytheists] stay true to you, stay true to them. Indeed, God loves those with *taqwa*" (9:7).

Taqwa does involve virtuous behavior, but it is not just an external thing. It also involves intentions. It is the internalization of God's will. *Taqwa* is the willing choice to allow one's conscience to be guided by God, expressed externally through goodness and charity. That willing submission to God will inevitably express itself through righteous behavior – and the combination of a well-formed conscience and honorable actions will preserve the believer from real danger – the danger of eternal punishment.

But how does one develop such virtue? Scholars and lawyers can help guide understanding and actions. But making God's will your own requires spiritual practice. This inward, spiritual aspect of Islamic practice, Sufism (Arabic, *tasawwuf*), is often called "interior Islam." It can also be described as mature Islam. Whereas a child is motivated to do good and avoid evil based on the promise of reward and the threat of punishment, a mature believer experiences personal gratification through virtuous deeds, and finds evil deeds personally repugnant. Sufi teachings and practice grew in Islam as a way to help people develop this ability to take joy in virtue.

Sufism has its roots in the earliest centuries of Islam. During the lifetime of Prophet Muhammad, the community benefited not only from religious and political leadership, but also from his personal example. Muhammad lived a life fully motivated by the desire to do the will of God. He was a prophet, of course, but he was also a man, and distinguished between those two aspects of his life. He cautioned people that there was a difference between those of his choices that were inspired by God and those that were simply based on his best judgment. On matters of revelation, the words he spoke were not his own; they had the unquestioned authority of their divine origin. But on everyday matters, he sought the advice of his community when needed, as guided by the Quran (see 3:159 e.g.), and displayed great humility. For example, when people asked him questions about planting their crops, he advised them that he knew no more about it than they did. This principle of consultation (*shura*) established a basis for democratic governance in Islam according to many modern interpreters. But even so, the Quran says that Muhammad set the best example of Islamic behavior. His personal choices, the way he conducted his life, and the way he treated people all served as examples that inspired his community to piety. But his death left a void in this regard. True, reports of Muhammad's actions in various circumstances circulated in the community and were eventually recorded in order to provide guidance for people. But reports are different from the personal, lived examples of piety. As the scholars and other officials established the details of Islamic legal and governmental institutions, the challenge of providing living examples of spiritual development was often taken up by individuals – some scholarly, some not – who simply gained a reputation in the community for their ability to inspire and guide others on the path to piety.

There were exemplars of the simple, pious lifestyle among Prophet Muhammad's companions and in the generation that succeeded him. Hasan of Basra (d. 728) is often mentioned in this regard. Known for his ascetic lifestyle, he is said to have worn the same wool cloak every day and still, when he died, it was sparkling clean. Indeed, the name "Sufi" – the term used to describe a Muslim who seeks in-depth spiritual development – comes from the term for wool (*suf*), as a symbol of simplicity and humility. The habitual use of prayer beads as a way to "remember God always" – a Sufi refrain – is also attributed to Hasan. As well, Hasan's lack of regard for the affairs of this world and focus on the path to eternal life inspired many. But among the most effective ways to inspire piety was through telling stories about the Prophet and his family. Some preachers became extremely popular for their ability to move audiences with uplifting stories of the Prophet's virtue, wisdom, and extraordinary devotion to prayer, attracting audiences of spiritual seekers from far and wide. Gradually, it became common for people to gather for extra devotional practices, "remembrance" (*dhikr*) of God through recitation of verses of the Quran, and discussions of religious themes in groups called "circles" (*halaqat*).

From informal beginnings such as the *halaqat*, Sufism developed into a diverse global phenomenon, with a number of distinct expressions. One was a distinctive intellectual tradition, as religious scholars were drawn to the path of spirituality. Harith bin Asad of Basra (d. 857), for example, was given the name al-Muhasibi, "the introspective one," for his emphasis on examination of conscience to ensure that one's motives for all actions are pure and honorable. This introspection, he taught, would yield ever deeper spirituality, and habitual virtue. Scholars like al-Muhasibi, who worked in Baghdad, attracted many students, forming early schools of thought. Al-Muhasibi is known as the founder of the Baghdad school of Sufi thought, known for such luminaries as Junayd of Baghdad (d. 910) and Ali al-Hujwiri (d. 1077), whose tomb in Lahore is a popular shrine even today. Al-Hujwiri's *Kashf al-Mahjub* (The Unveiling of the Veiled, or Revelation of the Mystery) is among the first systematic treatments of the developing Sufi tradition, and remains an important source of our understanding of early Sufis' lives and ideas.

The notion of progressive levels of spiritual development was soon formalized into a set of steps or "stations" of practice (maqamat) and accompanying psychological "states" (ahwal). The steps are derived from the Quran's encouragement to practice repentance, self-control and moderation, patience, gratitude, and trust in God. Ideally, these steps take the spiritual seeker to a condition of joyful, continuous awareness of the Divine Presence. As Sufi thought developed, some scholars began to identify the final stage of the spiritual journey as a kind of absorption or extinction (fana') of the self in the overwhelming experience of Divine Presence. The Egyptian Dhu'l-Nun (d. 859) and the Persian Bayezid (or Abu Yazid, in Arabic) al-Bistami (d. 874) are associated with this stage of the formalization of the Sufi way. Reflecting the experience of absorption or annihilation of the ego, al-Bistami is said to have proclaimed, "Glory to me; how great is my majesty!" Al-Kharraz (d. 899) of the Baghdad school put it another way. For him, the goal was "survival" or "subsistence" (baqa') in God. Perhaps the most renowned expression of this experience was that of the tenth-century Persian al-Hallaj (d. 922): "I am the Truth." Unfortunately for him, this claim was considered the height of blasphemy. Claiming to be "the Truth" (al-haqq) is equivalent to saying, "I am God," since "the Truth" is one of the divine names. Al-Hallaj was famously executed by dismemberment culminating in decapitation, and then burned, his ashes thrown into the Tigris river.

In response to such exuberant expressions of mystical rapture, other scholars encouraged moderation. The Persian Abu Nasr al-Sarraj (d. 987) and his contemporary Abu Bakr al-Kalabadhi (d. ca. 995) each wrote books describing Sufi practices of their day, and both cautioned against those who only pretended to have achieved special awareness of the inner meanings of things; these "charlatans" could lead innocent believers away from the path of true piety. Both books are valuable resources for understanding the early development of Sufi thought and practice, and show that Sufism was gaining popularity and spreading geographically. Al-Kalabadhi wrote in Bukhara (in modern Uzbekistan). But their works also indicate that the development of Sufism was not without conflict. Among the reasons for concern is that the highest state of spiritual awareness is sometimes described as allowing a special kind of knowledge (*ma'rifa*), a kind of direct intuition of Ultimate Reality (or the nature of things, or even of God). This special knowledge is described as going beyond mere belief in matters of faith, and beyond even the rational understanding of things for which traditional religious scholars are known; *ma'rifa* provides immediate understanding, and brings with it absolute certainty that this understanding is of divine origin. That kind of certainty leaves little room for argument – for example, from religious scholars who might understand things differently. It may even allow for the possibility of bypassing Shariah. For these reasons, scholarly Sufis like al-Kalabadhi not only cautioned moderation in Sufi practice, but also sought to demonstrate that Sufism is consistent with mainstream Islamic belief and practice.

Al-Sarraj's and al-Kalabadhi's work was followed by others' efforts to "mainstream" Sufism, including al-Qushayri (d. 1072). Al-Qushayri's *al-Risala* (Epistle) presents the biographies of dozens of the most influential Sufis and a manual of their belief and practice, specifically in order to demonstrate Sufis' respect for the Shariah.[13] But the scholar most commonly associated with integrating Sufi belief and practice into mainstream Islam is Abu Hamid al-Ghazali. In his magnum opus, *Ihya' 'Ulum al-Din* (Revival of the Religious Sciences), al-Ghazali describes the various religious sciences as they relate to worship and daily life. These are *fiqh* (jurisprudence or legal studies) and *kalam* (rational study of revealed truths; theology), and he says they are absolutely essential for all religious seekers, including Sufis. These fields of study provide the foundation-for all correct belief and practice. But, he says, they do not necessarily lead to the kind of deep piety identified as "closeness to God." The ultimate goal of correct belief and practice is to overcome the human tendencies that keep one from closeness to God, such as anger, greed, and lust. These negative traits must be replaced with the positive traits described above: repentance, moderation, patience, gratitude, and trust in God. The ultimate goal, then, is not a special kind of knowledge, as some Sufis had claimed, but rather the interiorization of virtue for the purpose of salvation. For al-Ghazali, the Sufi way was directed toward deeper awareness of and motivation to follow the revealed will of God. Al-Ghazali's autobiography, *al-Munqidh min al-Dalal* (The Deliverance from Error), demonstrated that he spoke from experience. He was a trained legal scholar of the Shafii school, and had studied both theology and philosophy in depth. But these intellectual pursuits left him unfulfilled. Sufism allowed him to move beyond mere obedience and imitation to the "life of the heart" where true faith is found.

Other scholars took a more philosophical approach, attempting to give a rational explanation for the mystical experience of absorption into Ultimate Reality. Among them was Shihab al-Din al-Suhrawardi (d. 1191). Al-Suhrawardi described existence in terms of light; all individual existents ("creatures" in ordinary language) are like rays, emanating from the One, Pure "Light of Lights," God. The further from this Source a being was, the paler its manifestation or share of Light. The goal of spiritual development was to move ever closer to the Source, gradually expanding one's participation in Light/Existence, and eventually losing all individuality by being absorbed into or reunited with the Source. For this reason, al-Suhrawardi is called a philosopher of illumination (*hikmat al-ishraq*). His teachings were judged by orthodox scholars to blur the distinction between God and creatures. He was therefore put to death, and so is often called al-Maqtul, "the Killed." But his Illuminationist thought was later taken up by the Persian Mulla Sadra (d. 1636), who remains one of Iran's most influential philosophers.

Among the best known of the Sufis who gave philosophical expression to Sufism is the renowned Spanish mystic Ibn al-Arabi (d. 1240). Ibn Arabi claimed famously that although it may appear that the world is full of endlessly diverse and discrete existents, in fact, all existence is One. This is the doctrine of the "oneness of being" or "unity of existence." Ibn Arabi explained this unity of existence by using a Neoplatonic theory of "emanation," very common in his day and still accepted by some mystical thinkers. According to this theory, God is Ultimate Existence or undifferentiated Absolute Reality. From that undifferentiated Absolute Reality is generated lower existents in a kind of cascade of descending degrees of perfection. This process of generation or emanation begins with divine awareness of its own perfect attributes: Truth, Beauty, Love, and so on. These Divine Attributes or Names of God then become externalized in the phenomena of nature: the celestial spheres, earth, human beings, the lower animals, and nature. Thus, all existence is an effect or manifestation of the Divine, a "theophany." But what has thus been externalized can likewise be internalized – in effect, reabsorbed into the Oneness of Ultimate Reality. And this, again, is the goal of the religious seeker, for Ibn Arabi. Using the terms *fana'* and *baqa'*, Ibn Arabi explains that human beings may, through careful practice and contemplation, ascend the levels of existence to be reunified with their source.

Ibn Arabi describes the experience of being reabsorbed into Ultimate Existence poetically: For example:

> My Beloved, joy of my eyes
> You are me as Myself,
> there where I am My companion at every moment –
> May God be glorified –
> You are my essence.
> Hand in hand let us enter together into the presence
> of the only Beloved.
> Let there be no more distinction between us
> Becoming One in Reality.
> Oh, how wonderful a thought
> and what subtle blending:
> The transparency of the glass, the purity of its contents
> become identical, causing confusion:
> Is it the glass or is it the wine that we see?
> All life in the universe vanishes.
> Moons are eclipsed, the sun disintegrates,
> the stars explode.
> We are thus thrice annihilated,
> similar to annihilation itself.
> And we attain to the three degrees of Permanency
> following the example of Permanency itself.[14]

Indeed, poetry became a far more popular means of expressing the mystical sense of the undifferentiated oneness of all existence than philosophy. A characteristic expression was that of the great Persian poet Jami (d. 1492):

> Neighbor and associate and companion –
>   Everything is He.
> In the beggar's coarse frock and in the king's silk –
>   Everything is He.
> In the crowd of separation and in the loneliness
>   of collectedness –
> By God, everything is He, and by God, everything is He.[15]

Like al-Suhrawardi, mystic poets often use the metaphor of light to describe the perception of the oneness of Being, as in this excerpt from Farid al-Din Attar's (d. 1220) *Mantiq al-Tair* (Speech of Birds):

> Who in your Fraction of Myself behold
> Myself within the Mirror Myself hold
> To see Myself in, and each part of Me
> That sees himself, though drown'd, shall ever see.
> Come you lost Atoms to your Centre draw,
> And be the Eternal Mirror that you saw:
> Rays that have wander'd into Darkness wide
> Return, and back into your Sun subside.[16]

Water, as well, was a common metaphor for the ebbing and flowing of undifferentiated Being, as in this excerpt from the same poem by Farid al-Din Attar:

> As Water lifted from the Deep, again
> Falls back in individual Drops of Rain
> Then melts into the Universal Main.
> All you have been, and seen, and done, and thought
> Not You but I, have seen and been and wrought:
> I was the Sin that from Myself rebell'd:
> I the Remorse that toward Myself compelled …[17]

Similarly, the incomparable Jalal al-Din Rumi (d. 1273) uses water to symbolize Being, and the inevitable return of raindrops to the sea as a metaphor for the creature's quest to return to the source of creation:

> Happy was I
> In the pearl's heart to lie;
> Till, lashed by life's hurricane,
> Like a tossed wave I ran.
>
> The secret of the sea
> I uttered thunderously;
> Like a spent cloud on the shore
> I slept, and stirred no more.[18]

The individual seeker's desire to return to the Source of All Being is often described in terms of profound longing, as if the perception of individuality is a burden. The liberation of the Sufi from what twentieth-century existentialist Gabriel Marcel would call the "the wound I bear within me which is my ego" was clearly a cherished goal of many Sufi seekers. But, as noted, claims of the oneness of all Being seemed to blur the distinction between the Creator and creatures, and thus would be seriously challenged, even by other Sufis. (See Chapter 4 for further discussion of critiques of Sufism.) But not all Sufism was expressed in this kind of ecstatic "God-intoxication," as it was sometimes called. Parallel to the development of the Sufi intellectual tradition, and arguably far more influential, was the development of popular Sufism. This took the form of various methods or "ways" – *tariqas*, sometimes translated as "orders" – toward spiritual development, each attributed to a specific acclaimed Sufi master. The search for spiritual development is clearly a personal one but, as the example of al-Hallaj demonstrates, it is one best pursued with guidance lest one become delusional. The recognition of this need developed into a regularized pattern whereby the spiritual seeker would submit to the tutelage of one who had already demonstrated success in the Sufi way. The student (the *murid*, *darwish*, or *faqir*) affiliates with a guide – *pir* (in Persian, *sheikh*; in Arabic, *murshid* or *muqaddam*) – to receive careful instruction in the steps along the spiritual path. As al-Ghazali explained:

The disciple must of necessity have recourse to a director to guide him aright. For the way of the Faith is obscure, but the Devil's ways are many and patient, and he who has no Shaykh to guide him will be led by the Devil into his ways. Wherefore, the disciple must cling to his Shaykh as a blind man on the edge of a river clings to his leader, confiding himself to him entirely, opposing him in no matter whatsoever, and binding himself to follow him absolutely. Let him know that the advantage he gains from the error of his Shaykh, if he should err, is greater than the advantage he gains from his own rightness, if he should be right.[19]

Some of the great Sufi guides were recognized as saints or "friends" of God (sing. *wali Allah*). These were people who had gained reputations for extraordinary piety that was often recognized as a kind of spiritual power. They subsisted in such intense awareness of the Divine that they seemed to have supernatural gifts. Being in their presence was transformative. They seemed to be able to read people's souls and know their innermost thoughts. Some seemed to evince the very spiritual energy that kept the world spinning as it should. As early as the ninth century, Sufis developed the notion that every generation has such a spiritual "axis" or "pole" (*qutb*), although they are not always recognized as such. The reputations of the great saints of Sufism spread quickly, often enhanced by graphic stories about their spiritual powers. Not every great Sufi was a *qutb*, but the spiritual gifts of many were often described in miraculous terms. Their closeness to God, their sainthood, was evidenced by their spiritual power or "blessing" (*barakah* or *karamah*). Many Sufis believed that this blessing allowed such saints not only to read people's minds, but often to know the future, bi-locate, withstand extraordinary physical duress, cure illnesses, and prescribe remedies for various afflictions. As well, this spiritual power was often believed to survive the saint's death, so that the tombs of saints became important pilgrimage sites for people seeking spiritual favors and even intercession with God.

But most important was the reputation of the saints' ability to guide people on the path to spiritual development. There were – and continue to be – many routes to spiritual development, with varying emphases on such practices as asceticism, contemplation, and prayer. Some stress solitude while others encourage social interaction. Some involve living in extreme simplicity; some incorporate rhythmic chanting, music, and/or dance. Sufi "ways" range from "rustic" to "ecstatic," but most fall between those two extremes. One of the oldest identifiable *tariqas* is the Qadiri, named after Abd al-Qadir al-Gilani (d. 1166). As a youth al-Gilani showed such intelligence and devotion that he was sent to Baghdad to study, and quickly became an expert in philosophy and law. But he also became known for his inspiring sermons advising Muslims how to go beyond mere obedience to fully spiritual religious practice. Instead of focusing on self-denial, as some teachers did, al-Gilani stressed simple piety, charity, honesty, and sincerity. His own life was a model of the kind of spiritual search that leads people to the spiritual path. The story is told of his trip to Baghdad as a young student. His mother had sewn his money into the lining of his clothes so that he would not lose it on the trip. But on the way to Baghdad his caravan was waylaid by robbers. The thieves demanded that everyone give them their money and jewels, but they overlooked the ragged-looking boy. When he realized what was happening, al-Gilani told the robbers that he had some money, too. The criminals were so moved by the boy's honesty and sincerity that they converted on the spot and went on to live virtuous lives.

As with many spiritual leaders, stories about the power of al-Gilani's piety spread quickly. The Qadiri *tariqa* and its offshoots spread throughout the Middle East, westward across North Africa and eastward to China and South Asia. Unlike some orders that devised their own sets of rules, Qadiris were advised to simply follow Islamic legal codes and internalize them through spiritual practice. The Qadiri order was also relatively informal; unlike some orders that required strict initiation rites and distinctive rituals, the Qadiris remained flexible so that local customs in various regions could be accommodated. Sometimes local customs or practices came to dominate a *tariqa*'s practice in a particular region so that they generated a sub-*tariqa* with a unique identity. This was the case, for example, with the Muridis, established in the late nineteenth century in Senegal and Gambia. Although the order was strongly influenced by the Qadiris, its founder Ahmadu Bamba stamped it with its own characteristics. Still, the Qadiri *tariqa* remains among the most widespread orders in the world today. Al-Gilani's tomb in Baghdad is still a popular pilgrimage site.

Another example of a localized order is the Badawi or Ahmadi, named for Ahmad al-Badawi (d. 1276), especially popular in rural Egypt. The miraculous works of its founding saint achieved such notoriety that his birthday is celebrated annually across Egypt. However, its other festivals are connected with the seasons of the Nile river and are timed in accordance with the pre-Islamic solar calendar of the Copts rather than the lunar calendar of Islam.

Similar to the Qadiri order in its simplicity, the Shadhili order began in Egypt under the inspiration of Abu'l-Hasan Ali al-Shadhili (d. 1258). The Shadhilis focus on carrying out their daily responsibilities in a state of prayerful gratitude to God. In fact, they emphasize spiritual wakefulness so strongly that they introduced the use of coffee in order to stay awake during long prayer sessions. The Shadhili order's popularity has spread across North Africa and Sudan.

In contrast to this kind of sobriety is another early order from Iraq, the Rifai, named for Ahmad al-Rifai (d. 1182). The Rifais' *dhikr* sessions are so loud that they are known as the "Howling Dervishes." Their loud chant, combined with intense, rhythmic head-shaking, is meant to induce a state of ecstasy that leaves them impervious to physical pain. This condition may then be demonstrated by skin piercings and other similar forms of self-inflicted torture.

The Rifai order, with its extravagant *dhikr* practices, spread westward into Egypt, northward into Turkey, and eastward into Asia. As noted, the Qadiri *tariqa* also spread far and wide, including eastward into central Asia and the Indian subcontinent. The Suhrawardis, named after Abu Najib al-Suhrawardi (d. 1168) of Persia and developed by his nephew Umar Suhrawardi (d. ca. 1235), is another early order that became prominent in South Asia. The Suhrawardis are a "sober" order, stressing the Sunni Shariah, regular prayer, and active community involvement.

Some orders are associated more extensively with Turkey, such as the Bektashi. The Bektashi originated perhaps as early as the thirteenth century in central Asia. They spread westward into

Turkey and the Balkans, as well as into South Asia. Their orientation is far more eclectic than that of the Suhrawardis, involving both Shii elements such as veneration of the descendants of Prophet Muhammad and Ali, and Christian elements, such as the use of bread and wine in some rituals and the full participation of women in all ceremonies. They are also known for their highly developed tradition of poetry. The Naqshbandi, named for Baha al-Din al-Naqshband (d. ca. 1390), originated in Bukhara (in modern Uzbekistan) and are quite the opposite: they are a notably "sober" order. Rejecting music, chanting, and dance, they stress instead "silent *dhikr*." Rather than encouraging self-deprivation to control carnal desires, the Naqshbandi focus on spiritual education through mindful simplicity, concentrating on God, and cultivating a sense of solitude even in a crowd. Nevertheless, the Naqshbandis also produced some great mystical poets, including Jami, cited above.

The Naqshbandis spread widely, including into South Asia, the home of the majority of the world's Muslim population. But one order in particular is associated primarily with South Asia, the Chishti *tariqa*. Named for Mu'in al-Din Chishti, who died in northern India in 1236, the order may well have begun far earlier in what is now Afghanistan. Among the most beloved of Sufi saints, Mu'in al-Din is known as Gharib Nawaz, "Friend of the Poor." He taught his followers to cultivate three virtues, attributed to al-Bistami: "a generosity like that of the ocean, a mildness like that of the sun, and a modesty like that of the earth."[20] The order itself reflected these virtues. Its lack of discrimination made its community centers extremely welcoming, especially in the environment of India's hierarchical caste system. Mu'in al-Din's teaching would later be summarized in the phrase *sulh-i kul*, "peace with all," by the Mughal emperor Akbar (d. 1605; see Chapter 4). Another enormously attractive aspect of popular devotion often associated with Chishtis is *qawwali* music. Still today, popular *qawwali* performers attract thousands to their highly evocative and often lively performances of songs of praise. Mu'in al-Din's tomb at Ajmer remains a popular pilgrimage site.

Other orders are perhaps better known in the West, such as the Mevlevis or "Whirling Dervishes." The Mevlevis incorporate a

Figure 2 Mevlevis or "Whirling Dervishes". © *Ian Berry/Magnum Photos*

rhythmic spinning into their prayer recitals. The spinning motion makes their full white robes fan out in a dramatic display. That spectacle, accompanied by music, has earned the Mevlevis invitations to demonstrate their ritual around the world, including at Carnegie Hall. The founder of their order, Jalal al-Din Rumi, cited above, is also well known in the West. His exquisite poetry is among the bestselling poetry in America today.

Among the most enduring themes of Sufism, and the basis of its universal appeal, is the emphasis on love. That was the theme of Sufism's first saint, a young woman from Iraq named Rabia (d. 801). According to legend, she was born into poverty and sold into slavery. But her piety so inspired her owners that she was freed, so that she could inspire others to lives of utter devotion and absolute, selfless love of God. Numerous verses, attributed to her and passed down through the ages, still have the ability to inspire. She confesses to God, for example, that she has two kinds of love for Him. She does nothing but think of God all day, but she says that is a selfish kind of love because it brings her so much happiness. The love that God deserves, she says, is one that strips away all separation between herself and God, so that she is no longer even aware of herself. Elsewhere, Rabia asks God to let her burn in hell if her devotion is motivated by fear of hell, and keep her out of heaven if she is only motivated by hope of reward. Her goal – like that of other Sufis – is to love God without external motivation:

> My peace, brothers, is in my aloneness
> Because my Beloved is alone with me there – always.
> I've found nothing to equal His love,
> That Love which harrows the sands of my desert.
> If I die of Desire, and He is still unsatisfied –
> That sorrow has no end.
> To abandon all He has made
> To hold in my hand
> Proof that He loves me –
> That is the name of my quest.[21]

The teaching of the scholars is important, but it is only a first step toward spiritual awareness, in the Sufi view. As Rabia puts it, "The real work is in the Heart."[22] Even the sober al-Sarraj (d. 987) proclaimed: "Love is a fire that has been lit within the breasts and hearts of the lovers. It burns and turns to ashes everything but God."

But it is Rumi who is best known for expressions of ecstatic love. His poetry beautifully expresses the yearning for spiritual freedom that characterizes much of Sufism. It is a desire to be released from the bonds of selfishness, desire, and greed, to be completely absorbed in divine goodness and beauty. Like Rabia, Rumi encourages people to go beyond the externals of religious practice, and seek deeper personal awareness:

> For years, copying other people, I tried to know myself.
> From within, I couldn't decide what to do.
> Unable to see, I heard my name being called.
> Then I walked outside.

The key to spiritual awareness, says Rumi, will not be found in books:

Today, like every other day, we wake up empty
and frightened. Don't open the door to the study
and begin reading. Take down a musical instrument.
Let the beauty we love be what we do.
There are hundreds of ways to kneel and kiss the ground.[23]

Instead, true happiness is to be found in the intoxicating love of God:

> God has given us a dark wine so potent that,
> drinking it, we leave the two worlds.
> God has put into the form of hashish a power
> to deliver the taster from self-consciousness.
> God has made sleep so
> that it erases every thought.
> God make Majnun love Layla so much that
> just her dog would cause confusion in him.
> There are thousands of wines
> that can take over our minds.
> Don't think all ecstasies
> are the same!
> Jesus was lost in his love for God.
> His donkey was drunk with barley.
> Drink from the presence of saints,
> not from those other jars.
> Every object, every being,
> is a jar full of delight.
> Be a connoisseur,
> and taste with caution.[24]

So popular is spiritual poetry that even today, for example, Muhammad Iqbal (d. 1938; see Chapter 4), although he was a profound philosopher and is the "Father of Pakistan," is most beloved for his poetry. And he begins his masterpiece, the *Javid Name*, with a tribute to Rumi:

> Tumultuous love, indifferent to the city –
> for in the city's clangour its flame dies –
> seeks solitude in desert and mountain-range

or on the shore of an unbounded sea.
I, who saw among my friends none to confide in,
rested a moment on the shore of the sea:
the sea, and the hour of the setting sun –
the blue water was a liquid ruby in the gloaming.
Sunset gives to the blind man the joy of sight,
sunset gives to evening the hue of dawn.
I held conversation with my heart;
I had many desires, many requests –
a thing of the moment, unsharing immortality,
a thing living, unsharing life itself,
thirsty, and yet far from the rim or the fountain,
involuntarily I chanted this song.[25]

Conclusion

The extraordinary accomplishments of the medieval Muslim
world stand as a tribute to the dynamism and creativity in the
service of God and humanity that many see as the true spirit of
Islam. Many Muslims see them as a reflection of the Quran's
unique commitment to intellectual endeavor. The Quran commands even Prophet Muhammad to seek knowledge (20:114).
But as Ibn Khaldun observed, no empire lasts forever. Muslims
soon faced the challenges of epidemic disease, internal conflict,
and external attacks that would eventually shake the empire to
its very core. But the law, science, and spirituality developed in
the medieval world would survive, and serve as a foundation for
reorganization and renewed growth in the Muslim world, until it
was ultimately subdued by European colonization.

Chapter 3

Division and Reorganization

The Crusades and Other Disasters

Among the catastrophes that struck the Muslim world in the late Middle Ages was the Black Death. That was the name given to the bubonic plague, a gruesome, deadly disease that swept Europe in the mid-fourteenth century, killing up to two-thirds of the population in some places. In England alone it reduced the population by half. But the plague hit the Muslim world equally hard. From the Black Sea, trading ships spread it throughout the Mediterranean, including Islamic North Africa and Spain, killing more than half the population in some cities.

Unfortunately, the plague was not the only disaster to hit the medieval Muslim world. It was also besieged by European invaders who believed they were fighting a holy war for Christianity. By the tenth century Europe had become mired in corruption and conflict. Much of it stemmed from the competition for supreme power between the Holy Roman emperors and the popes. This was not a struggle between secular and sacred, or earthly and heavenly authority. The competitors did not believe they were in the process of dividing up spheres of influence (even though that is how it turned out in the long run). Both the emperors and the popes were struggling for overall authority on earth, sanctioned by heaven. At the end of the eleventh century, Pope Urban II was determined to reassert church leadership, not just in the spiritual realm but in the earthly one as well. A request from the Byzantine emperor in Constantinople (in modern Turkey) for assistance in his struggle against the growing power of the Muslims in the Middle East provided the perfect opportunity. The chance for Rome to help Constantinople had the added bonus of demonstrating that the pope was leader of both Western and Eastern Christians. Pope Urban II therefore called a church council and challenged his Christian warriors to rise to the occasion.

Christians were already prone to be suspicious of Muslims. They had heard that they were "infidels," and followers of a "false prophet." St. John of Damascus (d. 749) had described Islam as a heresy derived from Christian sources.[1] Eulogius, the bishop of Cordova during the ninth century, when Cordova was the capital of Islamic Spain, did not help matters. He claimed that when Muhammad died Muslims expected angels to come and take him to heaven. Instead, he said, dogs consumed his body and therefore Muslims conduct an annual slaughter of dogs. Clearly, fear of Muslims was growing in Christian Europe. By the end of the tenth century the story of a minor battle between Charlemagne and the Basques at Roncesvalles in the eighth century had been transformed into one of France's earliest epics, the "Song of Roland." In this telling of the story, Charlemagne's enemies were not the Basques but the Muslims of Spain. The Muslims, so the story goes, had colluded with a disgruntled French soldier and killed one of France's noblest knights. The poem was the source of another version of the story of Muhammad's death, this one with pigs consuming the Prophet's body. This story was used to explain the Muslim prohibition of the consumption of pork. Other interpretations explain that Muhammad was killed by the pigs while he was drunk; that, Christian audiences were told, was why Muslims also prohibit drinking.[2]

According to the increasing rumors in Europe about Muslims, not only were they infidels, but they were ruthless killers determined to take over the world. They had already taken over most of Spain, along with parts of southern France and Sicily, not to mention the formerly Christian Byzantine lands in the Middle East – including the "Holy Land." Such stories prepared the ground for the papal call to arms, issued in 1095. Pope Urban II is reported to have contributed to the hysteria about Muslims as he tried to encourage his faithful at the Council of Clermont to join in his holy war. His exaggerated stories of hideous torture of Christians, including brutal circumcisions, aroused fear and hatred, of course. But vengeance was hardly a Christian virtue, and killing was still considered a mortal sin. It was a violation of both a sacred commandment and the example set by Jesus. Since the fourth century, when Christianity had become politicized under the emperor Constantine, Christians had been called upon to serve as soldiers, but they still had to do penance if they killed someone. But with the Crusades came the transformation of Christianity from a pacifist religion to one that fully condoned war under certain circumstances. Pope Urban II told his flock that killing people in wars declared just by the church was not a sin. It was virtuous, in fact, and any sincere fighter who died in the process became a martyr. All punishment due in the afterlife for sins committed in the here and now would be waived; the martyr was assured immediate entry into heaven.

Thus it became both a Christian duty and a quick route to "present and eternal glory"[3] to join in the holy war against Muslims, and many Europeans responded to the papal call enthusiastically. Rich and poor, professional and amateur, European Christians joined the call to retake the Holy Land. Wave after wave, they went into Muslim lands, killing Jews and Christians as well as the Muslims who were their main target. The first army of crusaders captured Antioch and Jerusalem, killing all their inhabitants. They then established their own "crusader states" in Jerusalem, Tripoli, Antioch, and Edessa. The second crusade, called by Pope Eugenius III in 1144, failed in its effort to take Damascus. Eventually, Salah al-Din ("Saladin," d. 1193) succeeded in organizing the Muslims sufficiently to fight back against the European invaders. An Iraqi Kurd who served the Muslim ruling family in Syria and Egypt, he led the campaign to recapture Jerusalem in 1187. The Europeans continued their invasions periodically over the next two centuries. But their last stronghold in the area, Tripoli, was retaken by Muslims in 1289. The ruins of crusader castles remain in the Middle East, as does the chilling effect of the term "crusade." It recalls the brutality of the Christians and the utter contempt they showed for anyone who did not share their European Christian identity.

To this day, the treachery of the European invaders is recalled with horror. When the Muslims conquered Jerusalem, taking it from the Byzantines in 638, Caliph Umar guaranteed the security of its Christian inhabitants, their property and churches. When the European Christians took Jerusalem in 1099, according to their own accounts, their leaders promised security to those who surrendered. But, except for a few men who had barricaded themselves in a tower, the Christian soldiers slaughtered all the inhabitants, men, women, and children, Muslim and Jewish. Then the Europeans disemboweled the corpses, to get at the gold coins they believed the Muslims had "gulped down their loathsome throats."[4] In Jerusalem's al-Aqsa mosque alone, according to Muslim sources, the crusaders killed "more than 70,000 people, among them a large number of Imams and Muslim scholars, devout and ascetic men who had left their homelands to live lives of pious seclusion in the Holy Place."[5]

The plight of the victims of the European crusaders was known throughout the Arab Muslim world. One of the historians at the time, Ibn al-Athir (d. 1234), quotes the lament of an Iraqi poet of the era:

> We have mingled blood with flowing tears, and there is not room left in us for pity.
> To shed tears is a man's worst weapon when the swords stir up the embers of war.
> Sons of Islam, behind you are battles in which heads rolled at your feet.
> Dare you slumber in the blessed shade of safety, where life is as soft as an orchard flower?
> How can the eye sleep between the lids at a time of disasters that would waken any sleeper?[6]

Despite the sympathy for the crusaders' victims, and the strong desire to rescue them, Muslims are proud to recall the valor and restraint shown by Salah al-Din as he rescued Jerusalem, in contrast with the crusaders' butchery. It took nearly a century for the Muslims to regain Jerusalem, but eventually the European leaders surrendered the city and asked for general amnesty for all its inhabitants. Otherwise, they said, they would kill all their wives, children, prisoners, and animals, and destroy the Islamic holy places. Salah al-Din granted them amnesty and allowed them to be ransomed by their people. Even though the Christian leader of Jerusalem looted both the Christian and Islamic holy sites, Salah al-Din let him go and had him escorted to Tyre. The Muslims were horrified that the ancient holy site, al-Aqsa mosque, had been used by the Christians as a storeroom and latrine, yet Salah al-Din did not rescind his amnesty. He simply ordered the shrines to be cleansed and restored to their original use.

In fact, Salah al-Din was not always so magnanimous. There is a horrific eyewitness account of the treatment received by two groups of religious warriors – the Templars and the Hospitallers, who had terrorized Muslims for years. Salah al-Din had some 200 of them beheaded, and the onlooker who gives us the gory report claims that the soldiers who carried out the executions received great praise. This was a violation of Islamic norms which forbid killing prisoners of war. Obviously, Salah al-Din believed that even as prisoners these soldiers were a threat to the survival of the community; he treated the other captive knights with dignity and allowed them to be ransomed later. But most Muslims are unaware of this deviation from Salah al-Din's standard policies. To this day, in recognition of his nobility in victory at Jerusalem, Salah al-Din is eulogized as a model of Islamic virtue: "just, benign, merciful, quick to help the weak against the strong." He was generous, courageous, steadfast, humane, and forgiving.[7] Salah al-Din's valor and nobility had saved Islam from the Western invaders. Their subsequent campaigns – and there were many – were ultimately failures.

A third disaster then struck at the heart of the Muslim world. No sooner had the European invaders been vanquished than the Muslims were attacked from the other direction. Beginning in 1220, waves of Turkic tribesmen, called Mongols, came riding in from central Asia, conquering everything in their path. Led by Genghis Khan, these nomads had no regard for settled, urban life. But they did depend upon some of the products of the civilized populations of Islam's great trading cities along the Silk Road, and these became desirable targets for the mighty Mongols.

The Silk Road, made famous by Marco Polo in the thirteenth century, was the ancient trade route established in Greek and

Roman times across the Middle East to China. It stretched from the Mediterranean to the Great Wall, crossing Syria, Persia, Afghanistan, Pakistan, India, and central Asia. Along the route travelers had to contend with treacherous deserts and mountains, including the highest in the world – the Himalayas, the Hindu Kush, and Karakorum; excruciating heat and sub-zero temperatures; and bandits of every variety. Yet trade along the route thrived until sea travel was developed enough to make it more efficient than land travel over great distances. The silk traded by the Chinese gave the route its name, but it was not the only commodity of value for the thousands who engaged in Silk Road commerce. Precious metals, ivory, oils, skins, ceramics, glass, and spices were some of the other desired products. As well, explorers, missionaries, and conquerors used the route on their adventures. Afghanistan and Pakistan were at the crossroads of the various trails that made up the Silk Road. Alexander the Great traveled to this region in the fourth century BCE. To this day, some residents of modern Afghanistan and Pakistan claim to be descendants of Alexander's troops. Buddhists from India came into Pakistan and Afghanistan in the first century CE, establishing their religion and leaving monuments, including the magnificent sculptures at Bamiyan that were destroyed by the Taliban in 2000. Nestorian Christians fled eastward from Roman authorities who had declared them heretical, in the fifth century, and two centuries later, Muslim traders and teachers along the Silk Road brought Islam as far as China, where it remains a significant presence today.

The Silk Road was for centuries the most important bridge between the East and West. Along its route were some of the most magnificent cities of the ancient world. Bukhara, for example, in present-day Uzbekistan, was established at the site of an oasis by the first century CE. Built around a central fortress, the city provided both protection from the dangers of the road and a trading site. Its inhabitants' gold embroidery and metalwork were valuable commodities in the East–West trade. In the early eighth century it was conquered by Arab Muslims and became a regional capital known for his beautiful mosques and many schools. One of the two leading *hadith* collectors, in fact, Abu Abd-Allah Muhammad ibn Ismail (d. 870), was from there, which is why most people know him only as al-Bukhari. But Bukhara was attacked and destroyed by the Mongols, under Genghis Khan, in 1220, and twice thereafter in the next century. Ibn Battuta, the Islamic Marco Polo, visited the city in the 1330s and said, "Its mosques, colleges, and bazaars are in ruins ... There is not one person in it today who possesses any religious learning or who shows any concern for acquiring it."[8] Samarkand, also in present-day Uzbekistan, was another ancient city of central Asia. Originally called Maracanda, Samarkand was established at the crossroads of the India and China routes on the Silk Road. Alexander the Great captured it in 329. When it was conquered by Muslims in 711, the city was renamed Samarkand and remained an important and prosperous regional center. Bukhara and Samarkand were considered among the most beautiful cities in the Muslim world, but, like Bukhara, Samarkand was also destroyed by Genghis Khan (1221).

Under Genghis Khan's successors, the Mongols continued their advance through the Muslim world. In 1258 they reached Baghdad and burned it to the ground. Unlike other Islamic centers like Mecca, Jerusalem, and Damascus, Baghdad was not an ancient city. It was a planned city, established on banks of the Tigris river on the site of a Persian village in 762, as the Abbasid capital. Its architects set up Baghdad around the caliph's palace and a great mosque, with three concentric walls surrounding it and four roads leading out from the center to the four corners of the empire. Markets and suburbs were built outside the walls. Nicknamed Madinat al-Salam (City of Peace), Baghdad quickly became the center of the empire's economic and cultural life. It was described in the *Thousand and One Nights* as one of the world's treasures. Ships from around the Indian Ocean and as far away as China visited its harbor. The city had known conflict in the years following the reign of Harun al-Rashid, but it was still thriving when Hulegu Khan, Genghis' grandson, and his troops descended upon it.

Some of the cities destroyed by the Mongols did recover. In Baghdad, the old Abbasid palace survives, as does the Mustansiriyyah, a school of higher Islamic learning built in 1234, but the city did not regain its greatness until the modern era.

Timur Lang, or Timur the Lame (Tamerlane, d. 1405), inherited the conquests of the Mongols. A Muslim born of Turkic parents near Samarkand, he took it upon himself to make Samarkand the most splendid capital of a reconstituted Mongol empire. He brought in experts to build great mosques and schools. His buildings were typically large, with domes and arched doorways and decorated with marble and mosaics, many with gold and precious stones. They are still among the greatest architectural monuments of the Islamic world.

The Mongol invasions traditionally mark the end of the political unity of Islam. It was also, for all practical purposes, the end of the Abbasid caliphate. While Baghdad burned, the Abbasid caliph packed up and moved to Cairo. His successors continued to be recognized as Islamic leaders, if in name only, until the last one (al-Mutawakkil III) was taken by Ottoman conquerors to Istanbul in 1517. However, many areas of the Muslim world reorganized eventually and went on to great power and prestige. We will examine the rise of three of them: the Ottoman Turkish and Arab world, Safavid Persia, and Mughal India.

The Decline of the Abbasids and Rise of the Ottomans

Egypt had already become autonomous. It was always difficult for the Muslim leaders to control Egypt from their capitals in Medina, Damascus, and Baghdad. Rebellions in Egypt had marred the reign of the third caliph, Uthman, and there were sporadic uprisings against taxation and religious discrimination thereafter. By the ninth century, the caliphs had begun to grant tax revenues to people they appointed as administrators to this rich region. They also chose as administrators for these "tax farms" people with no tribal ties in the area, primarily Turks who had been purchased as slaves, in an effort to maintain loyalty to the central government alone. These Turkish administrators soon established themselves firmly enough to become independent, too, including setting up their own slave army. The architect of this independence was a governor named Ibn Tulun. Through careful management of agriculture and taxation, his administration grew rich and powerful, and was even able to take control of Syria from the caliph. He also built the famous Mosque of Ibn Tulun, still standing in a Cairo suburb. Ibn Tulun's son then extended Tulunid control to Iraq. The Tulunids were overthrown by other foreign administrators, this time from central Asia, who were then taken over by the Shii Fatimid dynasty (909–1171).

The Fatimids were a formidable force. They were from a branch of Shii Islam (see below). Their name comes from that of Prophet Muhammad's daughter Fatima, since they believe that only Muhammad's descendants through the marriage of his cousin Ali to his daughter Fatima were legitimate imams (in Shii usage, "rulers"). The Fatimids therefore considered themselves not just independent of the Sunni Abbasid caliph, but the rightful holders of his position. From their original base in Yemen, they were able to establish sovereignty all across North Africa, as well as in Sicily, Syria, and western Arabia. They were fiercely committed to their cause, and gained the loyalty of many Muslims discontent with Abbasid rule. They quickly became wealthy and powerful. It was the Fatimids who established the city of Cairo in 969, and built it into a splendid center of military – including naval – power. Cairo was also a magnificent cultural center: the Fatimids established al-Azhar University there, which was the first university in the Western world and is still thriving. But the Fatimids had their own problems with the question of succession. A group broke away from the rest of the Fatimids in 1094: its members believed that the legitimate successor, Nizar, had been unfairly passed over in favor of his younger brother. Known by Islamic historians as the Nizaris, this group plunged the regime into civil war. The group is known by European historians as the Assassins, because they fought the crusaders so fiercely. (The name "Assassins" comes from the Nizaris' alleged use of hashish to prepare themselves for battle; they were called the Hashishin, "those who use hashish.")

The Fatimids were in power in Egypt when the crusaders first descended upon Jerusalem. Many people believed that the Fatimids' lack of cooperation with Baghdad weakened the overall Muslim effort against the Europeans. They were the ones that Salah al-Din overthrew in order to return Egypt to the Sunni fold so that he could create a unified front against the crusaders. But

Salah al-Din also established an independent dynasty in Egypt, the Ayyubids (1171–1250). With the powerful army he established in Egypt he was able not only to defeat the crusaders and gain control of Jerusalem and the Holy Land, but also to gain control over Syria, Iraq, Yemen, and western Arabia (Hijaz). Despite the stability and prosperity his victories brought to Egypt, power struggles developed. Like the Abbasids before them, the Ayyubids sought to maintain a loyal army by staffing it with slaves ("mamluks," from the Arabic term for slave), mainly Turkish. The idea was that, as foreigners, these slaves would have no local loyalties that could develop into rival power structures. But by the end of the ninth century, mamluk soldiers had gained control of the Abbasid caliphate. Abbasids remained caliphs, but mamluks were the real rulers (sultans), and even they did not control the entire Muslim world. The caliph was acknowledged as the spiritual leader of the Muslim world but Egypt was autonomous. By the mid-thirteenth century, Ayyubid mamluks became Mamluks – in effect, a dynasty in its own right, in control of the Egyptian empire that Salah al-Din had established.

Not all Mamluk sultans placed their sons on the throne, but all were from a particular branch of former slave soldiers. And to ensure that they were recognized as legitimate rulers, the Mamluks invited the Abbasid caliph who had been deposed by the Mongols from his palace in Baghdad (1258) to take up residence in Cairo. By this time, there were no pretensions of combined religio-political rule. The caliph had no earthly power whatever. He was a symbol of Islamic unity, and gave legitimacy to the political rulers.

Making use of their own military, the Mamluks were effective rulers for the first half of their two-and-a-half-century reign. They became heroes by defeating the sixth crusade, and repulsed an early Mongol invasion (1260). But they were not able to fully protect their lands. By the fourteenth century, the plague had hit Egypt and decimated its population. What is more, the Europeans came back, this time not as warriors but as traders. Portuguese traders developed safe and efficient sea trade routes around the Indian Ocean, bypassing the overland routes that had been a significant source of revenue for the Mamluks. And the Mongols came back, too. After they had taken over the Abbasid capital in Baghdad, they established a number of regimes throughout central and South Asia, and the Middle East (Southwest Asia). By that time, the Mongols had become Muslims themselves, at least in name. The famous Timur Lang (Tamerlane), who would rebuild Samarkand and make it his splendid capital, tried to unify all the Mongols. He subdued the local khans (rulers) in central Asia, the Crimea, Persia (which at that time included what is now western Afghanistan), and Mesopotamia (Iraq), and raided as far as Delhi in India. He was brutal beyond belief. Stories are told of entire cities' populations being massacred. His troops gained a reputation for being expert riders and archers who built towers of the skulls of their thousands of victims. But he was also successful, amassing the great wealth he used to rebuild and beautify Samarkand, for example. Inevitably, he turned again toward the Arab world. In 1401 he defeated Egypt's Mamluk army and took control of Syria and Iraq. Damascus was taken and Baghdad was once again destroyed.

By the time Timur died (in 1405, on his way to China), Mamluk power was on the wane. The Mamluks continued to rule Egypt, but they never recovered the country's economic prosperity or military might. Another of the autonomous forces during Abbasid times with whom the Mongols tangled were the Seljuks (also spelled Seljuqs), a dynasty named for the leader of one of the nomadic Turkic tribes from central Asia. They began as border guards for a semi-autonomous Persian family (the Samanids; see below) in the ninth and tenth centuries. By the mid-eleventh century they were in control of Baghdad, ruling in the name of the Abbasid caliph.

The Ottomans were another Turkic dynasty. Like the Seljuks for whom they originally worked, they had begun as border warriors, guarding the northwest frontier against invasions and launching their own attacks against the Byzantine forces in the name of Islam. The power struggle between the Seljuks and Mongols weakened the Seljuks sufficiently to allow the Ottomans to firmly establish their power in Anatolia (present-day Turkey) in the thirteenth century. Their armies became a magnet for men seeking employment – both Muslims looking for work as *mujahiddin* (warriors in the struggle to spread Islam), and Christians looking for work as mercenaries. By the fourteenth century they had established a regular cavalry and an infantry – called the "new troops" or Janissaries, consisting mainly of converted Christian conscripts from the Balkans. By the end of that century, the Ottoman chief Bayezid had managed to establish sovereignty in the Balkans. The name of the Ottomans came to symbolize hope for a reunified Islamic empire; the nominal Abbasid caliph in Cairo began to call the Ottomans sultans of Islam, rather than the Mamluks under whose protection they were living.

By this time, the ferocious Timur Lang felt the challenge. Although he was busy expanding his sovereignty from central Asia toward India, he decided to stop the advancing Ottoman powers. The two most powerful forces in the Islamic world at the time were competing for dominance. It was Timur's forces that triumphed in battle, at Ankara in 1402. But the result was not reunification of the empire. Timur's power would continue to be felt in the eastern regions, while the Ottomans continued their consolidation of power in the west.

The Europeans also began to worry about Ottoman expansion, and even organized a new crusade (1444) to try to drive the Ottomans back across the Dardanelles (the straits that separate Europe from Asia at Istanbul). But it failed, largely because of the loyalty of the Serbian Christian rulers to the Ottoman sultan. In 1453, under Mehmed (Muhammad) II, "the Conqueror" (r. 1451–81), the Ottomans put an end to the Byzantine empire, capturing Constantinople. Under its new name – Istanbul – it became the new Ottoman capital.

By the turn of the sixteenth century, Ottoman forces had subdued rival Muslim rulers in the region and expanded Ottoman sovereignty further in the Balkans – including Serbia, Bosnia, and Albania, as well as Crimea – and were well on their way to establishing naval superiority in the eastern Mediterranean. The idea of a reunified Islamic world may have been out of the question, but reunifying former Byzantine lands under the banner of the Ottoman sultan was not. The Ottomans simply had to oust their Seljuk cousins from Syria and Egypt. That was accomplished by Sultan Selim II (r. 1512–20), who was just the man for the job. He had killed his own brothers and nephews, and four of his own five sons to make sure no one interfered with his hold on the throne. By 1517 his forces had swept away the remaining impediments to Ottoman dominance in the Arab world, including the conquest of Syria and Egypt. The Ottomans then claimed that the last Abbasid caliph had transferred the rights to the caliphate to them.

The way was thus clear for Selim's hand-picked – i.e., only surviving – successor, Suleiman, to become "the Lawgiver" (r. 1520–66). Suleiman's predecessors had established a stable administration. The practice of granting land in return for service – the source of weakness in so many administrations of the time – was replaced with uniform taxation throughout Ottoman domains – avoiding another traditional source of discontent. Islamic law was guaranteed as the law of the land, but only part of the law. In a move that would have significant consequences in the modern era, the Ottomans devised a legal system whereby their legitimacy was maintained. The Ottomans enforced Islamic law, but at the same time they retained the right to issue their own laws for matters not yet developed in Islamic courts. Islamic law, identified as Shariah, was in force side by side with Ottoman law, called Kanun (Arabic: qanun). The application of Islamic law was effectively limited to ritual and personal matters (the proper ways to cleanse oneself, pray, give charity, fast, or perform pilgrimage, for example, as well as the correct procedures for marriage, divorce, and inheritance) – which were the most highly developed aspects of Islamic law at the time. That left the Ottoman bureaucracy considerable leeway in developing law for administrative, commercial, and other areas of vital concern to the government. Non-Muslim religious communities – Jews and Christians – were given autonomy, precluding dissent on grounds of religious discrimination.

The stability achieved during this period of Ottoman history allowed for enormous prosperity. Ottoman wealth can perhaps best be measured in its artistic achievements, chief among which are its architectural monuments. Ottoman architecture reached its high point during the reign of Suleiman, a generous patron of the arts. His chief architect was Joseph Sinan (d. 1588), a

Greek Orthodox citizen drafted into service in his early twenties, who designed hundreds of mosques, palaces, schools, public baths, and poorhouses, in addition to bridges, fountains, and granaries. Many of his works are still counted among the most spectacular in the world. Two of the most famous are the great mosques of Suleiman (Suleymaniyya) in Istanbul and Selim in Edirne (Selimiyya). Sinan's buildings are supremely light and elegant. Their enormous central domes and walls are pierced with dozens of windows, and their walls are covered in light colors, inlaid with beautiful tile and mosaic designs. The mosque of Selim is probably Sinan's greatest achievement. It went beyond his previous technique of achieving lightness and spaciousness through minimal internal supports, to designing a building without any internal supports whatsoever. It is not only a monument to architectural beauty; it is an engineering masterpiece.

The stability and prosperity of Ottoman administration also allowed for further expansion. From their base in Egypt, the Ottomans expanded their authority over the numerous autonomous regimes in North Africa (the Maghreb). By the end of Suleiman's reign their empire included Libya and Algeria (Tunisia would be included soon afterwards). To the Europeans, Suleiman came to be known as "the Magnificent," as he continued Ottoman expansion in their direction. Belgrade fell to Ottoman forces in 1521, and twenty years later so did Hungary. By 1529 Suleiman's army was besieging Vienna. Although Suleiman's westward expansion was stopped at Vienna, the Ottomans were powerful enough to take advantage of Europe's divided politics. The sixteenth century was a time when Catholics were battling Protestants, and ruling families were competing for control of the disintegrating Holy Roman Empire. The Habsburgs, still holding the title of Holy Roman emperors, reigned supreme in Austria, the Netherlands, Luxembourg, Burgundy, and Spain. France, naturally, felt surrounded, and was therefore happy to support Suleiman's efforts in the East, hoping it would weaken the Habsburgs. It was this combination of circumstances that allowed Suleiman's forces to take Belgrade in 1521.

Figure 3 The mosque of Selim complex (1557) in Istanbul. © *Chris Hellier/Corbis*

The Habsburgs and Ottomans continued to compete for Hungary for another twenty years, and Europe continued to fear the Ottoman expansion right through the seventeenth century, when the last attempt to take Vienna was turned back. By that time, the Ottoman empire was well into its declining years, although it would survive until the end of World War I, and with it, the caliphate. The last person to be named caliph, Abdulmecid II, died in exile in Paris in 1924; the office of caliphate was officially abolished in 1924. But despite the caliphal title, and the greatness achieved by the Ottomans, the Muslim world never again achieved political unity. From their stronghold in Anatolia, the Ottoman Turks consolidated control only over the Arab world. The Persian world was organized independently.

Persia: The Safavid Empire

While Ottoman expansion was halted in Europe at Vienna, its eastward push was stopped in Persia, which would establish the second great Islamic empire of the middle period. It is arguable that if Suleiman had concentrated all his efforts in the Islamic world instead of pushing into Europe, Islamic political reunification might have been possible. But as it was, Suleiman ended up fighting on two fronts. In the east, he pushed beyond Syria, taking Iraq and parts of Azerbaijan. There he ran up against an the expanding power of the Persian shah (king) Esmail and his son Tahmasp I.

After the destruction of Baghdad (1258), various Mongol dynasties established their regimes in the region, and competed for control the area after the death of the last Il Khanid, Abu Said in 1335. Not surprisingly, it was Timur Lang who came out on top, taking Khurasan and eastern Persia by 1385. From there he continued to consolidate his holdings in the region, as we saw above. But while the warrior Seljuks were able to gain dominance in Baghdad and Syria, giving way eventually to the warrior Ottomans, in Persia it was the descendants of a religious order, the Safavids, who were able to oust the Mongols. This would give a very different character to Persian history from that of the Turks and Turkish-dominated Arabs.

The Safavids were a Sufi order that originated in Turkic Azerbaijan in the fourteenth century. Identifiable by their red turbans (which is why they were known as Kizilbash, or "Red Heads"), the Safavids attracted followers from throughout Iran as well as its surrounding territories (Syria, eastern Anatolia, the Caucasus and beyond). As their influence grew, their ideology also developed. During the fifteenth century, they highlighted their distinction from their primarily Sunni neighbors by identifying themselves as a specifically Shii order. Basing their legitimacy on the main branch of Shii Islam, they became more and more powerful, and gradually overcame other local rulers. By the turn of the sixteenth century, they had evicted the Mongols from northern Iran and declared themselves sovereign.

As Safavid influence spread northwestward into eastern Anatolia, the Ottomans decided they had to stop them. As champions of Sunni orthodoxy, the Ottomans considered the Shii and Sufi Safavids to be heretics. Several serious clashes between the Ottomans and Safavids took place in the early sixteenth century. The Ottomans took the challenge so seriously that when their own Sultan Bayezid (r. 1482–1512) began to be attracted to Sufi mysticism they deposed him. The ferocious Selim I then took up the struggle against the Shii Safavids. The Safavids were no match for his artillery-equipped troops. Still using archers, the Safavids were defeated in 1514 and sent back into their central Persian strongholds. But the Ottomans, also engaged in Europe, were unable to gain further victories against the Safavids. In a treaty signed at Amsaya (1555), Suleiman agreed to leave Azerbaijan and the Caucasus to Persia, and allow Persian pilgrims access to the holy cities of Mecca and Medina, and well as to Shii pilgrimage sites in Iraq.

The western Muslim world thus achieved equilibrium, delineated between the Sunni Ottomans (1517–1922) and the Shii Safavids (1502–1722). Shii Islam, now represented in a state, was free to develop its unique character. As noted in Chapter 1, Sunni and Shii Islam differ very little on essential doctrinal issues. The main difference between the two branches of Islam lies their respective theories of government and its relationship to prophecy. In Sunni Islam, the death of Prophet Muhammad marked the end of prophecy and the beginning of human beings' responsibility to find ways to implement the Quran's demand for justice, inspired by the Prophet's example, in ever-changing circumstances. In Shii Islam, the death of the Prophet marked the end of prophecy, but not the end of prophetic guidance. According to Shii thought, divinely inspired guidance continues through the family of Prophet Muhammad. His descendants were therefore the only legitimate successors to the Prophet's earthly leadership. His descendants were not themselves prophets, but their interpretations of scripture were authoritative. By contrast, in Sunni Islam legal scholars were charged with the responsibility of interpreting scripture for application in daily life, and the profession of scholarship was open to anyone willing to undertake the requisite training. As it happens, Shiis did not always agree on which descendant of the Prophet should rule. Shiism split during the seventh century over this issue; there had been other disputes earlier, and there were other minor splits later on. But the major branch of Shii thought (the Twelvers, *Ithna'ashari* Shiis) believes that the line of Prophet Muhammad's descendants eligible for community leadership ended by the ninth century. The last imam (whether he is identified as Ismail as the Seveners/Ismailis believe, or as Muhammad al-Muntazar, as the Twelver Shiis believe, or as one of the other candidates identified by smaller branches of Shii Islam) will return before the end of the world as the Mahdi, "guided one." The Mahdi will then lead humanity in creating a just society before the end of time and final judgment. Until that time, the last imam exists in a hidden or spiritual form (often called "occultation," *al-ghaibah*, in Arabic), and continues to offer guidance to the community through the legal scholars. Until the Mahdi returns, Shii Muslims are instructed to cooperate with their governments and follow the guidance of the scholars.

In the absence of the imam, Sunni and Shii theories of government, therefore, are not terribly different. Shii Islam, however – particularly Twelver Shiism – did develop an ethos or overall character different from that of the dominant Sunnis. This character stems primarily from the fact that the Shii were persecuted by the early Sunnis. The Prophet's grandsons, championed by the Shii, were harassed by the Sunni Umayyads, and the younger grandson, Husayn, was ultimately martyred. As a result, from its earliest days Shii Islam was a voice of vigilance and protest against injustice, and suffering for the cause of justice. As Mohammad Khatami, former president of Iran put it:

> In the Muslim world, especially in Iran, whenever oppressed people have risen against tyranny, their activism has been chan-neled through religion. People have always witnessed the fiery and bloodied face of religious revolutionaries who have risen to fight oppression and despotism.
>
> Our social conscience is replete with memories of the clash of true believers with hypocrites who have used religion to justify

people's misery. Our part of the world has witnessed the historical antagonism between truth- and justice-seeking religion and the oppressive and misguided views of religion that have been the tool of oppressors.
Is it not true that in the history of Islam, religion has opposed religious and secular tyranny?[9]

It was during the Safavid period that Twelver Shii Islam's ethos of suffering in the struggle against injustice was institutionalized. The martyrdom of Imam Husayn in 680 by Umayyad troops took place at Karbala on the 10th of Muharram (the first month of the Islamic calendar). Karbala, in Iraq, became – as it remains today – a major site pilgrimage for Shiis. The month of Muharram became a time of mourning (ta`ziyyah), similar to the Christian period of Lent, in memory of the suffering of the martyrs. It is still marked by poetry recitations and reenactments of the martyrdom of Husayn, similar to Christian Passion plays.

Safavid Persia also became a place of high cultural achievement. As in Ottoman Turkey, the peace provided by political equilibrium allowed for prosperity and cultural productivity. By the time Islam came to the Persians, they already had a long history of urban society and efficient bureaucracies. In fact, it was a Persian family who organized the Abbasids' bureaucracy for them. The Safavids therefore readily developed an efficient state administration, which was headquartered in Isfahan. The great Safavid Shah Abbas (r. 1588–1629) made Isfahan his capital and set about beautifying it with parks and fountains, and architectural monuments unrivaled to this day. The city is centrally organized around an enormous plaza surrounded by bazaars (bazaar is the Persian word for "market"), parks, palaces, schools, and other public buildings. It is dominated by mosques, including the magnificent mosques of Shah Abbas and Lotfallah. The Lotfallah mosque is considered one of the world's most beautiful religious buildings. Its facade is covered with tiles of various shades of blue; its graceful Persian-style dome is decorated with an elegant turquoise floral design on a white background. People who visit the mosque say its overall effect is so awesome as to inspire spirituality even in unbelievers. Shah Abbas also patronized other arts, including one of Persia's most unique contributions, the painting of miniatures. Among the oldest surviving examples of this exquisite art form are those from Isfahan. Works by the city's undisputed master, Reza Abbasi, are on display at New York's Metropolitan Museum of Art.

Eventually, Safavid leaders succumbed to attacks from powerful neighbors. Interestingly, the last Safavid king was overthrown by an Afghan tribal leader, Mahmud of Kandahar (1722). Later, another Persian dynasty would rise, the Qajars (r. 1794–1925), and they would be replaced by the Pahlavis in the twentieth century. But the influence of Safavid culture remained dominant. Among the first tasks undertaken by Reza Shah Pahlavi (r. 1925–41) was the restoration of Isfahan's architectural beauty. Persian culture was also undoubtedly influential in shaping the culture of the third great center of Islamic life in the middle period, Mughal India.

India and the Rise of the Mughals

On the eastern borders of Persia was the autonomous Ghaznavid empire. It had arisen during the decline of Samanid control of western Afghanistan. The Samanids were a Persian family who had gained autonomy under Abbasid rule and taken control of much of Afghanistan as well as the great Silk Road cities of Khurasan, Samarkand, and Bukhara, their capital. They were powerful and their reign was prosperous, known for great art and culture. By the eleventh century, the Samanids' border guards, the Seljuks, had taken control and begun expanding westward. On the eastern side of the empire, another of their former slave guards (Sebuktegin, d. 997) had broken away and established himself as the ruler of Ghazna (present-day Ghazni, Afghanistan). His son Mahmud (d. 1030) then expanded his control. As the Samanids' power decreased, Mahmud took temporary control of parts of Persia, but his major impact was in the other direction. After a series of brutal raids, he gained control across present-day Pakistan. To that Hindu and Buddhist region he brought what would become the permanent presence of Islam. His raids, particularly those on Hindu temples, also brought him vast wealth. (Mahmud, like Timur after him, was decidedly intolerant of other religions. He perhaps even set an example for the modern-day Taliban in his destruction of other people's religious icons.) He used this wealth to finance cultural development in his realm, particularly Persian high culture. Although he was of Turkic background and anti-Shii religiously, he established Persian as the language of culture in his realm. He also brought famous scholars such as the scientist al-Biruni and the poet Firdawsi to his court; the final version of Firdawsi's famous epic *Shah Nameh* (Book of Kings) was dedicated to this ruthless ruler. Written in verse form, the *Shah Nameh* tells the story of Persian history from ancient times to the Arab conquests. It remains a classic of Persian literature.

Successors to Mahmud's power-base moved the capital to Lahore, the great ancient city of the Punjab, having lost eastern ground to Persian powers. There they remained for some time, and much of the region became Muslim. Then, around 1190, the Persian Ghurid rulers who had taken control of Ghazna, began raids into Indian territory. They ousted the last of Mahmud's successors at Lahore and within ten years began a military campaign right across northern India. It was the slave-warriors (mamluks) who worked for the Ghurids who ultimately established what would become Islam's lasting power-base in India: the sultanate of Delhi.

As Mahmud had done in Ghazna, once they had established peace the sultans of Delhi introduced Persian-influenced Islamic high culture. Poets and artists were welcomed there, and merchants found ready markets. Sufi missionaries brought their mystical teachings, becoming the major source of Islamic religious learning in India. Indigenous Hindu society in the region was divided along caste lines and well established in their localized realms. Muslim rulers had more expansive territorial designs. Free of caste restrictions and offering religious freedom to their subjects, the Muslims became in effect a ruling class. The sultans of Delhi built on the prosperity offered by trade and local agriculture, and were able to expand their sovereignty during the thirteenth and fourteenth centuries. By 1350 they had gained dominance throughout much of the Indian subcontinent.

The sultanate of Delhi was effectively ended by another of Timur Lang's infamous attacks. This one was particularly brutal. Timur considered the Delhi sultans' policy of religious freedom to be unconscionable. For Timur, unlike most Muslims, religious freedom was not an essential feature of Islam; in fact, he was mortally opposed to it. In 1398 his troops destroyed Delhi and massacred its inhabitants. Fortunately for all concerned, however, Timur was dead by 1405, allowing Islam in India to recover from his near-fatal blow. Autonomous Muslim rulers outside Delhi survived, and eventually Islamic power was reconstituted in Delhi, under the Lodi sultans, from the highlands of Afghanistan, in the late fourteenth century.

What would become the great Mughal (i.e., Mongol) empire in India was begun by Babur (d. 1530). Babur had inherited Timur's Mongol power in Kabul and, in true Mongol fashion, began to look beyond his borders. In 1526 he defeated the Lodi sultans (at the battle of Panipat) and took control of Delhi. But Babur's Mongol successors would overcome their heritage of intolerance. They would foster a culture of inter-religious respect that would allow them to maintain dominance in India until the British took control in the eighteenth century.

The architect of the Mughals' ecumenical culture was Babur's grandson Akbar "the Great" (r. 1556–1605). As we have seen, the stability and prosperity of the Ottoman and Safavid empires were established despite the challenges posed by the ferocious Timur. Akbar was the only ruler of the middle period who was a direct descendant of Timur (as well as of Genghis Khan). But, defying his intolerant heritage, he was among Islam's most enlightened rulers. Inheriting control of virtually all of northern India, including parts of present-day Pakistan, Bangladesh, and Afghanistan, Akbar found himself not only a cultural minority but a religious one as well. Muslims were and would remain a minority in India, along with dozens of other minorities – including Christians, Jews, and Zoroastrians. But Akbar welcomed religious diversity. He established a uniform tax system that did not discriminate against non-Muslims, and incorporated Hindus into his administration. In order to preclude divisive and destructive religious discrimination, he promoted respect for a non-sectarian monotheism (called *din-i ilahi*, "divine religion"). Allowing full expression of the rich cultural heritage of his many diverse subjects, Akbar thus gave rise to one of the most unique and culturally productive regimes in Islamic history.

Although Islamic rule in India ended over two centuries ago, and hostility between the Hindus and Muslims remains, Mughal architecture still offers enduring and cherished evidence of its legacies. The planned city of Fatehpur Sikri, for example, built by Akbar, is a wonder of sixteenth-century engineering. Its monumental gateway clearly reveals the combined Hindu and Islamic styles. It is ornately carved with multiple arches over a post and lintel structure, and opens directly into the Great Mosque of Fatehpur Sikri. Unfortunately, Akbar and his technicians overlooked one essential aspect of life in their planning: water. The city had to be abandoned for lack of this vital resource, but it remains a popular tourist attraction. A massive gate – the Delhi Gate – was a feature of another of Akbar's achievements, the Agra Fort.

Akbar's son and grandson provided even greater architectural monuments to India. Jahangir (r. 1605–27), who was born on the site of Fatehpur Sikri, added to the beauty of the Mughal landscape, creating the Shalimar Gardens in Kashmir, for example. But his greatest devotion was to art. He was a painter himself, and devoted enormous resources to patronizing the art. Earlier Mughal painting is known for its riotous colors and movement, but Jahangir's artists, known primarily for their portraiture, developed a more delicate, sedate, almost spiritual style. Jahangir's son Shah Jahan (r. 1628–58) continued to support art (in the UK, examples can be found in Windsor Castle library), but not to the extent that his father did. He will always be remembered for his architectural monuments. Among them are the Great Mosque and Red Fort at Delhi – again, a massive structure of red sandstone, with rows and rows of columns and arches under a flat roof. He also built the Shalimar Gardens of Lahore, eighty acres of lush gardens beautifully landscaped and accented by reflecting pools and fountains of white marble. But none is more famous than the Taj Mahal, the splendid mausoleum he commissioned at Agra for his wife Mumtaz Mahal. Its white marble dome and towers, complemented by its trademark reflecting pool, remain a symbol of love and spirituality for people of all faiths and none.

The respect for religious diversity institutionalized by early Mughal rulers certainly contributed to the peace and prosperity of the realm, reflected in its refined cultural achievements. The period is also noteworthy for its intellectual sophistication. In Mughal India science and scholarship continued to flourish. A unique reflection of this openness and sophistication is seen in the genre of humorous social satire, for example in the stories of Raja Birbal, Emperor Akbar's court poet. Birbal was a peasant from outside Agra who had helped the emperor find his way to Agra one day. In gratitude, the emperor told the boy to visit him someday in his capital. When he was a bit older, Birbal decided the time had come. He approached the guard at the royal court and found him skeptical, to say the least. He managed to convince him to let him in, but only by promising to share half of any gift the emperor might bestow on the young man. He entered Akbar's chamber and the king remembered him at once and was delighted he had come. "Ask for anything your heart desires and it shall be yours," he said. Birbal said, ""If [Your Majesty] pleases, my dearest wish is to be given fifty lashes of the whip!" Naturally, people thought he was crazy but when the king asked him why he wanted such a strange gift, Birbal explained that the guards would only let him in if he split any gift with them. "Are our people to be kept away by a greedy, wicked guard?" he thundered. "Send for the rascal!" The guard was sentenced to the entire "gift" of fifty lashes and never again tried to bully poor people who sought an audience with the emperor. And [the young man] was given a place at the court, with all the comforts that went with it. "We confer on you the title of Raja Birbal from this day on," the emperor declared. "And you shall stay near us and amuse and guide us henceforth!"[10] From then on, Birbal both entertained and gently criticized the mighty and meek alike.

Even more interesting as a reflection of the times are the stories of Nasroddin. Nasroddin was a legendary figure who symbolized both wisdom and foolishness, or perhaps wisdom and social commentary disguised as foolishness. Satire of any aspect of society could be clothed in a story about Nasroddin. If the story were cleverly enough presented, it might circulate far and wide as a vehicle of people's concerns.

One of the stories told about Nasroddin reveals a growing concern about the excessive mysticism in Indian popular religion. According to this story, Nasroddin was sent by the king to find out about the spiritual leaders who had become so famous in India at the time. Nasroddin traveled the countryside, interviewing members of the mystical communities, and listening as they outdid one another with stories of their leaders' wondrous and miraculous works. He then returned home and wrote his report for the king. It contained only one word: "Carrots." The king asked him what that was supposed to mean. What did carrots have to do with mysticism? Nasroddin explained that, like a carrot, most of the reality of mysticism is hidden from view; very few people recognize it when they see it growing; it must be cultivated and if it isn't, it will deteriorate; and "there are a great many donkeys associated with it."[11]

In fact, Indian Islam had traditionally been dominated by Sufi teachers, particularly those from the Chishti and Suhrawardi orders. Islamic political sovereignty in the Indian subcontinent was established by military force. But spreading the religion was left primarily to the Sufi preachers. As noted in Chapter 2, the Chishtis were deeply spiritual. Their preachers taught people to avoid materialism in all its forms. Poverty was considered a virtue and social involvement a distraction. The goal of spiritual life in Chishti thought was to achieve union with the divine One by transcending the self through chanting (*dhikr*). Chishti communal centers (*khanaqahs*) became major sources of Islamic teaching from the thirteenth and fourteenth centuries in northern India – for many people, they were the only source of Islamic teaching. The Suhrawardi order cultivated piety through *dhikr* based on the names of God. A number of other non-traditional forms of religious expression also developed on the popular level, such as those of the Qalandars. Less organized than Sufi *tariqas*, these "irregulars" often displayed unorthodox behavior and little respect for Shariah.

The Sufi approach to spiritual development allowed for a wide range of religious expression and was, as such, naturally tolerant. But it also gave rise to concern among scholars that the essential roots of Islamic teaching were being lost. They were afraid that Islam's core teachings were being replaced with a kind of amalgam of religious and spiritual teachings, and that many of them were distinctly un-Islamic – a development that was bound to displease the religious authorities. Beyond that, the mystical belief that all reality is in fact One seemed to be heretical. It was contrary to Islamic monotheism. Traditional religious scholars believed that it contradicted the Islamic view that God is the Creator of all individuals, and that there is eternally an essential distinction between God and creatures. To claim that human beings share in any way in divinity seemed to be not only heretical but blasphemous. In fact, this monism (belief that all existence is essentially unified) appeared to some scholars to be influenced by Hinduism. After all, Hindus, despite their multiplicity of gods, believe that ultimately there is only One, one reality in which all individual existents – inanimate, animate, divine – participate. Traditional religious scholars therefore began to feel the need to root out what they considered un-Islamic influences.

The concern for orthodoxy in Indian Islam showed itself as early as the sixteenth century, in response to the growing popularity of a new religion that seemed to combine Islam and Hinduism: Sikhism. There had been significant interaction between Hindu and Islamic spirituality. Many spiritual exercises of Hindu yoga practice – controlled breathing patterns, for example, and the use of meditation to achieve heightened religious awareness – found their way into Sufi practice, and Islamic monotheism found increasing expression in otherwise polytheistic Hindu thought. But Sikhism was a new religious movement that actively blended characteristically Islamic monotheism with Hindu monism. The Sikh religion was begun by Guru Nanak (d. 1539), a Hindu spiritual teacher from the Punjab (in northwest India). Nanak taught that there is only one God, but also that people undergo countless rebirths on the road to *moksha* (escape from the cycle of rebirth) and reabsorption into the divine One. He taught that people can escape this cycle through virtuous living and meditation on God's name. Both Muslim and Hindu scholars found fault with Nanak's teachings, but their popularity continued to spread under Nanak's successors, especially in the tolerant atmosphere created by Akbar.

But during the reign of Jahangir concern for religious orthodoxy began to gain political attention. At this time, leadership of the Sikh community had passed to Nanak's fifth successor, Arjun. In response to scholars' complaints, Jahangir demanded that Arjun remove from Sikh scriptures references that were offensive to either Muslims or Hindus. When Arjun refused, he was tortured to death (1606).

There were also Sufis who believed that some mystics went too far. Sheikh Ahmad Sirhindi (d. 1625) was one of them. He was a leader in another Sufi order, the Naqshbandis, a more reserved order from central Asia. Sirhindi was appalled by Emperor Akbar's religious initiatives, particularly his eclectic new "divine religion." He believed Akbar's and Jahangir's religious openness was dangerous to Islam, and did not even think that Shii Muslims should be tolerated. But his most vehement criticisms were directed toward Chishtis and anyone else who believed that all existence is really One. He taught that this belief in the unity of existence (*wahdat al-wujud*) was really just an illusion. He thought that such people achieved an altered state of consciousness through "artificial means" – various exercises such as chanting and rhythmic swaying. Sirhindi criticized the Sufis, saying that it only seems that all existence is One (*wahdat al-shuhud*, oneness of appearances); despite the appearance of unity in mystical consciousness, in reality creatures remain distinct from one another, as well as from the Creator. To claim that this perception is actually the way things are is heresy, since it equates God with his creatures. What is more, people who claim that all existence is One, and that everything that exists is really a manifestation of God, also do away with evil, since God is necessarily all good. For this kind of Sufi, then, evil is just a perception, too. In this context, Sirhindi says, the law of God becomes irrelevant. Straying from the Shariah, he concludes, people naturally fall into moral decline.

Jahangir thought Sirhindi's intolerance of Shiis was misguided. He had him imprisoned for a short time. But Sirhindi had obviously struck a sympathetic chord among many Muslims, and he became widely popular. He was declared Mujaddid al-Alf al-Thani, "the renewer of the second millennium" of Islam. Sirhindi also influenced some Mughals, in particular Akbar's great-grandson

Aurangzeb (r. 1659–1707). When Aurangzeb was young, Sufism was still highly influential among the Mughals. His own brother, Dara Shikoh (d. 1659) – next in line for their father Shah Jahan's throne, was among them. Drawn to mysticism, Dara Shikoh promoted the esoteric teachings of many religions. He surrounded himself with people of many faiths, and personally sponsored the translation of Hindu scriptures. Aurangzeb took it upon himself to champion the cause of orthodoxy, first within his own family. He and two other brothers – all provincial governors – fought with Dara Shikoh for the right to take control of the empire. Dara's troops defeated one brother's army, but after a series of battles Aurangzeb's imperial forces emerged victorious. Aurangzeb then had Dara Shikoh executed as a heretic; two other brothers were exiled and killed. Aurangzeb had himself declared emperor. His sickly father was imprisoned, where he died seven years later.

This violent beginning of Aurangzeb's reign was only a taste of what was to come. Like his predecessors, Aurangzeb insisted on expanding Mughal control militarily, leading to numerous and ongoing rebellions that drained the Mughal resources during Aurangzeb's long reign. Internally, Aurangzeb began a campaign to impose Islam, in its traditional form, throughout the realm. That meant reversing many of Akbar's policies that had led to peaceful relations with non-Muslim religious communities, especially Hindus. He reimposed the tax on non-Muslims, had many Hindu temples and schools destroyed, and prohibited the building of new ones or even the repair of old ones. He imposed economic policies that disadvantaged Hindus, and offered bribes to those who would convert to Islam. Naturally, these policies marginalized and alienated Hindus, severely weakening the social fabric of Mughal India.

Aurangzeb's relations with the Sikhs were no better than those with the Hindus. After Arjun's execution under Jahangir, the Sikhs had retreated from their pacifist stance and established themselves in a defensive position in the Punjab. In its largest city, Lahore, Aurangzeb built the colossal Badshahi mosque to symbolize the triumph of Islam. Aurangzeb also tried to force the Sikh guru Tegh Bahadur to convert to Islam. When he refused, Aurangzeb had him executed. This resulted in further militarization of the Sikh community, and further hostility toward the

Figure 4 Worshipers at Badshahi mosque in Lahore. © *World Religions Picture Library/Christine Osborne*

Muslim rulers. This hostility often flared into open rebellion against their Muslim overlords in the Punjab, resulting in a cycle of vicious reprisals.

Succeeding Mughal leaders thus inherited a mortally wounded realm. Continued efforts to impose Islamic dominance on a mixed population, with a Hindu majority, resulted in ongoing uprisings and inter-communal warfare in India. Indeed, it was these rebellions that allowed Britain to impose direct rule over much of the subcontinent in 1757. They held it until 1947, when it was partitioned into the Hindu-majority state of India and the Muslim-majority state of Pakistan.

Understanding Developments in Islamic History

Following the classical period of Islam, when its texts and ideals were formulated and its basic institutions established, Muslims were subjected to a number of attacks – by plague and disease, but, more importantly, by foreign invaders. The once unified Muslim community became fragmented. After the decline of the Abbasid caliphate, Muslims would never again live as a single political unit. A period of division and almost continuous warfare was followed by reorganization. The Muslim world reconstituted itself into the three empires discussed above – the Ottoman, the Safavid, and the Mughal – as well as several other autonomous Islamic communities in sub-Saharan Africa and South Asia. Muslim intellectuals felt the need to put these developments into perspective. Thirteenth-century historian Ibn al-Athir registered the concern of many that infighting among regional rulers was weakening the Islamic community. He believed that it was this infighting that allowed foreigners to be successful: "It was the discord between the Muslim princes ... that enabled the Franks [crusaders] to overrun the country."[12] There is no question that Ibn al-Athir was right. We have seen that the majority of the battles fought by the Ottomans, Safavids, and Mughals were against Muslims, as they jockeyed for position in the vacuum created by the decline of Abbasid power.

Yet we have also seen that – when stability was restored – Islamic society continued to be prosperous and enormously creative. Virtually all the great scientific and artistic advances described in Chapter 2 were achieved not under the unified Umayyad or Abbasid caliphates, but under the various regional units that developed after the demise of central authority. Many of the great thinkers and artists of the time ended up working under a number of different patrons, depending upon the political situation. There is the famous case of Nasr al-Din al-Tusi (d. 1274). Al-Tusi was the renowned Persian astrologer and mathematician who developed the most accurate table of planetary motion known to science at the time. He did it while working at the great observatory at Maragheh in Azerbaijan, which he himself commissioned to be built while he was a government minister under the Mongol leader Hulegu Khan. That was after he had worked with a branch of the Shiis known as the Ismailis. When they were attacked by the Mongols – some say with al-Tusi's assistance – al-Tusi, who was actually a Twelver Shii, joined the Mongols and encouraged them to destroy Sunni Baghdad in 1258.

The great historian Ibn Khaldun (d. 1406) also had experience working under a number of regimes, from Spain to

North Africa and Egypt. But he used this experience as a laboratory for understanding political and historical processes in general. As we saw in Chapter 2, Ibn Khaldun's *Muqaddimah* is often cited as the first work of historiography and the precursor of the modern disciplines of anthropology, sociology, economics, and political science. But he is perhaps best known for his theory of the cycles or patterns of power. In Ibn Khaldun's view, the rise and fall of regimes is perfectly natural. His analysis is based on the world in which he lived, which was divided between nomads of the deserts and settled peoples of the towns. In his view, nomadic communities have a natural solidarity (*'asabiyyah*) resulting from the strenuousness of their lifestyle. They have to cooperate and assist one another or they will not survive. When a group of nomads decides to give up their wandering ways and settle in towns, their natural solidarity and expectation of cooperation in the face of challenges serves them well. It translates into a commitment to fairness and mutual assistance, both necessary for the continued survival of the group. But that solidarity only lasts for one or two generations in a settled environment. The settled life is easier than the nomadic life, and people get soft. The first few generations remember how difficult life was in the desert and work hard to maintain balance and order within their new domestic environment. But as prosperity develops, the natural solidarity fades. People forget how important fairness and cooperation are, and begin to work for personal gain. This results in competition and rivalries that divide the community against itself and inevitably leave it weakened and open to conquest.

The world in which Ibn Khaldun lived was a perfect example of this cycle. He was surrounded by competing regimes – and survived a number of them. But unlike political analysts, Ibn Khaldun did not equate the strength of the Muslim community with political or military power. Instead, he identified the source of strength of the Muslim community as its commitment to justice. As long as the members of the community remained committed to justice – which consisted in an ethic of fairness and cooperation among community members – the community would remain strong. When community members turn against each other, putting their own interests above those of the group, the social fabric is weakened and eventually splits. "Injustice," he said, "brings about the ruin of civilization".

> Whoever takes someone's property, or uses him for forced labour, or presses an unjustified claim against him, or imposes upon him a duty not required by the religious law, does an injustice to that particular person. People who collect unjustified taxes commit an injustice. Those who infringe upon property commit an injustice. Those who take away property commit an injustice. Those who deny people their rights commit an injustice. Those who, in general, take property by force, commit an injustice. It is the dynasty that suffers from all these acts, inasmuch as civilization, which is the substance of the dynasty, is ruined when people have lost all incentive. This is what Muhammad actually had in mind when he forbade injustice.

Ibn Khaldun then concludes with a justification for the preservation of human rights in Islam, providing one the earliest listings of human rights in history: "This is what the religious law quite generally and wisely aims at in emphasizing five things as necessary: the preservation of (1) religion, (2) the soul (life), (3) the intellect, (4) progeny, and (5) property."[13]

For Ibn Khaldun, the ultimate purpose of the Islamic community was justice. God established the Muslim community and commissioned its members – as his stewards – to spread justice throughout the world, by protecting people's rights to religion, life, education, family, and property. Commitment to this purpose was to be the basis of their solidarity. When that commitment weakened among various rulers, inevitably their regimes fell into decline.

But Islamic civilization as a whole need not decline, provided people maintain their commitment to justice. Ibn Khaldun actually chastises people in his era who take a passive attitude toward establishing justice. These are the people who sit back and wait for the Mahdi to appear. Ibn Khaldun says that all Muslims believe that at the end of time a man from the family of Prophet Muhammad will appear and lead Muslims back to a just society. Because the society will be just, it will also be powerful. The Mahdi and/or Jesus will then overpower the Antichrist, ushering in years of justice before the final judgment. (The Mahdi is not mentioned in the Quran. Belief in the Mahdi comes from oral traditions, which are not consistent. That is why some people believe that Jesus will come after the Antichrist appears so that he can do away with him, while others believe that Jesus will come with the Mahdi and help him get rid of the Antichrist.) Ibn Khaldun notes that some scholars criticize belief in the Mahdi, although he himself does not. But he does criticize people in his own time who simply assume that injustice will be corrected soon, when the Mahdi appears.[14] He believes that all people must work for justice by maintaining their commitment to fairness and cooperation in all their social dealings. In the same way, he criticizes people who rely on fortune-tellers and astrologers to predict the future. (He uses as evidence of their unreliability the fact that, at the time of Prophet Muhammad, there were reports that the world would end 500 years after the coming of the Prophet. Ibn Khaldun was born 723 years after the Hijra.)

Instead of waiting for the Mahdi or allowing fortune-tellers to control their destiny, Ibn Khaldun says that people should use reason to understand their religion and the world, and figure out how to establish Islamic values in the world's ever-changing circumstances. Furthermore, he criticizes those mystics who believe that all existence is One, that only God exists, and that we are all a part of God. He says that this is just a passing perception, and it is foolish to trust such passing perceptions, like blind people who are not aware that there is an entire dimension of perception beyond their abilities.

Rather than trying to understand things beyond their perceptive abilities, people should concentrate on things they can understand. Ibn Khaldun then gives an elegant description of empirical science, the kind of understanding of their environment that human beings can develop through observation and reasoning in an orderly way. Pursuit of science has obvious practical uses that promote human wellbeing. Practical sciences can help us build better homes, for example, and grow better crops. But of all the kinds of science, law is the most important, since it details the ways to promote justice and prevent injustice. And this is the reason for which human beings were created.

Conclusion

Ibn Khaldun's analysis of the rise and fall of nations is brilliant. It became a classic of historiography. And his articulation of the source of strength of Islam is an eloquent tribute to Islamic values. But it still leaves unanswered the question of Islamic trauma in the modern era. How did the Muslim world – the world of Suleiman the Magnificent, Shah Abbas, and Akbar the Great, the world of universities and public libraries, great architects and artists, literature and learning – become part of what is today known as the Third World – weak, underdeveloped, and associated with unpopular governments? How did these magnificent states of the middle period of Islamic history become subjected to European powers? These are the questions addressed in the following chapters.

Chapter 4

Colonialism and Reform

The twentieth century was disastrous for the Muslim world. It opened with European powers in control of large portions of former Ottoman and Mughal lands, as well as other parts of the Muslim world, and dominating in Iran. World War I ended the caliphate and consolidated European control over most of the Muslim world. Muslims in all these regions therefore had to struggle with multiple challenges and against enormous odds. As the vitality of Muslim society declined, reformers had begun to work in many parts of the Muslim world. But their work was complicated by the threat of foreign domination. A number of trends thus emerged: agitation for reform in declining Islamic empires; the struggle for independence from growing European power; efforts to modernize Islamic societies and reform religious thought in order to deal with contemporary challenges. In this chapter we will survey the takeover of the Muslim world by European powers, and examine the early reform movements that were developed to deal with it.

Colonialism

By the early the twentieth century, almost the entire Muslim world was under the control of European countries. The French controlled North Africa and Syria; the British controlled Egypt, Palestine, Iraq, and India; the Dutch controlled Indonesia; and the Dutch and then the British controlled Malaysia. From this vantage point, it began to look like the Crusades were on again. But it took some time before the pattern of colonization became clear, because the process by which Europe gained control of these regions was actually gradual and, in some cases, subtle. It also developed sporadically, one city or region at a time, over a wide geographic range. Spain established a beachhead here; France set up control there; Britain took over areas in North Africa, the Middle East, and India; Italy and Holland operated at opposite ends of the Islamic world; and so on. European countries gained control of the Muslim world through a combination of strategies, including gradual assumption of economic power, playing off internal rivals against one another, and military campaigns when necessary. As a result, Europe's overall domination of the Muslim world did not become apparent to most people until it was almost complete.

After the Crusades, the first European inroads were by way of the sea, when the Portuguese took control of the Indian Ocean spice trade from the Arabs. As we saw in Chapter 3, this was a wound to the Mamluk economy from which it never recovered. Eventually, the Ottomans were able to overpower the Mamluks and take control of almost the entire Arab world. For centuries, the Ottomans had been a formidable force. They were strong enough to be able to play a role in Europe's pre-modern power struggles, when regional powers tried to assert themselves against the old imperial families who wanted to control the entire continent. We saw above how Suleiman the Magnificent was able to manipulate those struggles to Ottoman advantage in the Balkans. However, in the bargain Suleiman gave French subjects the right to travel and trade in Ottoman lands. French traders were also given the protection of French laws and courts even while they were in Ottoman lands; they were exempted from Ottoman laws, including taxes. Suleiman also granted the French king Francis I the right to control access to trade in the Middle East for other European subjects (in the Capitulations of 1536).

These special privileges (*imtiyazat*) were later demanded by the British as well, and expanded throughout the Ottoman empire. They assured the Europeans safety of life and property, and freedom of religion, but the exemption from Ottoman law and taxes also gave the Europeans distinct trade advantages. These advantages, later obtained by the Europeans in the Persian world as well, were often passed on to local Christian and Jewish communities. They proved to be the critical factor in the Capitulations. They allowed Europeans and their allies in the Muslim world to amass greater wealth than it was possible for local Muslims to obtain.

Obviously, the brilliant Suleiman would not have given the Europeans such rights if they had posed any threat at the time. But as it turned out French cultural and economic influence in Syria (which included Lebanon until after World War II) grew exponentially. Religious missions were founded by Roman Catholics, catering to the area's Christians and to others interested in the advantages provided by European learning. European merchants had established lucrative trade in Syrian cotton, silks, and handicrafts by the seventeenth and eighteenth centuries. But soon the balance of trade began to shift. European manufactured goods were being imported, replacing indigenous crafts and enriching those merchants with close relations to Europe. By the late nineteenth century, it began to appear to Syria's Muslim majority that the Christians (including the Orthodox, who had benefited from Russian missions) were developing a distinct advantage based on foreign support. Communal rioting was the result. It brought increased attention from Ottoman officials and Europeans, and foreign influence continued to expand. France built rail connections between Syria's three major cities – Damascus, Beirut, and Aleppo. The American University of Beirut (originally called the Syrian Protestant College) was established in 1866, and the French Jesuit Université Saint-Joseph opened in Beirut in 1881.

By the outbreak of World War I in 1914, Christians were among Syria's most highly educated and Western-influenced population, and France treated the region as part of its eminent domain. In the Treaty of Versailles in 1919 ending that war, France was granted a "mandate" of control over Syria that would not end until France itself was occupied by Nazi Germany in World War II and could no longer afford to manage its Syrian territories.

By the early twentieth century, France – locked in competition with other European colonial powers – had already taken control of Morocco, Algeria, and Tunisia. In 1830 France had attacked Algiers, technically part of the Ottoman empire but virtually autonomous. The French proclaimed that they had nothing against the people of Algeria, only their Turkish rulers. Their original complaint was against piracy, a venerable tradition in the Mediterranean, which had been practiced by the Greeks, Romans, and Carthaginians. The famous Barbary pirates (named after the non-Arab inhabitants of North Africa, the Berbers) followed the same practice, demanding tribute from ships seeking to pass through their waters and seizing them along with their crews and all their contents if they refused. This provided a ready source of funds in their efforts to maintain their independence from Istanbul. But it was not popular among the nations whose economies were increasingly dependent upon sea trade. The practice became so unpopular that European countries and the newly formed United States demanded a halt to it and fought several battles when the pirate states refused to give in. President Thomas Jefferson even sent in the American navy, which struggled with the pirates for four years (the Tripolitan War, 1801–5). The British had bombed Algeria in 1816 in an effort to stop piracy, and had largely been successful. Nevertheless, the French claimed that their goal in attacking Algiers in 1830 was to put a stop to piracy. Their attack was successful, and the Ottoman officials were sent packing. But the French did not leave. The region quickly attracted French settlers, and France appointed a "governor general of the French possessions in Africa," headquartered in Algiers. Resistance by Algerians began immediately, but it only intensified the French resolve to take full control of the area. After years of Algerian attacks on settlers' farms and French reprisals against Algerian villages, France declared itself the ruler of Algeria. In 1845 Paris appointed a "governor general of Algeria." By 1871 Algerian resistance had been crushed. Algeria was considered a part of France. It only regained independence after a brutal war (1954–62), in which an estimated one- tenth of the population lost their lives and another one-fifth to one-third were displaced (relocated by the French).

From its North African headquarters in Algeria, France was able to expand its control to include Morocco. Morocco had never been a part of the Ottoman empire, enjoying an independence that allowed it to be a refuge for Algerians fleeing the wrath of France. But Moroccan assistance to the struggling Algerian resistance brought on French attacks. The French military easily defeated the Moroccans in the 1840s. But the European powers were always in competition for colonial holdings, the source of enormous wealth for these industrializing powers. So, in the 1850s, Britain negotiated for special trading privileges in Morocco, promising to protect Moroccans from the French. Meanwhile, Spain claimed territories in the western portion of Morocco, and declared war to secure them. Morocco was quickly losing its independence under a succession of weak rulers in the late nineteenth century. This led to rebellions that further weakened the sultan and allowed the Europeans to press their own claims. In a classic example of European colonial gamesmanship, Britain, Spain, and Italy agreed in 1904 to let France take over in Morocco if France let England have Egypt and allowed Spain to exercise its influence over northwestern Morocco, and Italy to take Libya. A futile rebellion by the sultan's brother ended in the Treaty of Fez (1912) which declared Morocco a French protectorate.

Meanwhile, on the other side of Algeria, Tunisia also asserted autonomy from its nominal Ottoman overlords. But Tunisia also felt threatened by its much larger neighbor Algeria. So when the French came into Algeria in 1830, Tunisia accepted their offer to act as their surrogates in the rule of Algeria. When it became clear that France actually intended to take direct control in Algeria, Tunisian rulers recognized the threat to their own independence and desperately tried to strengthen themselves against the modern European power. But they could only attempt this by raising taxes and taking out loans – from Europe. Popular discontent erupted in rebellions that further strained government resources. The Europeans finally decided to take control of Tunisia's government in order to recoup their debts. The only real suspense was over which of Tunisia's major lenders – Britain or France – would take ultimate control. The European colonial powers each worried that the other was taking unfair advantage in placing their increasingly high-stakes claims in the disintegrating Ottoman empire. They came together at the Congress of Vienna in 1878 to deal with a number of related issues. One of the outcomes was that Britain gave France permission to take control in Tunisia. On the pretext of securing Algeria's borders, France set up a resident governor in Tunisia and assumed direct control in 1881. France kept control of Morocco and Tunisia until 1956, officially, but in reality kept control of certain strategic areas until the 1960s.

Meanwhile, Britain had been extremely busy establishing its global empire. India became the jewel in England's imperial crown by processes similar to France's occupation of Syria. By the end of the fifteenth century, as we saw, Portugal had achieved dominance in trade in the Indian Ocean, by virtue of the superiority of its sea routes over the Arab land routes. By the seventeenth century, the British, French, and Dutch were competing for trade advantage in the region. The British East India Company, established by royal charter in 1600 specifically to gain control of trade in India and points east, acted as more than a commercial enterprise. As with many of today's mega-transnational corporations, it is difficult to say whether the company acted as an agent of the home government or vice versa. Either way, the effect on India was the same. In order to achieve its monopolistic goals, the company required military force, as well as administrators to control foreign populations, and the government was happy to oblige. In 1612 British forces defeated Portugal in battle and won concessions from the Mughals to engage in trade in cotton, silk, indigo, and spices. A rival British company struggled with the East India Company, and in the early eighteenth century the two merged into the United Company of Merchants of England. This was during the period in which Mughal power was declining; the intolerant policies of the successors of Akbar were increasingly unpopular, and regional powers struggled to assert their autonomy. The resulting weaknesses in various regions of India provided opportunities for the United Company. It gained control of Bengal in 1757 and from there began to expand, defeating the forces of the Mughals, regional forces, and other colonial competitors and, overall, exploiting the weaknesses in the subcontinent caused by disputes among the Mughals and their Hindu enemies.

The British government soon acted to take control from the company of what was effectively its policy in India (the Regulating Act of 1773 and Pitt's India Act in 1784), and continued the policy of expanding British control. Decisive defeats of local forces in 1818 brought capitulations from other leaders. India was no longer the home of the Mughal empire; it had gradually shifted from being a British trade monopoly to being a British colony. In 1846 the British defeated the Sikhs, who had established a state in the Punjab (northwest India) in the late eighteenth century. They annexed Sikh territory in 1849. The final stage came in 1857. By that time, Britain controlled, either directly or through compliant local leaders, virtually all of India. A revolt erupted among Bengali troops employed by the British. The immediate cause of the rebellion reflects the widespread discontent among all Indians – Muslim and Hindu – caused by British disruption of traditional life and imposition of foreign values. The British had ordered the troops to use a new kind of rifle, but in order to load this rifle the ends of the cartridges had to be bitten off. The trouble was that the soldiers believed the grease on the cartridges was a mixture of both cow and pig fat, offending both Hindus and Muslims. The British were so unpopular overall, however, that the revolt quickly spread to Delhi and turned into a general rebellion against British rule. It took over a year, but the British were able to put down the rebellion – with extreme brutality – and institute direct rule of the subcontinent. By this time it was possible to say that "the sun never sets on the British empire." (Their colonial subjects explained that that was because God couldn't trust the British in the dark.) They did not leave until 1947, when they "partitioned" the subcontinent into the majority Hindu state of India and the Islamic state of Pakistan, consisting of two sections (East Pakistan and West Pakistan) separated by language and culture and over 1,000 miles of India. The status of Kashmir, a Muslim majority state ruled by a Hindu, has yet to be settled.

At the same time, Britain was gaining control of Egypt and Sudan. Napoleon had sailed into the port of Alexandria in Egypt in 1798, and announced to the Egyptian people that he was going to overthrow the Mamluks, who had regained autonomy in Egypt. He claimed that the Mamluks were unworthy to rule Egypt because they were not good Muslims. He then told them that the French were better Muslims than the Mamluks, and his proof was that the French had destroyed the power of the pope, who had called the Crusades, and then evicted the notoriously anti-Muslim crusader knights from Malta. The French then occupied Egypt, saying that they were protecting the Egyptians from the Turks, too, whose greed had destroyed Egypt. Although Napoleon may have believed himself, it seemed to the Egyptians that his real goals were more mundane. They included protection of French trade, already well established there as it had been in Syria due to the favorable trade conditions provided to Europeans by the Capitulations. As well, the reliability of Egypt's annual grain production was attractive, given the periodic shortages at home. The French administrators of Egypt set about modernizing Egypt in their own image. From their new bureaucracy they established new tax policies and began confiscating Mamluk lands and redistributing them to those who would support their administration. They also built hospitals and made other contributions to the country, but they were still intruders, and their continued occupation met with stiff local resistance.

By 1801 the French had to vacate Egypt, after the Ottoman military defeated them in a series of battles, assisted by a British naval blockade. (They took with them the Rosetta Stone, which their archaeologists had discovered, providing the key to deciphering the pyramids' hieroglyphics. They took other ancient Egyptian artifacts as well, which would become the inspiration for a new style in French design motifs: art deco.) One of the leaders of the Ottoman campaign, Mehmed (Muhammad) Ali (d. 1848) was then put in control of Egypt. He tried to reorganize the country in ways that would allow Egypt to regain its pride of place among the world's nations, and secure it against foreign invaders. He centralized control of the economy and government, executing the Mamluk chiefs who competed for power and confiscating their properties as well as those endowed through religious foundations (*waqf* properties). He revived and modernized the country's irrigation system, and introduced improved crops for export. He modernized the education system, using French instructors and advisors and encouraging Egyptians to study abroad. And he modernized the military, initiating a draft so that Egyptians could defend themselves rather than rely on Ottoman troops.

Mehmed Ali also gained independence from Istanbul by using his military to help out in their campaigns against the rebellious Wahhabis. The Wahhabis were a narrowly traditionalist reform movement in Arabia, bent on reviving the strength of early Islam by wiping out "innovations" such as Sufism and art. They were also militant. In their view, contrary to that of other Muslims since the first century of Islam, Muslims who violate their strict rules – for example, by visiting the tombs of holy people and praying for their intercession – were declared infidels who must be fought. The movement is based on the teachings of Muhammad ibn Abd al-Wahhab (d. 1791), and spread by the Saudi family with whom they allied in the mid-eighteenth century. The combined Wahhabi–Saudi forces gained dominance in the Arabian peninsula. When they began to spread northward into Iraq and Syria, the Ottoman sultan asked for and received Mehmed Ali's assistance in confining the movement to the peninsula. Autonomy in Egypt and Sudan, the eastern portion of which he had already conquered, was Mehmed Ali's reward.

Mehmed Ali's successors, though more conservative, continued efforts to develop Egyptian economic power. They wanted to keep their independence from Istanbul, and knew they needed outside help to continue developing. But they were suspicious of Europe's growing influence in the region, so they switched back and forth from the French to the British for assistance. The British built a railway from Alexandria to Suez (1858), which allowed them a faster route to India, for example; the French then built the Suez Canal (1869), making the trip even easier. But all this development was expensive, and much of the capital was borrowed – again, from European sources. Many of the reforms did improve Egypt's financial status. For example, its long staple cotton became extremely valuable when the American Civil War eliminated American cotton from the world market. But when the war was over, Egypt was again faced with mounting debt – which would ultimately end the country's independence. By 1875, the Egyptian ruler was forced to sell his shares in the Suez Canal to Britain. The following year an international commission was set up to deal with Egypt's debt – one of the world's first international debt crises. The commission put all Egyptian finances under the control of a British and a French agent. When the Egyptians protested, France and Britain induced the Ottoman sultan to oust the Egyptian ruler (1879). The Europeans took over again, infuriating the Egyptians. Opposition groups organized within the National Assembly, which had been established in 1866, and the military, resulting in the establishment of Egypt's first political party, the National Party (al-Hizb al-Watani). The French and British sent naval forces to Alexandria in 1882 to protect their investments. Riots erupted, and British ships responded by bombing Alexandria and occupying Cairo. Britain kept control of Egypt, declaring it a British "protectorate" at the beginning of World War I, and installing a compliant monarch at the end of the war. Officially, Egypt was independent, but the monarchy implemented British policy. Actual independence was not achieved until a military coup overthrew the monarch in 1952.

Further east, the Dutch secured their hold over Indonesia and, for a time, Malaysia. Islam had been introduced to the Malay peninsula and the islands that would become Malaysia and Indonesia by Indian traders in the thirteenth and fourteenth centuries. By the early sixteenth century, Portuguese merchants were well established in the region's Moluccan Islands, the "Spice Islands." But within a century the Dutch East India Company outmaneuvered both the Portuguese and local traders and gained control of the region. Apart from a brief interlude of French control (1811–16, when France had conquered Holland and incorporated Indonesia into its empire) and Japanese control (1942–5, during World War II), the Dutch remained in power in Indonesia until 1949. They were ousted from what would become Malaysia (as well as Singapore) by Britain in the mid-nineteenth century. Except for the Japanese occupation during World War II, Britain kept control of Malaysia until 1957.

Even Italy got into the colonizing act. Like other North African provinces of the Ottoman empire, Libya had gained semi-autonomy during the eighteenth century. But the Ottomans reasserted direct control in 1835. Meanwhile, Italy began its efforts to compete with other European colonial powers. Britain's theory of colonial expansion tended to focus on coastal areas. Capitalizing on its naval superiority, Britain established bases around the "rims" of continents. France favored a north–south approach, establishing its colonial outposts directly south of its own territory. Italy favored the latter approach and chose Libya as a target for its colonial aspirations. After establishing a number of financial interests in the country, Italy secured direct control of Libya by defeating Ottoman forces in 1912. Italy consolidated its power in 1932, after destroying Libyan resistance, but it then lost control of Libya to British and French administrators, until independence was granted by the United Nations in 1951.

The Outcome of World War I

This pattern of commercial and political domination played out across the Muslim world as Europe expanded its control. But Europe did not operate as a unit, following a pre-planned scheme to take control of the whole Muslim world. Individual European countries used the rest of the world – including the Muslim world – as a kind of Monopoly board to play out their colonial competition. As one European power moved into one region, another moved into a neighboring region in an effort to block its opponent's expansion. European countries bargained with one another and traded countries in an effort to gain strategic advantage – with utter disregard for the rights and welfare of the countries being traded. The best examples are to be found in the Middle East, particularly Iraq. The land between the two great rivers, the Euphrates and the Tigris, has a long and illustrious history as Mesopotamia, part of the famous Fertile Crescent. But the modern state of Iraq was created by the Europeans from parts of three Ottoman provinces: most of Basra province in the south with its primarily Shii Arab population, Baghdad in the center with its predominantly Sunni Arab population, and parts of Mosul in the north, with its Sunni Kurdish population. (Kurds are an linguistic/ethnic group distinct from Arabs, Persians, or Turks.) The region had come under Ottoman rule in the sixteenth century but, as we have seen, Ottoman power was in steep decline by the beginning of the twentieth century. The Persian Gulf had been familiar territory to European traders since the early seventeenth century. But the discovery of oil in Iraq sharpened competition for this corner of Ottoman territory.

By the early twentieth century, the Ottoman sultan had been dubbed "the sick man of Europe." He was pictured in cartoons as a carcass, over which European-named vultures circled. Among those predators were Britain, Holland, and Germany – or, more precisely, British Petroleum, Royal Dutch Shell, and the Deutsche Bank. In 1914 these three companies formed the Turkish Petroleum Company, and began negotiations for the rights to develop Iraqi oil reserves. Local rulers were relatively autonomous by this time but still weak. They were therefore happy to trade the rights to this subterranean mineral for hard cash. But the outcome of World War I forced a slight modification in Europe's commercial and colonizing efforts. Germany's defeat in the war resulted in its exclusion from the company, and Britain took control of its shares. Britain also landed a military force from India. The British took over control of Basra and Baghdad provinces by 1917, claiming they were not planning to stay; they only wanted to help the Iraqis get rid of their unpopular rulers.

European colonial competition had proceeded unabated during the war. Britain had sought Arab cooperation in the war, knowing they were increasingly unhappy under Ottoman Turkish rule. Arab leaders had been agitating for independence, as we have seen, both from the Turks and the Europeans who had gained dominance in Arab lands despite Turkish rule. Debate often centered on strategy: should they work for reform of the Ottoman system and greater autonomy, or for full independence? If they chose independence, should they struggle against the foreigners first and then the Turks, or vice versa? The offer of British assistance against the Turks seemed risky but worthwhile. It had come in the run-up to the war from British administrators in Egypt to the leading family of Mecca – the Hashemites, descendants of Prophet Muhammad ("sharifs") and traditionally in charge of Islam's two holiest cities, Mecca and Medina. The British knew that the Turks had been modernizing, largely with German help. They realized that in the impending war, the Turks would no doubt ally with Germany against the British, French, and Russians. They therefore looked for a way to weaken Turkish forces.

Exploiting Arab discontent with Turkish rule, the British offered to recognize Arab independence in all liberated territories, in return for the Arabs' assistance in the war. They were to rebel against the Turks, effectively opening a second front in the war and preventing the Turks from providing significant assistance to Britain. This was a lot to ask, given that the Ottomans were not only the political rulers of the Middle East but also technically the spiritual leaders of the Muslim world. It was a momentous decision; among the earliest rules established in Islamic law was the prohibition on collaborating with non-Muslims against Muslim rulers. Nevertheless, after consultation with regional leaders, the Hashemite leaders decided to trust the Europeans. That, as it turned out, was a monumental misjudgment.

Along with the famous Lawrence of Arabia – the British officer assigned to work with the Arabs – the Arabs fought the Turks in the Middle East. They thus undoubtedly assisted in the defeat of the Germans and their allies. But after the war, instead of granting the Arabs independence as promised, the Europeans distributed Arab territories among themselves. This was what they had agreed secretly to do, at the same time as they were publicly promising the Arabs independence.[1] In the secret Sykes–Picot Agreement (1916), France was designated "protector" of Arab Syria and the Kurdish Mosul province. Britain would "protect" Baghdad and Basra provinces, and the Palestinian portion of traditional Syria, as well as what would be called Transjordan (the land on the eastern side of the Jordan river, all the way to Iraq). (Russia's claims, for example that the west bank of the Jordan river, from Gaza to Tyre, should be international, were ignored as a result of the 1917 Bolshevik Revolution.) The treaties ending World War I established the independent state of Turkey, but ignored the promises made to the Arabs. Instead, they imposed the provisions of the Sykes–Picot Agreement, changing only the term "protectorate" to "mandate." But France now wanted a share of the company that was exploiting Iraqi petroleum resources. So France traded Mosul to Britain in exchange for defeated Germany's share in the Turkish Petroleum Company. (Later, America became annoyed that its companies were excluded from the deal. So in 1928 the Exxon, Mobil, and Gulf petroleum companies were incorporated into the company, and it was renamed the Iraq Petroleum Company.)

Now Britain could put together Iraq: Mosul was added to Baghdad and Basra provinces to form the country. But what about a leader? The idea of the mandates was that the Europeans were supposed to watch out for the interests of the countries they were assigned, helping them along until they were ready to assume independence. They were not supposed to be colonial overlords. So Britain and France had to find Arab leaders they considered suitable for their new countries. Fortunately for them, there was a family of leaders available for work: the Hashemites. Their betrayal at the hands of the Europeans left them with only their domains in western Arabia. (Around this time the Saudi family began to expand from its realms in central Arabia, to which it had been limited since Egypt's Mehmed Ali had driven it back from Iraq. The Saudis would eventually defeat the Hashemites and name all of Arabia after themselves.) The sons of the elderly Sharif Hussein vigorously protested the violation of the Arab trust by the British. Faisal went north to Syria and set up a government in Damascus. But when he refused to accept the French mandate he was forced out of Syria. Meanwhile, the Iraqis were rebelling against their British overlords. So the British offered the deposed Faisal the title of king of Iraq. He accepted, but only if the British changed their "mandate over" to "alliance with" Iraq, and with the concurrence of the Iraqi people (1922). Faisal finally had a throne, and Britain had a compliant Sunni Arab ruler for its very diverse but oil-rich Iraq.

According to the treaty of alliance, Iraq was technically independent, but Britain got to run the army and appoint advisors to run the economy and foreign policy. And the pernicious Capitulations were reasserted, exempting the British from local laws and taxes. The fact that Iraq had not, in fact, been independent was made clear when in 1932, the League of Nations recognized its independence. But even then Britain maintained control of the economy and the military, and petroleum resources continued to be exploited by the foreign-controlled Iraqi Petroleum Company. Throughout this time, political opponents of the British-dominated monarchy were jailed, exiled, or executed, and insurrections were mercilessly suppressed. Perhaps most notoriously, Kurdish rebels in the early 1920s were suppressed with poison gas, and Shii uprisings resulted in the bombing of their villages. Foreign control of Iraq was not actually ended until a violent revolution in 1958.

The betrayal of the Arabs by the British and French resulted in the creation of other new states as well. Sharif Hussein and his son Faisal, when they were still in charge of western Arabia and Syria respectively (1918), decided to split Transjordan, that southern portion of traditional Syria situated between the east bank of the Jordan river and Iraq. But after Faisal's defeat in Syria and transfer to Iraq, the British decided to offer the rule of Transjordan to Faisal's brother Abdullah, provided he accepted their ultimate control, of course. Jordan got nominal independence in 1946 but, characteristically, Britain maintained control of the economy, the military, and foreign policy. In 1955 the sovereign kingdom of Jordan was admitted to the United Nations, but real independence came only with the departure of British military leaders in 1956.

As noted above, traditional Syria included Lebanon as well. Lebanon's mountains had separated it geographically from the rest of Syria and its long coast had opened it to cultural influences that had given the region a unique identity since the days of the ancient Phoenicians. Its strong local leaders had near-autonomy under Ottoman rule, but Lebanon was included in the French mandate over Syria. Under French control, the region was reorganized into a separate government, with a slight Christian majority. The government got its own constitution but, like Syria, was still controlled by France. Christian-dominated Lebanon was particularly pro-French; the language of administration and education was French, and the French dominated the economy. When France fell to Nazi forces during World War II, Lebanon and Syria were occupied by Vichy (pro-Nazi French) administrators. British and Free French troops defeated them and declared Lebanon and Syria independent, promising the locals the right to choose between separate countries or a united Syria. But in fact French administrators remained. In 1943 contending Lebanese factions agreed on a National Pact: the Muslims would accept a Lebanon independent of Syria, provided the Christians would commit to a Lebanon independent of France. The agreement was not put in writing, but it was accepted that the president of Lebanon would always be a Maronite Christian (a unique sect of Eastern Christianity, dating from the seventh century), the prime minister would be a Sunni Muslim, and the speaker of the National Assembly would be a Shii Muslim. Emigration of wealthy Christians to better economic fields abroad, and immigration of Sunni Muslims escaping war in Palestine/Israel would shift the demographic balance, severely straining communal relations in Lebanon.

The last portion of traditional Syria was given to Britain to rule, and it remains the most problematic place in the region: Palestine. The League of Nations granted Britain control of the area in 1922, and included the Balfour Declaration within the mandate. The Balfour Declaration had been issued in 1917 by the British foreign secretary Arthur James Balfour in response to requests by Zionist leaders for British support for their movement. In view of centuries of Christian persecution of Jews, leaders of the World Zionist Organization had given up hope that European Christians would ever allow Jews to live in peace and security, with equal civil and political rights. They therefore wanted to establish a homeland for Jews in Palestine, as the ancient Jewish homeland had been called by the Romans (after the name of its "Philistine" inhabitants). Lord Balfour wrote that the British government viewed

> with favour the establishment in Palestine of a national home for the Jewish people and will use their best endeavours to facilitate the achievement of this object, it being clearly understood that nothing shall be done which may prejudice the civil and religious rights of existing non-Jewish communities in Palestine, or the rights and political status enjoyed by Jews in any other country.[2]

Under British control of Palestine, the Jewish population increased exponentially, as Jews sought escape from intensifying anti-Semitism in Europe. According to Ottoman statistics, there were around 24,000 Jews in Palestine in 1882. By 1914, there were some 60,000. The British census in 1922 recorded 83,790 Jews, about 11 percent of the population. Within nine years, that number had increased to 174,610.[3] Arab leaders supported limited Jewish immigration on

Figure 5 The Dome of the Rock (687–91) in Jerusalem. © *Sheila Blair and Jonathan Bloom*

humanitarian grounds, but having been betrayed by the British and lost their autonomy in their own homelands, they were not surprisingly bewildered that Britain had now decided to distribute these lands to Europeans.

As Nazism grew in Europe, threatening the very survival of the Jewish people, more and more European Jews emigrated to Palestine. Native Palestinians began to rebel against this mass immigration into their land. Zionist activists in Palestine became anxious to evict the British and form a sovereign state. The British Mandate authorities in Palestine thus faced Arab uprisings against increased foreign immigration, and Zionist terrorism against both Arab opponents and the British presence. The pressure on Britain became too much, especially with its economy at home devastated by World War II. By the late 1940s, the British had to give up their troublesome colonial holdings. They made plans to leave not only India but Palestine as well. They handed the problem of Palestine to the United Nations. And, as Britain had done in India, the United Nations decided to partition Palestine. There were to be two states, one for Jews and one for Arabs, with the Jewish state receiving 55 percent of the land. The partition plan was rejected by the people whose land was being partitioned, of course, but it was passed anyway. Immediately, Zionist leaders declared Israel a state (May 15, 1948), and Arab leaders declared war. The Arabs were no match for the zealous European refugees. As a result of their defeat, some 800,000 Palestinians became refugees. Today, two wars (1967 and 1973) and countless United Nations resolutions later, Palestinians remain stateless.

The Effects of Colonialism: The Challenge of Islamic Reform

The cumulative effects of colonialism were enormous. The sense of betrayal and humiliation were succinctly expressed by Ayatollah Khomeini, the leader of Iran's Islamic Revolution in 1979: "The government has sold our independence, reduced us to the level of a colony, and made the Muslim nation of Iran seem more backward than savages in the eyes of the world!"[4] Interestingly, Iran was among the few countries that had avoided direct colonial control. Nevertheless its modern history is defined by the same kinds of commercial concessions and colonial competition (in this case, between Britain and Russia) that led to such disastrous results for other Islamic states.

Iran's first oil concession was granted in 1901, giving the right to exploit all of Iran's petroleum and natural gas for sixty years to the founder of British Petroleum (originally called the Anglo-Persian Oil Company, then the Anglo-Iranian Oil Company; it became British Petroleum [BP] in 1954) – in return for a cash payment of £20,000, a relatively small annual fee, and less than one-fifth of the annual profits.[5] At that time the Qajar family dominated Iran. They had already sold the rights to develop Iran's tobacco to a British firm. That had caused a major protest in the 1890s, but the Qajars were undeterred. They were intent on modernizing the country, inviting Europeans to build telegraphs and railroads, establish a banking system, and modernize the bureaucracy and the army. Oil revenues had not yet begun to flow, so the Qajars were forced to rely on foreign loans to finance their projects. Protests among the Iranians against growing foreign influence increased. Despite their confiscation of religious properties, the Qajars could stop neither the clergy-led protests against their policies nor the country's growing subjection to foreign interests. Protests turned into revolution in 1906. The British intervened and the Qajar shah (king) was forced to establish a constitutional government. But Russia intervened to strengthen the shah, lest the new government assert too much independence and reject Russian influence on the government. But with the Bolshevik overthrow of the Russian tsars, Britain became the dominant foreign influence over the Qajars. Opposition increased and again turned into revolution. The Qajars were overthrown by a man from the modernized military, Reza Shah Pahlavi (1925).

The new king was intent on continuing modernization according to Western standards, but also on maintaining independence from foreign powers. He decided to take control of Iran's oil production, but a British fleet of warships and the League of Nations convinced him to simply accept a higher percentage of profits in the company. With the increased profits, the shah was able to increase the rate of industrialization, which often meant forcing new lifestyles on people who were perfectly comfortable with their traditional ways. Nomads were forced to adapt to settled life, and people who had always been farmers found themselves living in towns, or moved to different agricultural areas to make way for new industrial developments. The shah even banned traditional Persian dress, insisting that men wear European-style hats and women remove their veils. Opponents to these perhaps well-intentioned but over-zealous plans were ruthlessly suppressed. As the shah's popularity at home waned, his fascination with fascism increased, leading to conflict with the Allied powers. During World War II, America, Britain, and the Soviet Union agreed to occupy the country and depose the shah. In his place they put his son, Muhammad Reza Pahlavi. The new shah agreed to be compliant with Western interests, and the Westerners agreed to withdraw their troops from the country (1942).

Following World War II, Muhammad Reza Shah continued the industrialization and Westernization of Iran, with the same results as his father's policies. British Petroleum maintained sole control of petroleum production in the country – its revenues were so high that the portion paid to the shah of Iran made him enormously wealthy and allowed him free rein in his country. But the rapid pace of change and introduction of foreign practices continued to result in social dislocation and unrest. Protest, whether voiced by religious or secular leaders, brought severe repercussions. By 1950, Iranians had become anxious to end the shah's undemocratic regime and gain control of their own resources. In 1951 the Iranian parliament, led by Muhammad Mosaddeq, called for the nationalization of Iran's petroleum industry. The popularity of this policy led to Mosaddeq being named prime minister and the shah seeking exile outside the country. The Iranian government offered to buy out BP, including an offer to compensate the company for a certain amount of future revenues. BP refused. It led a boycott of Iranian oil, and enlisted the assistance of the United States' Central Intelligence Agency to engineer a coup that ousted the nationalist government and reinstated the shah. BP then opened Iranian oilfields to other companies, including American ones and the National Iranian Oil Company, which would receive half the profits from Iranian oil.

From this time on, America gradually increased its influence in Iran, replacing Soviet and British influence. As a result, the shah's continued Westernization, financed by ever-increasing wealth, became associated with American influence. As opposition grew, so did the shah's intolerance. Extrajudicial arrests, imprisonment, and torture at the hands of the dreaded secret police SAVAK were common. Rumors of tens of thousands of deaths by torture were no doubt exaggerated, but they were effective in spreading fear and loathing of the regime. Yet the shah's popularity in America increased. He was interviewed sympathetically on American television and was named one of Mr. Blackwell's "best-dressed men," along with several Hollywood figures. The final straw was perhaps a symbolic one. One New Year's Eve (a western holiday), the shah was toasted with champagne (a forbidden drink) by an American president, Jimmy Carter, as a great humanitarian. The next year, 1979, the shah was overthrown in the Islamic Revolution.

What this story demonstrates is that added to their humiliation and sense of betrayal was the frustration of a colonized people's hopes for true independence and empowerment. In addition, the Muslim world experienced a leadership crisis. Not only was there a backlash against traditional leaders who had advised trusting in Europe in the first place, but the region lost many qualified people through the emigration of the wealthier and better-educated classes to regions where they could live in greater freedom and prosperity. Military governments often took the place of civilian leadership, a result of the fact that force was required to evict colonial powers. But ultimately the military governments were no more popular than the colonial ones. As a result, formerly colonized countries often experienced increased militarism and totalitarianism as they protested against their own dictators. At the same time, poverty deepened as colonized and formerly colonized peoples struggled in a fiercely competitive world market, at the cost of self-sufficient traditional economies. This typically led to rapid urbanization: the mass migration of rural people into cities in search of work. But work was often unavailable, leading to growing unemployment and underemployment. The migration to cities also led to the breakdown of traditional family structures as men left home in search of work and women were forced into single parenthood. Men unable to fulfill their traditional role as protectors and providers often experienced shame and despair, while women – burdened with running the family alone – began to question their traditionally subservient role.

Thus economic, political, and social crises were the cumulative effect of colonialism in the Muslim world, as elsewhere. These effects have influenced developments in the Muslim world since the end of the nineteenth century. Since that time, the challenge facing Muslims has been to understand how their society plunged from the heights of affluence and influence, culture, and learning in the Middle Ages to the depths of subjugation and despair, and then figure out what to do about it. But it would be a mistake to think that reform in the Muslim world began solely as a reaction to colonialism. In fact, voices of reform began to be heard as early as the thirteenth century. A century before Ibn Khaldun discussed the cycles of political life, another thinker living in strife-torn

Mamluk times discussed the challenges facing the Muslim community – the famous legal thinker Ibn Taymiyya (d. 1328).

Ibn Taymiyya believed that many of the problems of the Muslim world in his time resulted from leaders' efforts to keep that world politically unified. Ideally, he said, the community was united, but in reality it was divided into regional units. But lack of political unity need not compromise the strength of Islamic society, because that strength was based on shared moral commitment rather than on political leadership. The entire Muslim community could be morally united, cooperating throughout history to carry out God's revealed will, regardless of time or place. Differences of language, ethnicity, and culture paled in light of a shared commitment to Islamic principles. Although Arabs had the advantage over non-Arabs in that their native language was Arabic, the language of the Quran, all believers are equal in the eyes of God. Ethnic and cultural diversity are part of God's plan, as the Quran confirms (49:13). Living in the wake of Christian and Mongol invasions, Ibn Taymiyya was very distrustful of non-Muslims. Still, he insisted on religious freedom and security for Jews and Christians, in accordance with the Quran. To do otherwise would violate the very purpose of the Islamic state: to establish justice. Like Ibn Khaldun, he believed that the goal of all revelation is to guide human beings in the struggle to establish justice and prohibit oppression. And that is a task in which all Muslims must cooperate.

Themes of Islamic Reform: Personal Initiative and Social Solidarity

In discussing this goal, Ibn Taymiyya brought up two issues that would become major themes of modern Islamic reform movement. The first is rejection of fatalism, passivity in the face of injustice, and relying on the intercession of saints rather than taking responsibility in one's society. Ibn Taymiyya argued forcefully against determinism, the idea that human beings have no free will. Through an odd series of events, determinism had actually become the dominant position among Muslim theologians by the time of Ibn Taymiyya. As we have seen, in Islam as in Judaism there is greater emphasis in daily life on correct action than on correct belief. Nevertheless, the basis of Islam was, as it remains, commitment to absolute monotheism. God is one and undivided in the Islamic perspective, absolute, all-knowing, and all-powerful, our merciful creator and judge, from whom we all came and to whom we all return. Acceptance of this ultimate reality is considered to the be basis of submission (*islam*), which will manifest itself in obedience or correct behavior which, in turn, will result in a just and peaceful society whose success is measured by the wellbeing of even the weakest members. In other words, Muslims' primary concern is with actualizing God's will, rather than defining or categorizing beliefs. Nevertheless, challenges to belief did arise from time to time, and scholars had to formulate responses. In the process, they developed a set of beliefs that became part of official Islamic teaching.

One such challenge came from the Kharijis. The Kharijis ("Seceders") were religious zealots who had supported Ali, Prophet Muhammad's cousin and son-in-law and thus closest surviving male relative, in his dispute with the dynastic Umayyads over who was the legitimate leader of the Muslim community. But the Kharijis had turned against Ali when he agreed to arbitration in his dispute with his opponents. They saw this decision on Ali's part as compromise with evil. They believed the Umayyads sought leadership of the community out of sheer greed. To the Kharijis, this was a betrayal of Islam, meaning that Ali himself and all his supporters, in their compromise with people whose behavior violated Islamic norms, also ceased to be true Muslims. They were convinced that true Islam/*islam* can only be manifested in correct behavior. Someone who acts unjustly cannot be considered Muslim because a *muslim* is someone who does the will of God. They took literally the Quran's directive that "Truth comes from your Lord, so let anyone who wishes to, believe; and let anyone who wishes to, disbelieve" (18:29). To the Kharijis this indicated ultimate individual responsibility, not only for belief but also for actions. If people behave badly, then it is their own choice and therefore their own responsibility. At the same time, the Kharijis believed, it is the responsibility of the righteous to make sure that those who are causing problems are stopped. They believed that the community had to be vigilant against those who did not live up to the Islamic model and who undermined the goal of establishing a just society. They believed it was especially important that Muslims rise up against an unjust leader. They therefore continued to fight Ali, forcing him into a battle (658) in which most of them were killed. The rest escaped to remote areas and carried out sporadic attacks against rulers who, they believed, acted in ways unbecoming of a true Muslim.

Unfortunately, it is difficult to maintain social order based on such a model of human perfection, and that is how the Khariji model looked to the majority of Muslims. The issue was particularly significant since excommunication had become a very serious matter in Islam. The Quran insists, "There is no compulsion in religion" (2:256). It stresses that a plurality of religious communities is part of the divine plan. "If your Lord had so willed, He would have made mankind one community, but they continue to be divided" (11:118). "For each of you [religious communities: Jews, Christians, Muslims] We have appointed a law and a ritual. If God had willed it, He could have made you all one religious community. But [He has not] so that He may test you in what He has given you. So compete with one another in good works" (5:48). This acceptance of religious diversity and freedom was reinforced when Prophet Muhammad established the constitution for the various tribes of Medina, some Muslim and some Jewish. "The Jews ... are a community along with the believers. To the Jews their religion and to the Muslims theirs."[6] Accordingly, as we have seen, religious pluralism was a basic feature of Islamic societies and, in fact, a source of much of their strength and dynamism.

However, the matter of apostasy – rejecting Islam after having accepted it – was something different. As the Islamic community developed in history, belonging or not belonging to the community became a political matter. A Muslim was someone who accepted not only the word and will of God, but also the chosen leader of the community. Thus, anyone who turned against the leader of the community was considered a traitor, a threat to the well-being of the rest of the community. As in medieval Europe, people believed that everyone who accepted a particular religion had to be part of the same political community. Like pre-modern Europeans, the early Muslim leaders believed that anyone who rejected their leadership was declaring himself an enemy. As a result, as we saw in Chapter 1, they made the decision to force the rebellious tribes to submit to their leadership or face death. This decision became a precedent in Islamic law. From that time on, the charge of apostasy was a grave matter. So when the Kharijis began labeling professed Muslims as apostates, it had to be taken seriously. After significant debates, the majority of Muslims asserted their commitment to the Quran's emphasis on divine mercy and forgiveness. They stressed the struggle for social justice and the need to do good works, but chose to leave judgment of individuals to God. In a characteristic verse, the Quran claims, "God lets anyone He wishes go astray and guides whomever He wishes" (35:8). To most Muslims this meant – as it still does – that only God can judge people's souls. If someone claims to be Muslim, the community must accept that. It has no right to declare a professed Muslim an apostate based on the person's actions. Only God can judge the sincerity of a believer's heart. This majority position was developed by religious scholars (`ulama') as a theory of divine judgment based on mercy and forgiveness. They were known as Murji'is ("Postponers"), claiming that if people identify themselves as Muslims, others must accept them as Muslims. In legal codes, the position was expressed by Abu Hanifa, who claimed that no one can judge a professed Muslim to be a non-Muslim based on his or her behavior.

The practical implications of this view were obvious. Khariji-style radicalism was marginalized, their rebellions were put down, and people could once again live in peace and security. But acceptance of this position had other implications in society. After accepting the position that only God can judge people, some scholars concluded that the Umayyads' victory in the battles against Ali and the Kharijis was itself an expression of God's will. Since God is all-powerful, nothing can happen without God's will. Therefore, if the Umayyads are in power, that must be the will of God, and people should not fight it.

This position may have resulted in political stability, but it also led to an attitude of fatalism about what happens in society.

Scholars continued to raise the question of people's moral responsibility. A central feature of the Quran's teaching is that people will be judged by God based on their actions. They will be rewarded for good choices and punished for bad ones. But if God has predetermined everything, including people's individual choices, then what about moral responsibility? What can we make of God's mercy and compassion if He is going to reward or punish people for doing things over which they really did not have control? In other words, what about free will? Muslims found themselves face to face with the age-old question of how to reconcile the notion of God's omnipotence (all-powerfulness) with human responsibility. This discussion gave rise to another school of thought among Islamic religious scholars, the Mutazilis. Known as Islam's rationalists, the Mutazilis chose to stress God's justice, rather than God's omnipotence. God revealed that He is just, and that He will judge people based on their choices. Therefore, we must assume that human beings have moral responsibility. But other scholars found this position offensive. They believed that the Mutazili position put boundaries on God, as if to say that God would be forced to judge in specific ways based on what human beings did.

There were many other issues involved in the scholars' discussions about the question of God's omnipotence and justice. But eventually the rationalist position was overruled, and the position of an anti-rationalist scholar, al-Ashari (d. 935) became official teaching. The Ashari rejection of excessive rationalism in religion became associated with fatalism and determinism. It was this that Ibn Taymiyya argued against. He found it particularly evident in Sufi mysticism, with its emphasis on personal enlightenment, rather than social issues. He considered determinism worse than heresy, because it makes a mockery of God's promises of reward for good behavior and punishment for evil. Ibn Taymiyya was not opposed to Sufism; he believed that their spirituality was essential to true morality. But he rejected some practices associated with Sufism, such as praying to saints rather than relying on God, personal initiative, and group cooperation in the struggle to create and maintain a just society. He was, in fact, an inspiration in this regard to the Wahhabis, although the Wahhabis would take the position further, rejecting Sufism altogether.

As we saw in Chapter 3, this theme arose again in seventeenth-century India, where Sufism was most dominant, with the reform movement of Sheikh Ahmad Sirhindi. Sirhindi was particularly concerned with the kind of Sufi teaching that undermined the significance of everyday reality. According to some Sufi thinkers, all reality is One, and external appearances are just illusions. Through meditation and other spiritual practices, people should rise above appearances and focus on the oneness of all reality. Sirhindi believed this attitude distracted people from commitment to following the law. Later, another Indian reformer, Shah Wali Allah of Delhi (d. 1762), taught that Sufis must purify their practice and conform to mainstream Islamic teaching in order to achieve the goal of a strong, just, and united Islamic society.

Themes of Islamic Reform: Ijtihad

The second major theme of Islamic reform stressed by Ibn Taymiyya is the need to keep Islamic law flexible through *ijtihad*. As noted in Chapter 1, Islamic law is the core of Islamic society. Because of Islam's emphasis on good works and the creation of a just society, concern with behavior, rather than concern with belief, is dominant. True belief is assumed to be an essential prerequisite to righteous behavior, but rational discussion of belief remained relatively marginal in Islam. For that reason, the focus of religious thought in the first several centuries of Islam was law. By the tenth century, four major schools of Sunni law had been established, and a fifth developed in Shii Islam. During the early years of Islam, Islamic law was open and flexible. Its goal was to provide ongoing guidance for the ever-expanding Islamic community regarding what was permissible in view of the Quran and the example set by Prophet Muhammad. Flexibility was especially important, given that the Muslim world quickly came to include multiple, diverse cultures. In addition, circumstances rarely remained static: new conditions arose as societies developed economically, culturally, and politically. Yet, by the tenth century, Islamic law began to lose its flexibility. The interpretive element of Islamic law is called *ijtihad*. Sometimes called "intellectual *jihad*" since the two terms share a single root (meaning "to struggle"), *ijtihad* was the means by which scholars derived legislation concerning new or changed circumstances from the sources: the Quran and the Sunna. But as we saw in Chapter 2, eventually the scholars added another source of Islamic law: consensus (*ijmà*) among the scholars concerning the legal implications of the Quran and the Sunna. And using that source, they determined that no new *ijtihad* would be needed.

There is no particular date for this decision, nor is any one person given credit for it. The agreement that "the gate of *ijtihad* is closed" seems to have developed gradually. But is was evident by the beginning of the tenth century, says historian of Islamic law Joseph Schacht:

> [T]he point had been reached when the scholars of all schools felt that all essential questions had been thoroughly discussed and finally settled, and a consensus gradually established itself to the effect that from that time onwards no one might be deemed to have the necessary qualifications for independent reasoning [*ijtihad*] in law, and that all future activity would have to be confined to the explanation, application, and, at the most, interpretation of the doctrine as it had been laid down once and for all.[7]

In place of independent reasoning as a means for developing Islamic law in changing circumstances, the following of precedent (*taqlid*) was recommended.

Presumably, the goal of the scholars in discouraging *ijtihad* and encouraging *taqlid* was to maintain continuity in Islamic law, particularly during the perilous years when the central power of the caliph was giving way to autonomous regional powers (see Chapter 3). But in the view of many reformers the cessation of *ijtihad* makes Islamic law inflexible and unable to deal effectively with change, with deleterious results. First, Islamic law was marginalized. Political authorities began to legislate independent of the legal scholars, to suit their own needs. As we saw, Suleiman the Magnificent was known as Suleiman the Lawgiver at home, because of his penchant for legislation. But his law was not based on the Islamic sources; it was not called Shariah. Suleiman's law was called *qanun*, civil law as opposed to religious law. This pattern was followed by many other regional rulers, and especially by the European colonial powers. As non-Muslims, European citizens were exempt from Islamic personal law, and the Capitulations made them exempt from Islamic civil law. When European powers took control of Islamic governments, they continued the process of marginalizing Islamic law, setting up their own systems of economic, commercial, and civil law.

A related consequence of ending *ijtihad* was that people were left without religious guidance on new developments as they arose. In classical times, Islamic legal scholars (*fuqaha'*) were the bulwark of civil society. They were the people's protection against the autocratic tendencies of the caliph or sultan (ruler). Religious authority was the only protection against the sultan's awesome power. But the less flexible Shariah scholars were, the more people turned to secular law for guidance. By the modern era, religious law was restricted to ritual and personal matters – prayer, fasting, pilgrimage, charity, marriage, divorce, and inheritance. Shariah was considered a closed set. If Muslims wanted guidance on other matters, they would have to seek elsewhere.

Ibn Taymiyya recognized the danger of this trend even in the fourteenth century. He argued that *ijtihad* must remain active, lest Islamic law become irrelevant. Even during his day, the tendency was to consider Islamic law as a closed code rather than a dynamic process of deriving guidance for human life from divinely revealed sources. For this reason, Ibn Taymiyya stressed the difference between Shariah and *fiqh*. Shariah is God's will for humanity, revealed in nature, in history, in the Torah and the Gospels, but revealed most perfectly in the Quran and the example set by Prophet Muhammad (the Sunna). It is eternal and changeless, and many specific regulations have been made explicit in it. These include regulations concerning ritual, some dietary restrictions, and major moral issues such as murder, theft, and usury. But human beings must use reason to derive legislation from the revealed sources for circumstances not specifically dealt with in revelation. The regulations derived in this way by human beings are the realm of *fiqh*, and they are not changeless or infallible. Ibn Taymiyya was appalled that people equate *fiqh* with

Shariah. "Indeed, some of them think that Sharia is the name given to the judge's decisions; many of them even do not make a distinction between a learned judge, an ignorant judge and an unjust judge. Worse still, people tend to regard any decrees of a ruler as Sharia, while sometimes undoubtedly the truth (*haqiqa*) is actually contrary to the decree of the ruler."[8] In other words, Muslims in every generation must continue to seek guidance from the revealed sources, rather than relying on decisions made by people in the past. Not only are people fallible, so that their interpretations must be reexamined in light of new evidence or circumstances, but the fact that a decision was suitable for a given time and place does not necessarily mean it will remain suitable for all times and places. Ibn Taymiyya therefore insisted that *ijtihad* was a religious duty, essential to the vitality of the Muslim community.

The call to renew *ijtihad* was echoed by Muhammad Ibn Abd al-Wahhab, founder of the Wahhabis, in the eighteenth century. He treated Sufi saint worship and other innovations from early Islamic practice as the result of following human beings' guidance (*taqlid*), rather than that of revelation. Several other scholars during the eighteenth and nineteenth centuries echoed the same theme, but the most articulate expression came from Egyptian scholar Muhammad Abduh (d. 1905). In his view, *taqlid* was equivalent to intellectual servitude. He says that the Quran:

> forbids us to be slavishly credulous and for our stimulus points [to] the moral of peoples who simply followed their fathers with complacent satisfaction and were finally involved in an utter collapse of their beliefs and their own disappearance as a community. Well it is said that traditionalism can have evil consequences as well as good and may occasion loss as well as conduce gain. It is a deceptive thing, and though it may be pardoned in an animal, is scarcely seemly in man.[9]

It was the creativity of *ijtihad* that had allowed the Islamic community to thrive, responding dynamically to changing historic circumstances and, within a few centuries after the death of Prophet Muhammad, become one of the world's major political and cultural forces. But when people began to simply imitate their ancestors, elevating tradition to the status of virtue, they lost their initiative and fell into obscurity. They became easy prey for more energetic forces.

Unfortunately, at the same time that Abduh and other Islamic reformers were advocating reform of Islamic law and life through *ijtihad*, European powers were in the process of imposing European law codes in their newly acquired territories. They found it very difficult to deal with Islamic legal codes, particularly in conducting their international financial transactions. Criticizing Islamic law as rigid and archaic, they simply bypassed it. But in the context of increasing foreign domination many people became defensive of traditional law. It was essential to their identity as Muslims. Ultimately, it became difficult to distinguish between Western attacks on Islamic law as inadequate and Islamic reformers' critiques of Islamic law as moribund. As a result, many traditional Islamic scholars denounced reformers such as Abduh as "Westernizers," trying to conform Islam to European standards. (It is this complex interplay of historic forces that led to Islamic fundamentalism. We will discuss this further in Chapter 5.)

Themes of Islamic Reform: Commitment to Learning

A related theme of Islamic reform developed in the twentieth century is the call for renewed commitment to the Islamic tradition of scientific excellence. It is based on the recognition that Muslims had lost their commitment to learning. Among the first to voice this theme was Abduh's one-time mentor, the famous Persian anti-imperialist Jamal al-Din al-Afghani (d.1897). Among the things that annoyed Islamic reformers the most about European imperialism was the fact that it was often rationalized on the basis of claims that Islamic culture was backward and unscientific. Afghani reminded his listeners that it was Islam's commitment to learning that had produced the highest scientific culture in the Middle Ages. Scholars in the Muslim world had pulled together the ancient traditions of Greece, Rome, Egypt,

Mesopotamia, Persia, India, and China, revising and developing them, and then transmitted them to Europe. Where would modern Europe be without Arabic numerals and algebra, for example? This is the way science works, he noted. It is "continually changing capitals. Sometimes it has moved from East to West, and other times form West to East." Science does not belong to any single culture; it is a world heritage to which various communities have contributed at various times. Muslims have made major contributions to science, as history demonstrates, and so the Europeans are mistaken when they claim that Islam is inherently unscientific or backward. In fact, he says, of all the major religions Islam is the most supportive of science. When Islam came to the Arabs, they had no science. But Islam encouraged study and the acquisition of knowledge, and that's why Muslims quickly developed the highest degree of learning known to the Western world.

However, Afghani also recognized that Muslims had lost their commitment to learning. They had lost the scientific spirit. They had passed it on to the Europeans and, he believed, that is why the Muslim world had been overcome by the Europeans. Afghani was particularly critical of people who called themselves religious scholars. He said that their minds were actually "full of every superstition and vanity." They were unable to even take care of their communities, but they were nevertheless "proud of their own foolishness." These scholars were "like a very narrow wick on top of which is a very small flame that neither lights its surroundings nor gives light to others." And then Afghani pointed out the defensiveness of their position. He said they have mistakenly "divided science into two parts. One they call Muslim science, and one European science." Having lost their commitment to learning, Muslim scholars did not even recognize their own scientific heritage when confronted with it in modern form. They thought it was all foreign. Similar to the way in which legal scholars had rejected their own reformers, accusing them of engaging in "Westernization," religious scholars had rejected modern learning as "un-Islamic." He concludes, "those who forbid science and knowledge in the belief that they are safeguarding the Islamic religion are really the enemies of that religion. The Islamic religion is the closest of religions to science and knowledge, and there is no incompatibility between science and knowledge and the foundation of the Islamic faith."[10]

Abduh related the need for reform of Islamic law through *ijtihad* to Islam's inherent rationality. He described the rationality of the universe as a reflection of divine unity. Rejecting the tendency to split the world into the spiritual (religious) realm and the physical (non-religious) realm, Abduh insisted that the divine is revealed through all creation. That is why the Quran frequently reminds people to examine the world and see the signs of God in it. Based on the Quranic command to "read the signs" and "seek knowledge," Abduh actually considered the exercise of reason to be essential to the practice of Islam, even a form of worship. Failure to exercise one's reason was a religious failing: "So the Quran directs us, enjoining rational procedure and intellectual enquiry into the manifestations of the universe, and, as far as may be, into its particulars, so as to come by certainty in respect of the things to which it guides."[11]

Conclusion

Islamic reformers in this period agreed that there is no distinction between religious and secular science. As Ibn Khaldun had pointed out 500 years earlier, human beings were created with reason; that is the difference between them and animals. They were then commissioned by God to use it in order to carry out the "trust," their divinely mandated task to create and maintain a just society. Whether scrutinizing revelation, history, or nature, reason is required on an ongoing basis. When Muslim scholars lost their commitment to careful reasoning, relying instead on the past and making a virtue of imitating it, the Muslim world began to lose its cutting edge. It fell into stagnation and became easy prey for foreign adventurers. Among the most eloquent expressions of this theme is found in the work of Indian reformer Muhammad Iqbal (d. 1938). Iqbal said that Islam had fallen into stagnation 500 years ago, when it substituted inertia for its essential dynamism and adaptability. Also an advocate of *ijtihad* as the key to Islam's ability to adapt to ever-changing circumstances, Iqbal also found its root in human rationality. He criticized the scholars for their conservatism and fear of change. Although deeply mystical himself, he also criticized Sufis for excessive concern with the inner meanings of things. Muslims must be concerned with the practical world. Like Ibn Khaldun, Iqbal also criticized those who take a passive attitude toward life, waiting for God to send a great man to lead the community properly. In Ibn Khaldun's case, it was the Mahdi that people were waiting for; in Iqbal's critique, it was the *mujaddid*, or renewer (someone God would send at the beginning of every century to guide people, a belief Iqbal traces only to the sixteenth century). Relating the exercise of reason again to *ijtihad*, he said the "closing of the door of *ijtihad* is pure fiction" resulting from "intellectual laziness ... If some of the later doctors have upheld this fiction, modern Islam is not bound by this voluntary surrender of intellectual independence."[12]

Muhammad Iqbal – the advocate of dynamic, adaptable, progressive Islam – is known as the father of Pakistan. But today Pakistan is one of the poorest nations in the world, with an illiteracy rate of nearly two-thirds, and a brief history dominated by military dictators. It is also one of the most conservative states in the Muslim world. And Pakistan is just one example. The Muslim world overall has made little progress toward its goals in the modern era. What happened to the movement to revive Islam's commitment to reason and progress, which had been developing for centuries? Is it still alive anywhere? These are the questions that will be addressed in Chapter 5.

Chapter 5

Obstacles and Prospects
for Islamic Reform

Reformers such as Afghani and Abduh viewed the superior strength of European culture as a temporary phenomenon. As we saw in Chapter 2, scholars in the Islamic world had developed the natural sciences to their highest level during the Middle Ages. Muslim mathematicians, astronomers, and physicians were among the world's most renowned scholars. But by the modern era little evidence of this greatness remained beyond some terminology that has become so familiar that it is hardly associated with Islam any more. Reformers were convinced that Islam's eclipse had resulted from Muslims' dereliction of duty and violation of their own principles. They had fallen into a comfortable traditionalism, following the paths of their ancestors rather than forging new paths and meeting new challenges with confidence. As discussed in the previous chapter, early modern reformers identified three areas of Islamic life in which this was particularly evident: some Sufi practices that resulted in passivity and superstition; the habitual practice of *taqlid* (following precedent) among legal scholars rather than *ijtihad* (independent reasoning); and the rejection of modern learning by some religious scholars. As a remedy, many reformers called for the renewal of Muslims' activism and commitment to learning and science. Jamal al-Din al-Afghani insisted that science was not just a luxury; it was the basis of power. "If someone looks deeply into the question, he will see that science rules the world." He recounted the stories of the Chaldeans, the Egyptians, the Phoenicians, and the Greeks, and concluded,

The Europeans have now put their hands on every part of the world ... In reality this usurpation, aggression, and conquest has not come from the French or the English. Rather it is science that everywhere manifests its greatness and power. Ignorance had no alternative to prostrating itself humbly before science and acknowledging its submission."[1]

The question inevitably arises: given the length of time that Muslims have been advocating renewal and reform, why have their efforts not resulted in the desired renaissance? The term "renaissance" or "rebirth" (*nahdah*) was, in fact, optimistically used in the nineteenth and twentieth centuries to describe the goal of both cultural and religious reform movements. As late as 1989 a Tunisian Islamic reform movement renamed itself the Renaissance Party (Hizb al-Nahdah). Now, in the wake of September 11, the fall of the Taliban government in Afghanistan, and the fall of Saddam Hussein in Iraq, Islamic recovery seems as distant as ever. In this chapter we will discuss what obstacles have impeded the progress of Islamic renewal, and survey prospects for the future.

Obstacles: The Impact of Colonialism

Obviously, the outcome of World War I (see Chapter 4) had a very negative impact on the Muslim world. Instead of the expected independence and opportunity to develop economically, socially, and politically, most of the Muslim world found itself burdened with further European domination, often more direct than it had been before the war, and with a strong sense of betrayal and humiliation.

In this context, the call for renewal and reform became even more widespread than it had been before the war, but it also changed in tone. The self-scrutiny and often biting internal criticism that characterized the discourse of early Islamic reform were replaced with a defensiveness and tendency to focus on the external factors contributing to Muslim societies' problems – the actions of the West in particular. As well, the rational analysis of early reform was overshadowed by emotional accounts of the suffering caused by Western governments and their allies within the Muslim world, and utopian descriptions of what is generally characterized as "the Islamic solution."

One of the results of this shift was a popular rejection of those reformers who drew negative comparisons of conditions in the Muslim world with those in the West. The case of nineteenth-century Egyptian reformer Qasim Amin is a good example. Amin joined in an ongoing debate about the need for reform in the status of women. Abduh, like other reformers, had insisted on the need for educational reform in the Muslim world. Also like other reformers, he added that women as well as men must be educated. The education of both sexes was essential to social development. At the same time, several reformers added, Muslims must reexamine their overall treatment of women. They must recognize that in many ways the standards of dignity and equality established by the Quran had been abandoned in the case of women. This was the theme developed by Qasim Amin. In a book called *Tahrir al-Mar'a* (The Liberation of Woman, 1899), he argued that women's education and improved status in marriage, including ending the seclusion of women, was a necessary component of the overall health of Islamic society. But Amin's criticisms took the form of an attack on traditional religious scholars. He said that they had absolutely no interest in science. They could discuss the grammar of a single phrase from the Quran "in no fewer than a thousand ways," he said, but if you asked them anything about history, geography, or science, "they shrug their shoulders, contemptuous of the question." Amin concluded that the religious scholars were greedy and lazy.[2] This, combined with sarcastic descriptions of how unattractive traditional Egyptian women are, naturally turned popular opinion against his reforms. His criticisms of Islamic society sounded just like the criticisms leveled by the Europeans.

For many people, as for the religious scholars themselves, the major issue facing the Muslim world was now less the need for reform than the need for loyalty. To agree too enthusiastically with demands for change appeared to be collaboration with the imperial enemies. And this was exactly how Amin's work was received. Dozens of extremely hostile articles appeared in the newly developing Egyptian press, some even accusing Amin of carrying out his "attacks against Egypt" under orders from the British colonial government. Even today Amin is described as an unrepentant Westernizer – in effect, a "self-hating Muslim." Actually, the reforms he urged were not revolutionary; many others before him had called for improvement in the status of women, in accordance with Quranic standards. But under the impact of colonialism, and because of the association of such critiques with the foreigners who had taken over, opposition to change took the form of defending traditional practices. In other words, calls for reform in the context of colonialism often had an effect that was the direct opposite of what was intended. They increased people's attachment to tradition.

A similar reaction was perceptible in the area of educational reform. There is no question that education was in need of renewal. Islam's traditional commitment to learning had been undermined when the great medieval empires began to fade, chiefly because of the way traditional Islamic education developed. Although the sciences continued to flourish in the Muslim world well into the sixteenth century, they did so generally under the patronage of wealthy sponsors. Scientific study was not institutionalized as part of Islamic education. It was left to private scholars supported by wealthy sultans and princes. The natural sciences sometimes produced unorthodox speculation, such as the possibility of the eternity of the world and the impossibility of the resurrection of a dead body. As a result, religious scholars spurned such studies and, as we saw in Ibn Taymiyya's fourteenth-century critiques, limited their own studies to what had already been done. They focused on complex discussions of the Quran's grammar, style, and meaning, and on discussions of the ancestors' commentaries on its grammar, style, and meaning.

In the nineteenth and twentieth centuries, reformers often focused on this phenomenon. They expressed deep concern that reverence for tradition, combined with a distaste for controversy, effectively precluded innovation in Islamic education. During Europe's "Dark Ages," Muslim religious scholars' lack of science did not appear to be a problem, and early reformers' critiques fell on deaf ears. But when the medieval Islamic empires fell into decline, they were no longer able to subsidize the sciences at their private institutes. At the same time, European scholars began to develop the very sciences they had inherited from the Muslim world. European colonization of the Muslim world made it very clear that the tables had turned. Muslim reformers again recognized the need for reform. If the Muslim world had produced the world's cultural leaders in the past, so the reformers argued, it could do so again. It was simply a matter of recovering Islam's lost dynamism and commitment to learning in the service of humanity.

But in the context of European colonialism, again, this process of internal critique was compromised. Some religious scholars may indeed have fallen into an inflexible traditionalism. But they remained the backbone of Islamic society, the symbol of Islamic identity. And that symbolic value increased proportionately with every step European powers made in the Muslim world. Colonial control brought European innovations into the streets of the capitals – automobiles, highways, telephones and telegraphs, European clothing and music, and public mixing of the sexes. The greater the displacement of traditional lifestyles by these developments, the more important symbols of tradition became to many people living under the European yoke. For their part, the traditional religious scholars had become accustomed to the status quo. True, a good percentage of their traditional financial support had been confiscated by the newfangled states. But the scholars still enjoyed the status of respected elders in society and undoubtedly felt a responsibility to their communities. In this context, the more Islamic reformers criticized the traditional scholars as an impediment to development and independence in the Muslim world, the more they sounded like the Europeans who justified their imperialism by claiming the Muslims were incapable of running their own affairs. As a result, many educational reformers, in fact, alienated people in their own societies. In the eyes of people already under the pressure of colonization, these internal criticisms – despite their good intentions – seemed to be betrayals. Not all religious scholars rejected reform, of course. But tradition was well entrenched. Muhammad Abduh could not even get his own university – the famous center of Sunni Islamic learning, al-Azhar University – to teach Ibn Khaldun's *Muqaddimah*. "It would be against the tradition of teaching at al-Azhar," he was told.[3]

Another effect of the sense of betrayal by Europe in World War I was an intense emphasis on self-reliance. This took the form of insistence that Islam alone was sufficient for all human needs. This new discourse served the dual purpose of appealing to the broadest possible audience in largely under-educated populations, and motivating them to become politically involved. Thus, rather than criticizing people's passivity and superstitions as the earlier reformers had done, the more populist post-World War I reformers focused on what could be called consciousness-raising. As in the American Civil Rights movement and certain quarters of feminism, listeners were regaled with accounts of the suffering they had undergone at the hands of an essentialized enemy and encouraged to rise up and assert their rights. (Interestingly, in all three cases, the stereotyped enemy was usually the same: white men.) At the same time, the new populist discourse marked a subtle shift in the focus of modern Islamic movements, from reform to revival. Earlier Islamic activists had noted Islam's strength in the past and placed their calls for reform in that context; Muslims had to reform in order to recover the strength inherent in Islamic societies. The new trend in Islamic movements was not to deny the need for reform, but simply to stress the inherent glories of the religion as the means to recover Islamic societies' lost strength.

A natural corollary of the emphasis on the absolute sufficiency of Islam was its politicization. Islam came to be characterized as more than mere belief and rituals, as Western Christianity appeared to be. Instead, Islam was a comprehensive worldview and set of values and principles designed to guide all aspects of life – personal, social, economic, and political. From the perspective of this politicized Islam (called political Islam or Islamism by scholars or, less accurately, fundamentalism), pre-World War I political organization, with its secular orientation, was inappropriate for Muslim societies. The new order they proposed would be wholly Islamic. Unlike the earlier political parties, generally populated by educated people from the cities who had often gone to European schools and were comfortable with modern life, post-war reformers represented the majority of people – still largely rural or newly urbanized and generally traditional in outlook. Motivating them to become politically active in order to achieve independence and good governance became a major task of the Islamists. Competing with secular governments with far greater resources, often supplied through close relations with foreign powers, the Islamists demanded that foreign models of government be replaced with authentic Islamic governments.

The first and still the most widespread of these religio-political organizations was the Muslim Brotherhood. It began in Egypt in the late 1920s and gradually spread throughout much of the Arabic-speaking world. Its founder, Hasan al-Banna (d. 1949), described his reasons for founding the Brotherhood in a story with characteristic emotional appeal. He told of a group of laborers working for the British on the Suez Canal who came to him and begged him to lead them to freedom. According to al-Banna's account, they said:

We are weary of this life of humiliation and restriction … we see that Arabs and Muslims have no status and no dignity. They are no more than mere hirelings belonging to the foreigners … We are unable to perceive the road to action as you perceive it, or to know the path to the service of the fatherland [*watan*], the religion and the *ummah* [Muslim community] as you know it … All that we desire now is to present you with all that we possess, to be acquitted by God of the responsibility, and for you to be responsible before him for us and for what we must do. If a group contracts with God sincerely that it live for his religion and die in his service, seeking only his satisfaction, then its worthiness will assure its success however small its numbers or weak its means.[4]

This appeal to the sentiments of his audience allowed them to empathize with the suffering of the weak and lowly members of society. The impact is then compounded by identifying the villain responsible for the tragic plight of these pathetic workers and, by extension, of the Muslim people as a whole. It is "the West." Like the Crusaders of yore, "The West surely seeks to humiliate us, to occupy our lands and begin destroying Islam by annulling its laws and abolishing its traditions."[5] Whether it is capitalist Europe or communist Russia, al-Banna tells his listeners, the West is degenerate. The West's intellectual freedom and democracy are good, and there is nothing wrong with capitalism as such, al-Banna explains, but the West is hopelessly materialistic, and always willing to oppress the poor for the sake of the wealthy. Similarly, communism's emphasis on social justice and solidarity is admirable, al-Banna says, especially by contrast to Europe's selfish individualism. But communism's atheism and tyranny (its "Red barbarism") are no better than tsarist Russia's degenerate culture. Altogether, he concludes, Western ideologies have resulted in "a deadening of human sentiments and sympathies, and ... the extinction of godly endeavors and spiritual values."[6] The solution to society's woes, then, is perfectly clear:

> We believe the provisions of Islam and its teachings are all inclusive, encompassing the affairs of the people in this world and the hereafter. And those who think that these teachings are concerned only with the spiritual or ritualistic aspects are mistaken in this belief because Islam is a faith and a ritual, a nation and a nationalism, a religion and a state, spirit and deed, holy text and sword ...[7]

The most popular ideologue of the Muslim Brotherhood, Sayyid Qutb (d. 1966), further developed the themes of al-Banna. Like al-Banna, he explained that the world is divided between two hostile blocs, the communists and the capitalists. Each of them is determined to control the world for its own benefit and with no thought for the well-being of anyone else. "[N]either the Eastern Bloc nor the Western Bloc gives any credence to the values they advocate, or consider us ourselves as of any consequence ... We will receive no mercy from either bloc. We are oppressed strangers in the ranks of both. We are therefore the tail end of the caravan regardless of the road we take."[8] In what would become a dominant perception among contemporary Islamists, Qutb claimed that the West seeks to destroy Islam. The reason for this hostility toward Islam? Qutb claimed that the West is "angered only because of the [Muslim] believers' faith, enraged only because of their belief."[9] The source of people's problems, then, is nothing less than the perennial struggle between good and evil, and the answer to all their problems is clear. Islam "is capable of solving our basic problems, of granting us a comprehensive social justice, of restoring for us justice in government, in economics, in opportunities and in punishment." There is no need to turn to any other system.[10]

Anyone tempted to follow Western models only has to look at the misery in which Western people live, according to Sayyid Qutb. They walk around in

grief, sorrow and uneasiness. [Western man] is miserable, distressed and prey to confusion. He seeks to escape from life. Sometimes he takes refuge in opium, hasheesh and wine and sometimes wishes to forget his inner anxieties through the craze of rapidity and idiotic ventures ... It seems as if it were a hoard of demons who were chasing man and he were trying to flee and evade it, but it were always taking hold of his neck.[11]

Obviously, then, people must avoid Western innovations. Islam is the only proper course for humanity. It is the "only path that grants man excellence, bestows on him true freedom, and saves him from the curse of slavery." Islam, by granting sovereignty over human beings to no one but God, is the only religion that truly liberates humanity from earthly bonds.[12]

Sayyid Qutb remains the dominant spokesman of this post-World War I approach to Islamic revival. He was influenced by and influenced Abu'l Ala Mawdudi (d. 1979), the founder of South Asia's dominant movement of Islamic revival, the Jamaat-i Islami, established in the 1940s. In Mawdudi's works Islam is again the ideal solution to all of society's ills. Unlike other systems, says Mawdudi, Islam does not allow one group to dominate another.

In fact, it is an all-embracing order that wants to eliminate and to eradicate the other orders which are false and unjust, so as to replace them by a good order and a moderate program that is considered to be better for humanity than the others and to contain rescue from the illnesses of evil and tyranny, happiness and prosperity for the human race, both in this world and in the Hereafter.[13]

Unlike Western secularism, Islam "is a complete scheme of life and an all-embracing social order where nothing is superfluous and nothing lacking."[14]

Eventually, over the course of the twentieth century, the Muslim world did gain independence from its various colonial overlords. But independence was achieved as a result of enormous struggle, leaving liberated populations exhausted, in social and economic upheaval, and without stable governmental structures. Often those who led the liberation struggles took political control after independence, by default. Throughout the formerly colonized ("developing") world, it would take decades for communities to develop suitable, representative governments. In the meanwhile, post-independence rulers remain frequently as unpopular as the colonial occupiers had been. As we saw in Chapter 4, Iran – though it had avoided direct colonial control – is a case in point. And the effectiveness of the new stress on politicized Islam was never more apparent than in the career of Ayatollah Khomeini. As noted in the previous chapter, Shah Muhammad Reza Pahlavi was returned to power after the American-led overthrow of the popular anti-shah prime minister Muhammad Mosaddeq in 1953. The shah then continued his efforts to strengthen central power and speed Iran's transition into modern secular statehood. His White Revolution, launched in the 1960s, involved land redistribution which shifted power from traditional landholders, the modernization and secularization of schools, and the expansion of women's rights. There was opposition from many – often conflicting – quarters, including communists and capitalists, intellectuals and peasants. But leadership of the opposition was taken over by those with the broadest authority – religious scholars – and Ayatollah Khomeini quickly came to the forefront.

Again, the popular speeches of Ayatollah Khomeini are a prime example of political Islam's motivational appeal. Like that of the founding ideologues of the Muslim Brotherhood and Jamaat-i Islami, the focal point of his discourse was justice for the suffering people of Islam. He often appealed to Shii heritage in ways designed to arouse emotion. In an address delivered after the shah's troops killed several students at a seminary in Qum in 1963, he reminded the audience of the deaths of women and children at the hands of the Umayyad rulers in the eighth century. Shii Muslims believe the Umayyads were usurpers, and that the grandson of Prophet Muhammad, Hussein, was the rightful leader of all Muslims. But the Umayyads massacred Imam Hussein and his followers. Khomeini compared the shah's attack on the seminarians to that of the Umayyads against Hussein and his followers, arousing powerful sentiments in the audience. He then described the attack as nothing short of an attack on Islam itself:

> What did [the Shah's regime] have against the students of theology? ... What had our eighteen year-old sayyid [a student who had been killed in the attack] done to the Shah? What had he done against the government? What had he done against the brutal regime of Iran? [The audience cries.] Therefore we must conclude that it wanted to do away with the foundation. It is against the foundation of Islam and the clergy. It does not want this foundation to exist. It does not want our youth and elders to exist.[15]

After capturing the sympathy of the audience, Khomeini characteristically shifted emotional gears, from pathos to anger. He focused the blame for the sufferings of Iranians on foreigners or on the shah's regime, described as merely a tool of foreigners. A typical example: "All of our troubles today are caused by America and Israel. Israel itself derives from America; these deputies and ministers that have been imposed upon us derive from America – they are all agents of America, for it they were not, they would rise up in protest."[16] Khomeini then directs the audience's anger, telling them to rise up against the "agents of the enemies of Islam" and expose the sinister and destructive designs of imperialism.[17]

The emotional appeal, the external focusing of anger, and the general call to action were all extremely effective in consciousness-raising. Building upon the work of his predecessors, such as Ali Shariati (d. 1977), Khomeini's skillful articulation of these themes resulted in a mass following. He was able to fill the streets of Iran's cities with hundreds of thousands of people protesting against the shah's regime. Ultimately, his followers brought so much pressure on the regime that it collapsed. This was the Iranian Islamic Revolution of 1979, replacing the shah's secular government with a government led by religious scholars.

The ability to clearly identify both a foreign source of all society's problems and a simple and sacred solution was no doubt more appealing than self-critical rational analyses calling for extensive internal reform advanced by scholars like Muhammad Abduh. It allowed a vent for the emotional energy aroused by the accounts of their own suffering. As noted, reformist themes were not eliminated from this discourse. Sayyid Qutb, for example, called for flexibility in Islamic governments, rather than a simple return to the past. He said, "The Islamic system has room for scores of models which are compatible with the natural growth of a society and the new needs of the contemporary age."[18] Government must be based on consultation, and there must be no discrimination based on ethnicity or gender.[19] The Jamaat-i Islami's Mawdudi was extremely conservative socially, believing a woman's place is in the home, obedient to her husband. He was also conservative politically, insisting that non-Muslims be excluded from Islamic governments, but even he expressed support for *ijtihad* in order to develop suitable legislation for modern societies. But reform is a long process, and reformers in the Muslim world have faced formidable odds from the outset. The majority of governments in the Muslim world are undemocratic. Most have some form of democratic institutions in place, but in most cases a strong military holds real power and little opposition is tolerated. Ironically, the success of the Islamic Revolution in Iran made reform elsewhere more difficult. It raised the hopes of Islamists everywhere, but it also raised the fears of governments throughout the Muslim world that they would be the next targets of Islamists. Suppression of Islamist movements therefore increased throughout the 1980s. Suppression, in turn, intensified the emotionalism of Islamist rhetoric. In countries supported by the United States, heightened anti-Americanism was the inevitable outcome of the growing sense of victimization.

Indeed, as the twentieth century drew to a close and the Islamic Revolution in Iran receded into the past, there were no further victories of Islamist reform movements. Islamist parties had made progress in some elections. In Algeria, for example, in 1991 the popular Islamic Salvation Front (Jabhat al-Inqadh al-Islami, in Arabic; usually known by its French initials, FIS) was poised to dominate in the first federal elections open to opposition parties since independence from France. But the military stepped in and stopped the elections, sparking a bloody civil war that lasted until 2005. In many parts of the Muslim world, conditions worsened. The conflict between Israelis and Palestinians remained unresolved, as did that between Kashmiris and Indians. In the case of Afghanistan, just as Iranians were celebrating the victory of the Islamic Revolution, the Soviet Union was launching an occupation that would plunge the region and, arguably, the world into a conflict from which it is still struggling to emerge.

Throughout the 1980s, Afghans mounted formidable resistance to the Soviet occupation. Globally, there was widespread sympathy for the Afghans' efforts at self-defense. In the Muslim world it was seen as a legitimate form of *jihad*, and resistance fighters were known as the Mujahideen (the plural form of the Arabic term for "holy warrior" or "one who fights *jihad*"). Many of the Mujahideen leaders took their inspiration from Islamist ideologues such as Hasan al-Banna, Sayyid Qutb, and Mawdudi. They were joined in their efforts by Muslims and others from around the world, including Osama bin Laden of Saudi Arabia and Ayman al-Zawahiri of Egypt. And they were strongly supported by US weapons, training, and finance. Ten years of brutal warfare left over 1 million Afghans dead, several million displaced, and ruined economies, including that of the Soviet Union. In 1989 Soviet troops withdrew, and two years later the USSR collapsed. However, following the Soviet withdrawal, Afghanistan also fell into a debilitating civil war. After tens of thousands more deaths, order was restored only by the Taliban. These were former refugees, many of them orphans who had grown up in camps in Afghanistan and Pakistan due to the devastation caused by Soviet occupation and the civil war.

The plight of all refugees of the war in Afghanistan was dire. The international community, especially America, had been very generous during the resistance to Soviet occupation. But America's interest in Afghanistan ceased following Soviet withdrawal. The refugees – numbering 4–5 million by the year 2000 – were left to the care of the already strained resources of the United Nations, host countries such as Pakistan and Iran, and non-governmental organizations. The Taliban gained their name ("students") because they were among the few refugees to receive any education at all. They received virtually no modern education, only fundamental religious education that was heavily influenced by puritanical tendencies similar to those of the Wahhabi Saudis, the source of much of the funding for this education. They became convinced that returning to the simplest lifestyle of early Islam and strictly adhering to religious rules would please God. In return, God would allow them victory over their enemies.

The Taliban set out to cleanse Afghanistan of what they considered non-Islamic practices. They were victorious in their native Kandahar, and received a great boost when they captured a massive weapons depot at nearby Spinboldak. With these armaments they were able to drive the warring factions northward and impose their strict rule throughout most of the country, capturing the capital Kabul in 1996. The relief of Afghanistan's population was at first palpable. After nearly two decades of war, the streets were once again safe to walk – provided one adhered to the Taliban's notoriously strict regulations. Women were removed from mixed company, men were forced to grow beards and pray regularly, alcohol and music and all graven images were destroyed – from Western videos and pornography to the massive Buddha sculptures that had stood at Bamiyan for fifteen centuries. But still prosperity did not appear. Despite being "students," these under-educated former refugees were unprepared for the demanding technical tasks necessary to rebuild Afghanistan. By the end of the 1990s their entire annual budget consisted of a few hundred million dollars, earned mainly by the resale of surplus weaponry left over from Soviet occupation, the smuggling of automobiles from the Gulf to Pakistan (avoiding Pakistan import duty), and heroin production. (The Taliban were opposed to drugs and attempted to stop cultivation of the opiate-producing poppies, but the country was undergoing a drought, and poppies were their only drought-resistant crop.)

In these conditions, the so-called "Afghan Arabs" found refuge. Following the Soviet withdrawal, many of the foreign volunteers had returned to their native lands. Some, however, found they were not welcome at home and stayed on in (or returned to) Afghanistan. Chief among them was Osama bin Laden. When his efforts to bring the Mujahideen home to Saudia Arabia to replace US troops (stationed there after the first Gulf War) were rejected, the Saudi regime became his enemy, and the Saudi government, in turn, revoked his citizenship. The opposition of bin Laden's close associate, Ayman al-Zawahiri, to the Egyptian regime left him likewise in need of political sanctuary. Bin Laden, al-Zawahiri, and other former Mujahideen determined to carry on their work. The struggle against Soviet occupation may have ended, but there were still many instances of oppression in the broader Muslim world. Bin Laden established a "base" from which to carry on these diverse struggles – in Arabic, *al-qa `idah*. Al-Qaeda then focused its efforts on a single set of enemies iden-tified as common to all global problems, identifying the US and Jews as the co-culprits. This was the origin of the International Islamic Front for Jihad against Jews and Crusaders [Western Christians], established in 1998. Al-Qaeda carried out a number of attacks against targets worldwide, culminating in the simulta-neous attacks on the World Trade Center and the Pentagon on September 11, 2001.

The United States immediately identified the source of the attacks and sought out bin Laden. The Taliban leaders refused to hand him over, offering instead to extradite him to a third coun-try in order to be tried according to international law. Apparently mistrusting the Taliban, the US rejected that offer and launched its war in Afghanistan on October 7, 2001, a war that continues today. The Taliban government was quickly replaced, but Taliban resistance has continued and indeed gained momentum. By summer 2008 it was clear that the conflict in Afghanistan was spreading beyond that country's borders and had reached deep into neighboring Pakistan.

Indeed, Pakistan provides a chilling example of how Islamic reform efforts have been thwarted in the context of colonial and postcolonial politics. Pakistan was created in 1947 when Britain partitioned India. It is one of the two states in the world established for a single religious group. (The other one is, of course, Israel, created when Britain withdrew from its World War I "mandate" over Palestine and the United Nations partitioned Palestine, also in 1947). It was to be an Islamic state, ruled in accordance with Islamic values. The idea of Pakistan was developed by the progressive reformer Muhammad Iqbal (see Chapter 4) in the 1930s. On the level of practical politics, however, the cause of Pakistan had been taken up Muhammad Ali Jinnah (d. 1948), still known today as the "Great Leader" (Quaid-i Azam). Jinnah was a highly sophisticated man, trained in law in England. When he returned to India he became a successful attorney and active in the independence movement, working with people like Jawaharlal Nehru in the Indian National Congress Party and Iqbal in the Muslim League to free India of British control. His original goal was for a united, democratic India. He was known as the "ambassador of Hindu–Muslim unity." His orientation shifted, however, when elections in British India in 1937 resulted in Hindu governments that excluded Muslims from provincial cabinets. This convinced Jinnah that Muslims, even in a democratic Hindu India, would be totally marginalized. He therefore adopted the call for a separate Muslim state, becoming leader of the Muslim League. But his vision for Muslim Pakistan was a progressive one, where there would be no religious test for citizenship. It was to be a democracy, where people of all faiths could live in freedom and equality. Within this ideal Islamic state, all people would be free to develop and contribute constructively to world culture.

The vision for Pakistan was, in fact, a template for a modern Islamic state which could be consulted by those involved in the ongoing debate about Islam and democracy. Some contemporary scholars claim that Islam is inherently authoritarian and therefore incompatible with democracy. They often cite as evidence claims made by some traditional Muslims that "popular sovereignty" violates the Islamic principle that God is the ultimate sovereign and lawgiver, and the lack of working democracies in the Muslim world today. But Jinnah's vision for Pakistan – the one that inspired the mass following that proved an unstoppable force even for imperial Britain – was clearly democratic.

Jinnah was elected the first president of the Constituent Assembly of Pakistan, which met on August 10, 1947 to begin the process of forming a government and drawing up a constitution. He died before that process was completed, however, without expressing a preference for parliamentary over presidential democracy, for example. There remains debate as well about Jinnah's orientation toward economic systems. He favored free enterprise and the right to private property but also supported broad social programs, prompting some to argue that he was a socialist. But there is no doubt that Jinnah insisted on constitutional democracy. When he became Pakistan's first governor-general upon the state's creation on August 15, 1947, Jinnah broke with imperial tradition. Instead of pledging allegiance to the British monarch, he vowed to "bear true allegiance to the Constitution."[20] In speeches to the Constituent Assembly, he stressed pluralism and popular sovereignty as the critical elements in the new state:

If you ... work together in a spirit that every one of you, no matter to what community he belongs, no matter what relations he had with you in the past, no matter what is his colour, caste or creed, is first, second, and last a citizen of this State with equal rights, privileges and obligations, there will be no end to the progress you will make ... My guiding principle will be justice and complete impartiality, and I am sure that with your support and cooperation, I can look forward to Pakistan becoming one of the greatest Nations of the world.[21]

Jinnah and his followers agreed that these principles reflected essential Islamic values, and that their democratic government would always be guided by Islamic principles. According to the Objectives Resolution passed in 1949, which has survived through the ups and down of successive Pakistani governments, Pakistan will be a democratic state whose power is exercised "through the chosen representatives of the people." This power is delegated by God to the people based on popular sovereignty and Islamic principles. Those principles are "democracy, freedom, equality, tolerance and social justice," as well as an independent judiciary.[22]

The mass popularity of Jinnah's plan combined with Jinnah's effective leadership convinced Britain to agree to an independent Pakistan. However, the state was inherently unstable: divided by over 1,000 miles between East and West Pakistan, and covering populations of widely divergent geographic regions, differing languages and cultures; deprived of the industrial infrastructure that had developed in India; and in some cases even left without control of its own water resources. These conditions created overwhelming challenges for the new state's leadership. The ideals of an enlightened Islamic society – nurturing human dignity, committed to learning, acting as a positive force for peace and social development – were utterly overwhelmed by the struggle to maintain stability under increasingly difficult circumstances.

Pakistan's military, organized by the British, was the most stable institution in the country, and it naturally stepped into the breach. By 1958 martial law had been imposed. A constitutional government had been established in 1956; a second constitution was adopted in 1962, and a third in 1973. But instability continued, including wars with India over the disputed territory of Kashmir and the 1971 civil war that resulted in East Pakistan's formation into the independent state of Bangladesh. The result of this instability was the recurrent suspension of democracy and the imposition of martial law. Islam – as represented by the traditional religious scholars – was the one thing held in common by the entire population (except for small minorities of Christians, Hindus, and Parsis). Therefore, it formed the natural counterweight to the military.

The first period of martial law was declared during extreme tension among various factions, including those in East and West Pakistan. The military ruler, General Muhammad Ayub Khan, tried to bring stability through economic development and a government that was better suited to Pakistan's diverse needs. Part of the latter effort included the establishment of the Islamic Research Institute. Its responsibility was to develop Islamic legislation suitable for a modern state. Qualified scholars would examine traditional Islamic legal codes and recommend *ijtihad* in cases in which circumstances had changed and traditional legislation no longer was suitable for the goals of the Muslim community. By the mid-1960s Pakistan had implemented a number of the institute's recommendations, including some reforms of traditional statutes. For example, the medieval law limiting the legitimacy of women's testimony in court was revised in accordance with Quranic teaching on human equality and recognition of the change in women's social status through education. Polygyny (the right to marry more than one wife) was also limited, and the medieval equation of *riba,* which is forbidden by the Quran, with any level of interest whatsoever, was revised. According to the new interpretation, *riba* was identified as usurious interest rates, which continued to be forbidden, while reasonable interest rates were determined to be permissible in order to allow Pakistan to participate in the global economy.

Although Ayub Khan's economic policies were initially successful, poverty and instability quickly returned and, with them, opposition to Ayub's policies. Ayub Khan responded to the opposition with greater autocracy. As political unrest escalated, people turned to traditional religious leaders for solace. The traditional religious leaders, in turn, asserted their prerogative over Islamic legislation. Among their first victims was the director of the Islamic Research Institute, Fazlur Rahman. The "modernist" legislation he had advocated was characterized as un-Islamic by the conservative Muslim leaders whose methods Rahman had criticized. As he summarized his arguments later, Rahman had said that Islamic education had grown stagnant and unresponsive to the needs of society. He said that rather than participating in *ijtihad,* scholars simply memorized texts and then argued about details of what they had memorized. This "fruitless ingenuity" was a "waste of valuable intellectual energies." The scholars could reproduce traditional commentaries on the Quran in all kinds of ingenious ways. For example, they might write their commentaries while limiting themselves to only those letters of the alphabet that had no diacriticals (such as the dot on the letter "i" or cross on the letter "t"), requiring them to use only about half of the letters of the alphabet. And they could write commentaries on traditional commentaries "where, by reading words horizontally or vertically or in some cases diagonally, in each case successively or alternately (or by reading lines and not words alternately) on each page, one simultaneously obtains readable texts of as many as five disciplines (say, grammar, theology, law, logic, and philosophy) and in as many as three languages – Arabic, Turkish (Ottoman), and Persian!"[23] But they could not produce legislation that would allow Islamic society to develop intellectually, socially, economically, or politically. Fazlur Rahman's exasperation with the traditional scholars was interpreted as an insult to Islam. Despite the fact that he was a devout Muslim, traditional scholars accused him of being anti-Islamic. Accused of participating in anti-religious activity, he went into exile in 1968.[24]

Again, the pattern emerges. As we saw above, the Islamic world had been deprived of its independence and resources by foreign powers who justified their actions by disparaging the cultures and abilities of the people they controlled. In this context, the reform movement that had been developing long before foreign domination began was stifled. Traditional religious scholars became the symbols of all that was sacred and secure in society. Calls for change from independent Muslim reformers sometimes became almost indistinguishable from the contempt toward Islam shown by the colonial powers. Islamic reformers could be, and often were, accused of un-Islamic or anti-Islamic behavior, even collaboration with the enemy. But in the aftermath of independence, this pattern became more complex. Traditional scholars became – in addition to being symbols of all that is sacred and secure in society – symbols of political legitimacy. In times of social strife, authoritarian governments often assume control. Often such governments accommodate traditional religious elites in a bid for legitimacy. Their stamp of approval could grant legitimacy to even the most non-traditional government. This is just what happened in Pakistan. As the country's economic, social, and political problems mounted, successive governments found themselves catering to religious figures calling for stricter adherence to Islamic law, a process sometimes called "Islamization." Among the major opponents of Fazlur Rahman was the Islamist Jamaat-i Islami's leader Abu'l Ala Mawdudi. As we saw above, Jamaat-i Islami is often called an Islamic reform group since Mawdudi called for renewal of Islamic society through *ijtihad*. For example, Mawdudi said that all Muslims have the right to participate in legislation in an Islamic state, not just the economic or religious elite. He rejected the term "democracy" in favor of "theo-democracy," since all legislation must conform with revelation, but he believed that legislation in an Islamic state must remain flexible and responsive to the needs of society.[25] But in fact the reforms advocated by Jamaat-i Islami are not directed toward Islamic law as such. They leave the traditional codes generally intact and advocate stricter implementation of them as a means to improve the country's wellbeing. And because of their emotional appeal within society at large, Jamaat-i Islami and other Islamist groups in Pakistan have been able to bring pressure on Pakistan's various governments. Neither Jamaat-i Islami nor similar, smaller, religious parties had been successful in federal elections. Until 2002 they never received more than 4 percent of the vote. But as governments have become less and less effective in dealing with real economic and political problems, and therefore less and less popular, the religious parties have been able to pressure successive governments into more and more emphasis on traditional Islamic legislation.

This trend has been evident since the Soviet occupation of Afghanistan in the 1980s. At that time General Zia al-Haq was in charge of Pakistan. A military dictator and close friend of the United States, Zia relied on the support of traditional Muslims for legitimacy. It was under his regime that, in the name of authentic Islam, most of the modernizing reforms of Islamic law made during the 1960s were revoked. Successive governments followed suit. In 1991, the Enforcement of Shariah Act was passed, reiterating that "Islam has been declared to be the state religion of Pakistan and it is obligatory for all Muslims to follow the Injunctions of the Holy Quran and the Sunna." Expressing the no doubt sincere faith of millions of Muslims, the Act simply concludes that Islamization will result in the elimination of "bribery, corruption, obscenity, vulgarity, social evils, false amputations, etc."[26]

The 1990s saw three civilian governments, one led by the Harvard- and Oxford-educated Benazir Bhutto (d. 2007), yet virtually no legal, political, or economic reform. Indeed, the government of Nawaz Sharif (1990–3 and 1997–9) actually undermined some basic elements of democracy, such as the freedom of elected representatives to vote according to their conscience or the will of their constituents. Under Nawaz, constitutional amendments were passed stripping the president of the power to dissolve the government and requiring that elected representatives vote with their party or be dismissed. In 1999 the unpopular Nawaz was ousted by yet another military coup, that of General Pervez Musharraf.

Initially, there was popular support for the coup, and hope for an end to corruption and a return to stability. Even at that time, there was concern in many parts of Pakistan that continued bad governance was giving rise to the "Talibanization" of Pakistan and the growing "street power" of the Islamist parties who supported the Taliban. For example, in the spring of 2000 Chief Executive General Pervez Musharraf attempted to revise the "Blasphemy Law" (Provision 295-C of the Constitution), which allows anyone accused of insulting Islam to be jailed. According to this law, which was passed during General Zia al-Haq's Islamization program, anyone found guilty of any sort of insult to Islam or Prophet Muhammad is subject to the death penalty. For the most part, the law has been used against minorities, primarily the Ahmadi sect of Islam and Christians. Many Pakistanis oppose the law, believing it is simply a tool used to silence people and therefore a violation of the principles of an Islamic state. Nevertheless, the religious parties brought pressure against General Musharraf, in the form of mass demonstrations, and the government was forced to back down.

But this kind of pressure has never produced tangible results for the people of Pakistan – no more efficient government, no better infrastructure, no clean water or sewage treatment plants, no better education to allow greater economic competitiveness, no power to bring about changes that would improve their standard of living or that of future generations. With a population of some 165 million (2007 estimate), an over 50 percent illiteracy rate, staggering foreign debt, extraordinary instability in neighboring Afghanistan and Kashmir, and the constant nuclear threat from neighboring India, it is not surprising that Pakistan has not had the leisure to develop an effective democratic political culture in its brief history. However, the longer economic, social, and real political development are put off, the more frustration spreads in those sectors of society without access to economic power or the intellectual or educational apparatus to figure out how to get it. As a result, Pakistan has been caught in a "catch-22." Those who advocate effective political reform are silenced, often by the very people suffering from lack of good governance. Without good governance, radicalization increases. Radicalization represents mounting impatience with seemingly endlessly deferred progress. Amid deepening poverty and notoriously undemocratic governments, demands for good governance and economic development become increasingly desperate.

And now the Taliban, reconstituted in Afghanistan to resist what appears to them to be a government imposed by foreigners (the US-led coalition), have spread their operations into Pakistan. As 2008 drew to a close, their activities in Pakistan were widespread. They had gained control of the Federally Administered Tribal Areas (FATA) and North West Frontier Province (NWFP). Their activities reached as far as the capital, Islamabad, with increasingly frequent attacks against minorities and foreigners, as well as the newly installed civilian government perceived to be yet another arm of Western influence. These are not the Taliban of the 1990s. They are the next generation of Taliban, not necessarily from Afghanistan and not necessarily students. Yet, like the old Taliban, they are driven by fierce opposition to foreign intervention and tolerate no opposition to their authority or deviation from their narrow view of correct practice. Again, the majority, longing for peace and stability, are intimidated into silence.

Prospects for the Future

There are some hopeful signs of progress toward reform in the Muslim world. In Afghanistan, work is progressing toward a new government suitable to the needs of the Afghan people. Although there is still a great deal of anti-Americanism and traditionalism, some religious scholars are showing a willingness to undertake serious self-criticism in the effort to develop a society that truly expresses Islamic values. A senior religious scholar recently criticized the Taliban for not understanding or properly applying Islamic law. Another religious authority condemned the indiscriminate use of extreme punishments, such as amputation for theft and stoning for adultery, and called instead for efforts to develop a society in which people's needs are fully satisfied. In Indonesia, following the October 12, 2002 terrorist attack that killed nearly 200 people at a Bali nightclub, Islamic leaders supported the government crackdown on militant religious groups. Indonesia's two most popular religious organizations are the Nahdatul Ulama and the Muhammadiyyah. Leaders from both groups – including former Indonesian president Abdurrahman Wahid of the Nahdatul Ulama – condemned the nightclub attacks as terrorism. In the fall of 2002, an Islamic party defeated Turkey's long-running secularist Republican People's Party. The Justice and Development Party (known by its Turkish initials, AKP), has a long history of challenging the military-supported secularists, only to find itself banned in a violation of democratic principles. But the popularity of its moderate platform, based on Islamic values of social justice, pluralism, and democracy, continued to grow. Following its unqualified victory in the November elections, it was allowed to form a government. As of 2009, the AKP remains popular. It is working assiduously toward Turkey's long-term goal of inclusion in the European Union, and showing commitment toward progress in resolving ongoing human rights issues in Turkey.

But the sentiments of the majority of Muslims are rarely expressed in the political arena. An exception was the election of Mohammad Khatami as president of Iran in 1997. The Islamic government Ayatollah Khomeini called for was established by 1981. Iran was to be an Islamic republic, and its government was to be overseen by legal scholars (*velayat-e faqih*). It had an elected National Consultative Assembly, in accordance with the Quran's advice to Prophet Muhammad to consult with his followers, as well as an elected president. Religious scholars had to approve of candidates and their legislation, making sure it was in accordance with Islamic principles. This was a novel form of government, the first working model of an Islamic democracy. But the religious scholars in charge were generally from the revolutionary generation, still motivated by concern to protect Islam from the West, especially America. The fear of America was heightened by US support for Saddam Hussein in his eight-year war against Iran in the 1980s. The Iranians were well aware of the tyranny and brutality of Saddam's secular regime, and suffered grievously under his attacks on their territory. They could only assume that it was contempt for them and/or for Islamic ideals that motivated the US to support him. Thus, religious officials generally maintained their single-minded commitment to a religio-moral righteousness, including strict social policies designed to protect people from Western-inspired decadence. But within twenty years of Iran's Islamic Revolution a new generation had grown up. Having been protected from Western decadence, they felt quite secure in their Islamic identity. But they still felt the need for reform within Islamic society, practical reforms that would allow them to develop and reintegrate into world culture. There was growing frustration with the isolation of the country and stagnation of the economy, and increasing discontent with the lack of personal freedoms among the populace. These feelings were expressed in the landslide election of Mohammad Khatami as president in 1997. Khatami focused on the need to establish what he called a "new Iran," clearly appealing to popular sentiment.

Mohammad Khatami was elected on a platform of comprehensive reform in Iran. His election showed overwhelming approval of his plan to reintegrate Iran into the family of nations.[27] In order to achieve this goal, he said Islamic society overall must transform itself.[28] Despite continued efforts, Islamic societies have not achieved development. Muslims are still struggling economically, socially, and politically. Khatami acknowledges in his writings that the history of colonialism is a factor in this situation, but argues that it is now up to Islamic society to deal with it effectively. Defensiveness and emotionalism, he says, are no help at all. Instead, Muslims must examine their own societies and find out what is necessary to remedy their problems. Khatami says that the first step is to develop the freedom of thought and expression necessary to carry out this analysis. "[T]ransformation and progress require thought," he says, "and thought only flourishes in an atmosphere of freedom. But our history has not allowed human character to grow and to be appreciated, and thus the basic human yearning for thinking and freedom has been unattended at best and negated at worst."[29] People must not just blindly follow their religious leaders, no matter how pious or brilliant they are, he says. They must develop their own intellects and knowledge in order to help guide society collectively. And they must be able to do so without fear of censorship or persecution.

In a radical departure from Islamist anti-Westernism, Khatami says that Muslims should learn from the West. Western history should serve as an example from which Muslims may choose what to emulate and what to avoid. There are positive strengths and achievements in Western society which Muslims should try to incorporate into their own societies. Again, breaking from Islamist patterns, Khatami says that modernity is not some god-less rejection of religion, as many have portrayed it. Rather, it is a rejection of "autocratic and whimsical rulers" who plagued the pre-modern West and continue to plague the Muslim world. He insists that it takes freedom of thought and expression to cast off the shackles of these autocrats who base their legitimacy on traditional interpretations of religion.

True, Khatami says, the West is hedonistic and greedy, but that is not because of its freedoms. And materialism is actually weakening the West. Khatami actually thinks Karl Marx was partly right about the West. He says that Marx "was a great pathologist of the capitalist order," even if Marxism itself was "an impractical and unrealistic philosophy."[30] But that does not mean that everything about the West is bad or that everything about Islamic society is good. They are both flawed and can learn from each other.

Khatami is convinced that freedom, including intellectual freedom, is an essential Islamic value. For that reason, it is particularly offensive to him that freedom has been suppressed by some revolutionary leaders in the name of religion or even tradition. In fact, he says, we have to be careful about what we call tradition. The mere fact that something is old does not make it tradition. Nor does the fact that something is traditional make it good. The only "good traditions" are the immutable laws of God – what Khatami calls the "laws governing existence." Human beings make mistakes interpreting God's law, so no human tradition should be considered sacred. Human interpretation must always be distinguished from divine law, he says, and that requires intellectual freedom. Returning to the perennial themes of Islamic reform, Khatami concludes that lack of freedom has resulted in fatalism and excessive mysticism, distracting people from their communal responsibilities. Once Islamic societies regain their freedom and intellectual momentum, they can work to develop into contributing members of the world community. But they cannot achieve their goals in a vacuum. The West must be constructively engaged, through "rationality and enlightenment," not fanaticism. That merely harms Islam. Islamic societies do not need martyrs; they need what he calls "religious intellectuals," able to explore new options and develop new ways to deal with a world traditional authorities could never have imagined.

Overall, Khatami envisioned Islamic societies with a tolerant, reasonable and flexible ethos, based on a holistic understanding of human beings. In other words, he envisions a society that meets both the material and the spiritual needs of its citizens. In his inaugural address, he described the ideal society for Iran. Iran should be a society that respects "social and individual security within the framework of the Constitution." It should have "clearly defined rights and duties for citizens and the government." Its government should "officially recognize the rights of the people and the nation within the framework of law." Such a government needs "organized political parties, social associations, and an independent free press." This is a society "where the government belongs to the people and is the servant of the people, not their master, and is consequently responsible to the people."[31]

The path taken by Iran in electing Mohammad Khatami as president clearly represented a very hopeful trend in modern Islam. Its rational self-critique stands in stark contrast to the stridently defensive and militant stance taken by the Taliban and their supporters. Both trends exist in Islam today, often in uneasy balance. Moderate and progressive Muslims struggle against formidable odds. Progress toward reform is inevitably slow. But even in Iran, despite the popularity of reformist President Khatami, many Muslims expressed frustration with his inability to overcome the opposition of the traditionalist religious leaders, and continued to agitate for a more open society. In the fall of 2002, a popular reformist scholar at Tehran University, Hashem Aghajari, became an overnight sensation when he argued for Islamic reformation. Insisting that Muslims go back to the scriptural sources, he said that they must "separate historical Islam from essential Islam through analysis." Among the non-essential historical developments, he claimed, was the clergy itself. Unlike Sunni Islam, Shii Islam developed a hierarchy of scholars recognized as the sole authorities in matters of religious interpretation. (The highest level is "ayatollah.") But Aghajari pointed out that this rigid hierarchy only developed in the last century. It was, therefore, not part of essential Islam. What was essential, he claimed, is that every Muslim "consider himself the direct recipient of the Holy Book ... We have the right to receive and interpret this message on our own and based on our own circumstances." To simply follow what the clergy says is regressive, said Aghajari. In fact, he said, it is "fundamentalist," and allows the clergy to declare, "Anyone who is not with us is our enemy." By contrast, Aghajari concluded, "Islamic Protestantism [reformist Islam] is intellectual, practical and humane and as such is a progressive religion."[32]

For his courage in confronting the traditionalist clergy, Aghajari was condemned to death for blasphemy. However, mass demonstrations forced the conservatives to back down, encouraging more scholars to speak out publicly for reform. They included supporters of elderly reformist Ayatollah Hossein Ali Montazeri. Ayatollah Montazeri was a senior cleric and the successor Ayatollah Khomeini chose for himself. But in the late 1980s Montazeri became critical of the Islamic government's ruthless suppression of its opponents. He was therefore replaced as successor to Khomeini. Later he was placed under house arrest by Khomeini's successor Ayatollah Khamenei, for calling for a more open government. Under enormous public pressure, including a petition signed by over 100 members of the Iranian parliament, Montazeri was released in early 2003. Although he has not been given a public platform, his views continue to circulate and increase in popularity via the internet.

Even Ayatollah Khomeini's granddaughter Zahra Eshraghi, sister-in-law of President Khatami, has publicly called for openness in Iran. She campaigned for President Khatami in 1997, and currently works promoting women's rights in the Interior Ministry. She rejects the veil, pointing out that people voluntarily wore it as a symbol of revolution against the imperious shah. But when the Islamic government forced it upon women, its symbolism changed. "We have only ourselves to blame," she says, echoing both the self-critical attitude of contemporary reformers and their frustration with the slow pace of reform.[33]

As these examples indicate, many Iranians were impatient with the slow pace of liberalization. In the spring of 2003 even former President Rafsanjani joined the movement for ending Iran's social and political isolation, supporting a call for reopening relations with the United States. But at the same time there were more conservative members of the clerically dominated government who were concerned that liberalization was premature. They maintained an abiding distrust of the West and cautioned that the US was expansionist and would never allow an independent Iran to prosper. These concerns were elevated when, in January 2002, US President George W. Bush identified Iran as a member of a worldwide "axis of evil." Fears rose to crisis level when the US launched its war in Iraq, another member of the "axis of evil," raising alarm that Iran would be the next victim of what was perceived as US aggression. Within two years Iranian presidential elections replaced the progressive Mohammad Khatami with the provocative, protectionist, outspokenly anti-American Mahmoud Ahmadinejad.

But Islamic teachings and values in the modern world are not represented by political struggles. Radicalized political Islam represents only a fraction of the world's Muslim population. It has been responsible for the terrorism that scars the name of Islam in the world today. This, despite that fact that terrorism has been resolutely and repeatedly condemned by virtually every Islamic authority of note around the world. Three days after the September 11 attacks, the leaders of the Muslim Brotherhood, Jamaat-i Islami, Palestine's Islamic Resistance Movement (HAMAS), Tunisia's Nahda (Renaissance) Movement, the Islamic Party of Malaysia (PAS), and forty other Muslim scholars and political leaders issued the following statement:

> The undersigned, leaders of the Islamic movement, are horrified by the events of Tuesday 11 September 2001 in the United States which resulted in massive killing, destruction and attack on innocent lives. We express our deepest sympathies and sorrow. We

condemn, in the strongest terms, the incidents, which are against all human and Islamic norms. This is grounded in the Noble Laws of Islam which forbid all forms of attacks on innocents. God Almighty says in the Holy Qur'an: "No bearer of burdens can bear the burden of another" (Surah al-Isra 17:17).

The same day the leader of Lebanon's Shii Muslims noted, "Besides the fact that they are forbidden by Islam, these acts do not serve those who carried them out but their victims, who will reap the sympathy of the whole world ... Islamists who live according to the human values of Islam could not commit such crimes." The next day, the chief religious authority in Saudi Arabia issued a similar statement through the kingdom's US embassy:

> Firstly: the recent developments in the United States including hijacking planes, terrorizing innocent people and shedding blood, constitute a form of injustice that cannot be tolerated by Islam, which views them as gross crimes and sinful acts. Secondly: any Muslim who is aware of the teachings of his religion and who adheres to the directives of the Holy Qur'an and the sunnah (teachings of the Prophet Muhammad) will never involve himself in such acts, because they will invoke the anger of God Almighty and lead to harm and corruption on earth.

Hundreds of such condemnations have been issued since then. In February 2008, in fact, the rector of the conservative Dar ul-Ulum madrasa in Deoband, India, often associated with support for the Taliban, organized an "Anti-Terrorism Convention," issuing the following statement: "We condemn all forms of terrorism ... and in this we make no distinction. Terrorism is completely wrong, no matter who engages in it, and no matter what religion he follows or community he belongs to."[34]

Unfortunately, these statements are overshadowed by the horrific effects of terrorist actions, not the least of which is the fear they engender. Indeed, both the targeting of civilians and suicide are violations of Islamic law. And attacks on random individuals is absolutely condemned, precisely because of the fear it engenders. Such attacks are violations of the law prohibiting *hirabah*. *Hirabah* is the only crime in Islamic law that carries a mandatory death sentence.[35] As well, the association of Islam with postcolonial political struggles and, in particular, authoritarian and highly conservative governments, has left the widespread impression that Islam itself is inimical to human rights, including the rights of minorities and women, and to democracy. There is ample evidence to the contrary.

Islam, Human Rights, and Democracy

The notion of human rights – rights that all people are entitled to, simply by virtue of their being human – is a modern development in the West. It was not until the 1948 Universal Declaration of Human Rights was promulgated that the phrase "human rights" became part of our vocabulary. But the concept of essential rights for all members of the community goes back to the very origins of Islamic law. As noted in Chapter 2, there are five dominant schools of legal thought, and within each of those there are broad ranges of opinion with long discussions to justify each of them. But there is agreement among scholars on the goals or purposes (maqasid) of Islamic law. The famous eleventh-century scholar al-Ghazali says that overall the purpose of law is to assure success in this life and the next. We find discussions of human rights in the category of the this-worldly purposes of Islamic law. In Islamic legal discourse, rights are divided into two kinds: the rights accorded to God (huquq Allah or `ibadat), and the rights of human beings or individuals (huquq al-`ibad). The rights of God have to do with ways of being worshiped: through prayer, fasting, pilgrimage, and so on. The rights of human beings are those we saw stressed by Ibn Khaldun in Chapter 3: religion, life, family, mind or intellect, and property. Establishing and protecting these rights is considered one the primary purposes of Islamic law.

The question then becomes: how are these rights to be established and protected? Traditionally, preservation of religion is described as making sure people are allowed to carry out their religious duties. Jihad is often described as the means for defending religion. Some scholars describe preservation of life (nafs – sometimes translated as "soul") as the most basic human right, taking precedence over even the rights of God. According to that line of reasoning, if a life is at stake, the requirement for prayer or fasting may be suspended.[36] Other scholars point out that preservation of religion has priority over protection of life, since people must potentially take lives and risk their own lives in a war justified on the basis of its protection of the right to carry out religious duties. In any case, human life is considered inviolable except in the case of a just war or duly adjudicated capital punishment. It is preserved by making sure people have enough to eat and the ability to assure good health, and it is protected by effective penalties for those who take life without legal justification. Preservation of family includes the right to legal marriage and inheritance, for example, and is protected by providing penalties for those who undermine those rights. Preservation of intellect includes the right to education and the prohibition of substances that interfere with the intellect (such as intoxicants). And preservation of property (*mal*) is tradition- ally interpreted as maintaining conditions for creating and increasing wealth, including the right to private ownership of property, and it is protected by implementing penalties for theft or misappropriation of wealth or property.

As Muslim countries struggle to develop effective governance consistent with Islamic principles, the ways to achieve the goals of Islamic law are under intense discussion. For example, some contemporary thinkers have extended the list of essential rights to include consultation – the right to participatory government. Some classify consultation as a duty rather than a right.[37] But either way – right or duty –the issue is traced to the Quran's insist- ence on consultative government, *shura*. In a chapter by that name (Sura 42), the Quran requires that people conduct their affairs in consultation with one another.[38] The Quran instructs Prophet Muhammad himself to consult with his followers on practical matters (3:159).

European scholar Tariq Ramadan is one of the contemporary scholars who writes on this theme. He cites the examples of Prophet Muhammad consulting with his followers in battle, for example, and the Prophet's companion and successor, Abu Bakr – who told the community, "If you see me in the right, help me;

if you see me in error correct me." Ramadan concludes therefore that any government conforming to Islamic principles must allow for communal consultation, including both men and women, through direct elections or representatives, and that the most efficient means of doing that today is through a consultative council made up of elected members. He also says that representatives must be chosen on the basis of competence in various areas pertinent to daily life, rather than heredity or some other unearned criterion. This competence allows them to exercise *ijtihad*, that is, to deliberate and formulate ways to achieve Islamic principles in today's novel circumstances – rather than relying on models appropriate to circumstances that no longer exist.[39]

Like many contemporary scholars, including Iran's former President Khatami, Ramadan also extends the discussion of rights to include freedom of conscience and expression. This is based on his reading of the Quran's prohibition of compulsion in matters of religion (2:256). Ramadan says that people must have the right to choose their leaders, express their opinions, and live – male and female, Muslim and non-Muslim – under equal protection of the law, as was the case in the Prophet's time. Ramadan also says that while there's no unique model of Islamic government, the basic principles have been provided, which he calls "a framework to run pluralism."[40]

Many contemporary Islamic thinkers also reject Islamic exclusivism and fully endorse pluralism – including full equality for non-Muslims living under Islamic governments. For example, Egypt's preeminent Islamic journalist Fahmy Huwaidy argues for equal rights for non-Muslim minorities based on the overall goals of Islamic law. It is a truism that the purpose of Islamic law, and by extension, the purpose of an Islamic government, is to establish justice. Huwaidy states that "even if the banner of Islam is held on high and its religious teachings adhered to but justice is not achieved, the message is emptied of content and the means have failed to achieve the ends."[41] In order to achieve justice in today's world, he continues, democracy is essential. Democracy has been shown to be effective in the West, and it is the most effective way to implement the Quran's command to govern through consultation (*shura*). While *shura* has been exercised in various ways throughout history, in order for it to result in justice today, it must be anchored in a government that recognizes the right of people to choose their ruler, and this right must be shared equally by all citizens.

The argument for equal rights for non-Muslim minorities involves as well articulating the separation of powers in an Islamic framework. Traditionalist Islamic discourse often coalesces legal and political systems, assigning political roles to legal scholars. In this view, all law comes from God and only God can legislate. Therefore, the state's role is to implement revealed law, and only properly (traditionally) trained legal scholars may determine the best way to implement God's revealed law. Mawdudi was an early proponent of this approach, as was the Muslim Brotherhood's Sayyid Qutb. The classic example of this approach put into action is the *velayat-e faqih* (government by legal scholar[s]) established by the Iranian Revolution of 1979. Extrapolating from the requirement that the identity of a government as Islamic is based on its implementation of Islamic law, Ayatollah Khomeini and his followers concluded that the government must actually be run by Islamic legal personnel. The implications for non-Muslims in such a polity are obvious: they may live securely as protected people (*dhimmis*), as they did throughout most of Islamic history, but they may not hold high political office. Opponents of this view insist on the distinction between the political and legal spheres in Islam. From their perspective, well grounded in classical *fiqh* (see, for example, Ibn Taymiyya's *al-Siyasat al-Shar`iyyah*), Islam requires no particular political system, only that, for any political system to be considered Islamic, its law must be Islamic. Thus, while Islamic law is rooted in sacred sources, governments themselves are not. As Kamal Abu'l-Magd put it, "Islamic government is a civil and not a religious government."[42]

Egyptian legal scholar Salim al-Awa agrees. Not only is government a civil matter, with authority resting with the people whose right it is to choose it, but all citizens have equal rights to choose. This includes women and non-Muslims. In governments that conflate executive and legislative branches, women and non-Muslims are traditionally excluded, based on the belief that neither should have the right to rule over Muslim men. Al-Awa says that when the distinction between executive and legislative spheres is recognized, along with the distinction between the divine sources of Islamic law and the practical codes on which they are based, then it becomes clear that all citizens share equally the rights and responsibilities of democratic government. "The only permissible distinction [between candidates] is according to ethics, character, public record, and ability to support what is right and deter what is wrong."[43]

American scholar Khaled Abou El Fadl argues similarly. In Abou El Fadl's analysis, Islamic tradition is pluralistic, and incorporates a number of concepts comparable to those of modern democracies. In addition to the need for consultation in government, for example, Abou El Fadl says that early Muslim jurists "agreed on the notion that government exists by contract ... between the ruler and ruled."[44] There were differences of opinion regarding the status of this contract, but agreement that there must be popular approval of the government in some form. This is based on the classical concept of *bayah* or pledge of allegiance. Based on the example of the Prophet, governments must receive popular approval in order to be legitimate. Jurists disagreed on how to go about getting this pledge, from whom it was necessary, and what to do if it was missing, but the principle of government by consent was agreed upon nonetheless. So government must be approved by the populace, and it must be participatory.

Abou El Fadl acknowledges that some Muslims reject the idea of democracy on the basis of the belief that God is the sole legislator. But he argues that this is "a fatal fiction ... indefensible," he says, "from the point of view of Islamic theology," because it assumes that some human beings have perfect access to the divine will.[45] No human being or group of human beings can claim to have direct access to the divine will other than through the guidance of revelation, Abou El Fadl insists. And as perfect a guide as the Quran is, it does not regulate everything human beings will ever do. The Quran gives guidance for all aspects of life, but specific rulings for specific contexts, aside from the basic regulations presented in revelation, are left for human beings to extract, guided by the Quran's own principles. These principles have been articulated by jurists through the ages; Abou El Fadl identifies justice and mercy as foremost among them. Whether through an advisory body of jurists, as in the Middle Ages, or an elected assembly of representatives, as in a modern democracy, Abou El Fadl says, people must struggle to implement a social order that is both just and merciful. To the extent that it is successful in establishing justice and mercy, it will reflect divine sovereignty. As Abou el Fadl puts it: "Principles of mercy and justice are the primary divine charge, and God's sovereignty lies in the fact that God is the authority that delegated to human beings the charge to achieve justice on earth by fulfilling the virtues that approximate divinity."[46]

What constitutes a just and merciful government in today's world? For Khalid Abou El Fadl, such a government is one that protects the basic human rights identified by Islam's classical jurists. But traditional interpretations of these rights are not always tenable in today's world. For example, early scholars interpreted the protection of religion as the prohibition of apostasy on punishment of death, and they identified the protection of intellect as the prohibition of alcohol. Nowadays, those interpretations would not achieve a just and merciful society, Abou El Fadl believes. He says that the means of protecting those rights must be "re-analyzed in light of the current diversity of human existence." In particular, he calls for equal rights of free speech, association, and suffrage. Any government that does these things reflects the divine mandate. By recognizing the human responsibility for articulating, executing, and adjudicating that government, divine sovereignty remains intact. In other words, he concludes, "democracy ... offers the greatest potential for promoting justice and protecting human dignity, without making God responsible for human injustice or the degradation of human beings by one another."[47]

The rights of women are generally included in discussions of human rights in contemporary Islam, but some scholars make women's rights a focal point. Amina Wadud, for example, admits that women's status in many parts of the Muslim world is distinctly beneath that of men, but unlike some outspoken Muslim women, Wadud refuses to accept that this situation is a reflection of Islamic values. She says that the fundamental Quranic ethos is "equity, justice, and human dignity" as derived from a holistic understanding of the Quran, and that ethos includes gender justice. For example, Wadud discusses traditional legislation pertaining to women's legal testimony (see Chapter 1). In verses discussing the permissibility of borrowing and lending, the Quran advises that such transactions may be undertaken but should be recorded and witnessed by two men. But "if two men be [not at hand] then a man and two women, of such as you approve as witnesses, so that if the one errs the other can remind her" (2:282). Wadud disagrees with the interpretation of classical jurists whereby the import of the verse is that women's testimony is only half as reliable as that of a man. She notes that the unreliability of women's testimony was specific to the historic context of the verse, rather than a universal principle:

> Since the testimony of a woman being considered of less value than that of a man was dependent upon her weaker power of memory concerning financial matters, when women become conversant with such matters – with which there is not only nothing wrong but which is for the betterment of society – their evidence can equal that of men.[48]

Wadud proceeds to apply the same kind of analysis to other major issues in the legal status of women, including men's authority over women, inheritance, the right to initiate divorce, and child custody in case of divorce. In all cases, she derives conclusions from the Quran, which she believes views women as "primordially, cosmologically, eschatologically, spiritually, and morally ... full human being[s] equal to all who accepted Allah as Lord, Muhammad as prophet, and Islam as *din*."[49] She argues that modern implementation of Quranic views of women would yield full equality and social empowerment for women.

Acting upon these conclusions, Wadud has become a highly controversial figure within the Muslim world. When she has challenged the traditional segregation of sexes in the mosque, she received widespread criticism, from both Muslim men and women. Nevertheless, her insistence on human equality in all matters, including gender, based on a holistic reading of the Quran, is broadly accepted among reformist thinkers.[50] Even her decision to accept an invitation to lead mosque prayer, traditionally a right accorded only to males, was supported by such scholars as Khaled Abou El Fadl. In his 2001 monograph *Speaking in God's Name*, he argues that women and men share full legal and ethical equality in Islam. He even issued a *fatwa* (authoritative legal opinion) in which he noted that the Prophet "on more than one occasion allowed a woman to lead her household in prayer – although the household included men – when the woman was clearly the most learned in the faith."[51] Therefore, he says, the exclusion of women is based only on custom and "male consensus." He then cites the standard legal position that the common good should take precedence over custom, and concludes that "a female ought not be precluded from leading *jumu`a* [Friday congregational prayer] simply on the grounds of being female."[52]

While the permission for women to lead prayers in the mosque may not have universal appeal in the Muslim world, the vast majority of Muslims undoubtedly support human rights in general and women's rights in particular. Progress in this regard is, not surprisingly, more rapid in the West. For example, in 2006 ISNA (the Islamic Society of North America), the largest organization of Muslims in North America, elected Ingrid Mattson as its president. Professor Mattson holds a Ph.D. in Islamic studies from the University of Chicago and teaches as the Macdonald Center for Islamic Studies and Christian–Muslim Relations at Hartford Seminary, directing its Islamic Chaplaincy Program. Support for human rights in Muslim-majority countries is also overwhelming. In 2008 Gallup World Poll published the results of the most extensive survey of Muslim opinion ever conducted, *Who Speaks for Islam?* The poll sampled views of over 50,000 Muslims in over thirty-five countries, over a period of six years. It demonstrates that the views of the scholars expressed above are actually representative of the majority of Muslims worldwide. They long for freedom, rights, and democracy, and believe that these are in fact Islamic values.

Islam among World Religions

There are well over 1 billion Muslims in the world today, nearly one-fifth of the world's population. Roughly two-thirds of them live in countries that were colonized by Europeans; they have been working for decades under challenging economic and political conditions, following often brutal struggles for independence. Some are embroiled in history's most intractable conflicts, such as the fight to control the Holy Land. Others continue to struggle in the aftermath of "Great Power" conflicts, such as in Afghanistan and Pakistan, or under unpopular governments that are nonetheless supported by Western powers, such as Egypt and Saudi Arabia. Many Muslims find it extremely frustrating that their religion is judged on the basis of political developments in these countries. The vast majority of Muslims, like the majority of people everywhere, simply try to live their lives in accordance with their values, working to meet the challenges of everyday life. They have no say in what the governments of self-styled Islamic states do, much less what the terrorists do. Yet they find themselves increasingly judged by the actions of these newsmakers.

Indeed, among the most pressing concerns of Muslims today is how to deal with the Western world's apparent disrespect for Islam. Some Muslims are convinced that Christians actually despise Islam and are determined to destroy it. This perception is a unique phenomenon. It is different from the very real concern of Jews about anti-Semitism. Christians over the centuries have tried to destroy Jews – in the Inquisitions, the pogroms, and the Holocaust. The target was not Judaism, however; Christianity incorporated Hebrew scriptures into its Bible, and its basic history and beliefs into Christian teaching. Christianity could hardly exist without the heritage of Judaism. Christians cannot ridicule Abraham or Moses, for example, without ridiculing their own heritage. Instead, Christians developed a fear and loathing of Jewish people. As a result, many Jews share the perfectly understandable conviction that Christians hate Jews. Ridicule of Jewish people is therefore a matter of grave concern.

The concern among many Muslims, however, is not that Christians hate Muslim people. Muslims themselves often make fun of Muslims. A good example is a quote attributed to the famed nineteenth-century reformer Muhammad Abduh: "The true Islam is hidden [from the world] by Muslims." But historical experiences have made Muslims extremely sensitive to ridicule of Islam, the religion, and its prophet, Muhammad. From its earliest history, Islam found itself dismissed as a false religion brought by a false prophet. Many Jews and Christians became Muslims, of course, and many others lived in peaceful respect for the religion. But many rejected the teachings of Prophet Muhammad. The Quran even records that they were rejected as sorcery or trickery. As noted in Chapter 2, there is a long heritage of Christian lore extremely demeaning to Islam and Prophet Muhammad. The Crusades were launched in order to reclaim the Holy Land for Christianity from the Muslims, who were described as infidels – people with no true belief at all, rather than believers in a different religion. Colonial activity in the Muslim world was often associated with the work of missionaries, and was therefore easily incorporated into the perception of Christianity's efforts to eradicate Islam. When author Salman Rushdie published *The Satanic Verses* in 1988, a novel that parodied Prophet Muhammad and his family in extremely insulting ways, the book was hailed as a masterpiece in England and America. This was taken as more evidence of the West's lack of respect for Islam.

This perception is heightened by claims made by certain American evangelical Protestant preachers that Islam is a religion of violence. The Reverend Franklin Graham, for example, called Islam "a very evil and wicked religion" on a news broadcast shortly after September 11. The Reverend Jerry Vines, past president of the Southern Baptist Convention, was quoted describing Muhammad as a "demon-possessed pedophile." In an appearance on the television program, *60 Minutes*, the Reverend Jerry Falwell described Prophet Muhammad as "a violent man, a man of war," concluding, "I think Muhammad was a terrorist." Within two weeks, Falwell realized his offense and issued an apology, saying, "I intended no disrespect to any sincere, law-abiding Muslim." Leading Sunni authority Shaykh Tantawi then issued a public statement accepting the apology. Shii scholar Ayatollah Hussein Mousavi Tabrizi agreed, stating that "a person courageous enough to apologize for his errors is worthy of praise. It's humanitarian and good Islamic behavior to accept an apology from a person who admits making a mistake."[53] Some authors of offending remarks issued statements vowing to reconsider their views, and President George W. Bush spoke out against those who misrepresent Islam as a terrorist religion and who insult Prophet Muhammad. But the damage had been done. Riots broke out in India, resulting in a number of deaths, and anti-American sentiment clearly escalated in Pakistan. Within days after Falwell's statements, another statement was issued in the name of Osama bin Laden, attempting to convince Muslims not to be fooled; in his view, the West really seeks to destroy Islam. The statement referred to the US-led "crusade against the Islamic world," and urged Muslims to unite in order to "defend the targeted faith, the violated sanctity, the tarnished honor, the raped land and the robbed riches ... [T]he Americans and the Jews ... will not stop infringing upon us except through jihad."[54] And in elections held in Pakistan in October 2002, for the first time in history religious parties received a plurality of votes, increasing their number of seats in parliament by a factor of ten. As one observer put it, many Pakistanis seemed to feel that a vote for the Islamist parties was a vote against America.[55]

What appeared to be Christian disrespect for Islam was again on display with the desecration of holy sites in Iraq. Sacred mosques were bombed, and the tomb of Abu Hanifa, founder of the oldest school of Islamic law, was raided. Countless artifacts and documents from some of the world's most ancient civilizations – Sumeria, Akkadia, Assyria, Babylonia – were lost. Included among them were religious relics and examples of the world's earliest form of writing. Undoubtedly most devastating, however, was the loss of sacred texts. Copies of the Quran dating from the first century of Islam had survived both the destruction of Baghdad in 1258 and Tamerlane's attacks in 1401. But they did not survive the US-led war in 2003. This made the Reverend Franklin Graham's participation in a religious service at the Pentagon on the most solemn day of the Christian calendar, Good Friday (April 18, 2003), particularly painful for many Muslims.

In September 2005 a Danish newspaper published a series of cartoons ridiculing Prophet Muhammad. When Muslims protested, the cartoons were reprinted in dozens of newspapers around the world. People in the West argued in favor of the right of free expression, but many Muslims were unconvinced. While they recognize the right of free expression, the cartoons seemed gratuitously insulting. They were taken as more evidence of the West's contempt for Islam and Muhammad, the prophet not simply revered but loved by Muslims everywhere.

America's steadfast support for Israel despite its violation of United Nations Security Council resolutions concerning the rights of people who happen to be predominantly Muslims, and ongoing military campaigns against Afghanistan and Iraq, have likewise been interpreted as part of a campaign to destroy Islam. That conviction has resulted in attacks against Christians in some parts of the Muslim world. In Pakistan – again, one of the poorest countries in the Islamic world, and one of the countries most deeply affected by America's policies in Afghanistan – churches have been attacked. In a particularly gruesome example, seven Pakistani Christians working for a Christian charity in Karachi were murdered in the fall of 2002. However, this radical reaction represented only a tiny minority of Muslims. The majority Muslim view was represented by the thousands who marched in the streets of Karachi condemning religious extremism. Kamal Shah, police chief of Sindh (the state in which Karachi is located) condemned the murders: "I would rate it as the most tragic terrorist incident since 9/11." The Catholic archbishop of Karachi, Simeon Pereira, expressed his solidarity with Islam: "No real Pakistani Muslim would ever think of committing such a barbaric attack."[56] Unfortunately, attacks on Christians and other minorities in Pakistan have increased with the radicalization spilling over from Afghanistan, including several killings in summer 2009.

In fact, the terrorist attacks on America on September 11, 2001 were committed by people convinced that the West intends to destroy Islam. Terrorist tracts invariably attempt to inflame emotions and recruit followers by recounting the suffering of Muslims at the hands of those who ridicule and want to destroy the religion. But again, the views of the majority of Muslims are represented in the unequivocal condemnations of terrorism by Islamic scholars around the world.

Emotions continue to run high on both sides, and the situation remains volatile. The conciliatory public statements by evangelical Christians, President Bush, and Islamic scholars have been effective in most quarters. But resentment of the West's insults lingers, and is compounded by a related phenomenon, that of the stereotyping of Muslims. The mass distribution of the DVD *Obsession: Radical Islam's War against the West* in the run-up to the 2008 US presidential election did not help this situation. The documentary specifies that it targets only the extremist minority. But the effect of the film and its mass distribution was clearly to intensify negative stereotypes of Muslims. As noted, Muslims have been negatively stereotyped since their earliest encounters with European Christians. But since the rise of terrorism over the past few decades the problem of stereotyping has become especially acute. Demonstrated perhaps most blatantly in the 2006 Oscar-nominated movie *Borat*, stereotyping Muslims has become pervasive in our society, so much so that scholars write about it and comedians joke about it. There is even a post-*Borat* indie movie about it. *Driving to Zigzigland* is the story of a Palestinian actor in Hollywood who can only get roles playing a terrorist – which he refuses to do. Based on real-life experience, the movie then traces the life of the actor as he supports himself driving a cab and is subjected to endless harassment when passengers find out he is Palestinian. The musical score includes the 2005 hit *Stereotypes*, by the Iraqi Canadian hip-hop group Euphrates.

While terrorists attempt to exploit stereotyping for their own purposes, the far more common reaction to ongoing conflict and misrepresentations of Islam is increased effort on the part of Muslims to represent Islam in ways they believe are authentic. They deplore the "hijacking" not just of jets, but of Islam itself by terrorists and radicals. They reject the right of fanatics to define Islam. Muslims living in the West particularly feel the responsibility to take the initiative to speak out against radicalism and in favor of Islamic values of peace, tolerance, and commitment to justice. Muslim scholars have been producing works in English and European languages for decades, generally for academic audiences. But since September 11, the need for discourse among everyday believers has become glaringly apparent, particularly in the United States. At countless interfaith gatherings in communities throughout the country, Muslims have attempted to present their faith to Americans whose only exposure to Islam has been the kind that makes headlines.

Typical of these efforts is a collection recently published by concerned Muslims: *Taking Back Islam.*[57] The collection includes essays by Muslims from all walks of life who felt they simply could not allow the "moral nihilism" of terrorism to be associated with Islam. Michael Wolfe explains the rationale for publishing the book: "We knew something had to be done or our religion risked being tarnished, even corrupted." He cites the frustration American Muslims feel when "anti-American fanatics quote the Qur'an to justify mass murder, and ... anti-Muslim bigots quote it back – both sides using bad translations and phrases out of context ... [W]e have sought to replace them with a truer interpretation: that Islam is a peaceful, progressive, inherently forgiving and compassionate religion. Anyone who believes otherwise misses the core values of Islam."[58]

The Interfaith Youth Core (IFYC) is another such effort. Founded in Chicago in 1998 by Dr. Eboo Patel, the IFYC organizes young people of diverse religious traditions to cooperate in their shared commitment to community service. As the IFYC website describes:

> There are millions of religious young people in the world interacting with greater frequency. That interaction tends either toward conflict or cooperation. Here so many of these interactions tend toward conflict, the Interfaith Youth Core aims to introduce a new relationship, one that is about mutual respect and religious pluralism. Instead of focusing on dialogue on political or theological differences, we build relationships on the values that we share, such as hospitality and caring for the Earth, and how we can live out those values together to contribute to the betterment of our community.[59]

Among the major problems that Dr. Patel struggles against within the Muslim community is the anti-Jewish sentiment that has arisen in the context of political struggles with Israel. "There is never justification for transforming an entire people into an object of ridicule and hate," says Patel. He says that anti-Jewish statements "blacken the heart of anyone who says or thinks or feels them, and I want my religious community to have nothing to do with those sick attitudes." Shaykh Hamza Yusuf, among the most prominent young American Muslim leaders, insists that Holocaust denial undermines Islam. Patel reports that the voices of people like Shaykh Hamza "are having an increasing influence within the American Muslim community for a very simple reason – they reflect the attitude of the majority of American Muslims, who have felt both sickened and silenced by the minority of Muslims who speak of anti-Semitism as if it were a core tenet of Islam."

Patel's claims are clearly supported by recent statements emerging from religious elders. On November 11, 2008, a consortium of 100 mosques, synagogues, and Islamic and Jewish cultural and community centers published a full-page ad in the *New York Times* stating, "We are children of Abraham. We are rabbis and imams standing side by side, knowing that our words and our actions will determine our future."

Muslim scholars and religious leaders and those of the Roman Catholic Church have likewise taken bold steps to strengthen interfaith solidarity and acknowledge shared values between Islam and Christianity. Welcoming Catholic and Muslim leaders to a seminar in November 2008, Pope Benedict XVI spoke of the need "to overcome past prejudices and to correct the often distorted images of the other, which even today can create difficulties in our relations." The group issued a fifteen-point declaration calling on Catholics and Muslims to renounce aggression and terrorism, and calling for the rights of religious minorities to be respected everywhere.

The great play of Islamic history outlined above – from the formative period, through the medieval flowering of Islamic culture, the decline, colonization, and modern recovery efforts – is fascinating in its drama and breathtaking in its scope. But it scarcely reflects the enduring faith of Muslims in everyday life. Many Muslims, in fact, bristle at the claim that Islam is in a period of recovery or reform. For them, essential Islam has always endured, regardless of the vagaries of history. It has endured as a daily, lived experience of faith in God's power, benevolence, compassion, and mercy. With that faith, Muslims face the struggles of

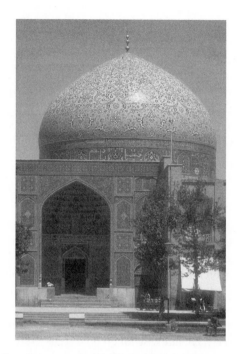

Figure 6 The mosque of Shaykh Lutfallah (1603–19) in Isfahan.
© *Peter Fraenkel*

daily life. The effects of centuries of political conflict and the impression of spectacular criminal acts will no doubt take time to fade. But the effort of devout Muslims to reflect their faith in daily life continues, guided by revelation – summarized eloquently in the popular Quranic verse cited above:

> It is not a matter of piety that you turn your faces to the East or West. Righteous is the one who believes in God and the Last Day, the angels and Scripture and the prophets; gives wealth, however cherished, to relatives and orphans, the needy and travelers and beggars, and for freeing slaves; and prays and gives *zakat*. And [the righteous] fulfill promises when they make them, and are patient in misfortune, hardship and trouble. These are the ones who are proven truthful and are pious. (2:177)

Notes

Preface

1   Office of the Press Secretary (Sept. 20, 2001). <http://www.whitehouse.gov/news/releases/2001/09/20010920-8.html>.

Chapter 1

1   W. Montgomery Watt, *Muhammad at Medina* (Oxford: Clarendon Press, 1956), 221–5.

Chapter 2

1   See al-Baladhuri, *Futuh al-Buldan*, ed. DeGoeje (Leyden: E. J. Brill, 1866); trans. Phillip K. Hitti as *The Origins of the Islamic State* (New York: Columbia University Press, 1916), 110–12; Daniel C. Dennet, Jr., *Conversion and the Poll Tax* (Cambridge, MA: Harvard University Press, 1950), 12ff.; C. Cahen, "Djizya," in John L. Esposito, ed., *Encyclopedia of Islam*, 2nd edn. (New York: Oxford University Press, 2009), 2:559; H. Lammens, *Études sur le regne du Calife Omaiyade Mo'awia Ier* (Beirut: Imprimerie Catholique, 1930), 226.
2   See N. J. Coulson, *A History of Islamic Law* (Edinburgh: Edinburgh University Press, 1964), chs. 2 and 3, upon which this account is based.
3   Fazlur Rahman, *Islam and Modernity: Transformation of an Intellectual Tradition* (Chicago: University of Chicago Press, 1982), 32.

4   Coulson, *A History of Islamic Law*, 37.

5   For a discussion of this claim, see Wael B. Hallaq, "Was al-Shafi'i the Master Architect of Islamic Jurisprudence?," *International Journal of Middle East Studies*, 25/4 (Nov. 1993), 587–605.

6   "He who holds what the Muslim community holds shall be regarded as following the community, and he who holds differently shall be regarded as opposing the community he was ordered to follow." Trans. in Majid Khadduri, *Islamic Jurisprudence: Shafi'i's Risala* (Baltimore: Johns Hopkins University Press, 1961), 287.

7   Trans. Bernard Lewis in *Politics and War*, vol. 1 of *Islam* (New York: Harper Torchbooks, 1974), 171–9.

8   Dennis Overbye, "How Islam Won, and Lost, the Lead in Science," *New York Times*, Oct. 30, 2001.

9   Philip K. Hitti, *History of the Arabs: From the Earliest Times to the Present* (New York: Palgrave Macmillan, 2002), 363.

10 Cited in E. B. Fryde, "History," *The New Encyclopedia Britannica* (Chicago, 1991), 20:566.

11 See, for example, Ronald Reagan, *Public Papers of the Presidents of the United States: 1981* (Washington: United States Government Printing Office, 1982), 745, 871.

12 Ibn Khaldun, *The Muqaddimah: An Introduction to History*, trans. Franz Rosenthal, ed. and abridged N. J. Dawood (Princeton, NJ: Princeton University Press, 1974), 11, 13, 23.

13 See Jawid A. Mojaddedi, "Legitimizing Sufism in al-Qushayri's 'Risala'," *Studia Islamica*, 20 (2000), 37–50.

14 <http://ibnarabisociety.org/>.

15 Annemarie Schimmel, *Mystical Dimensions of Islam* (Chapel Hill: University of North Carolina Press, 1975), 283.

16 Quoted in A. J. Arberry, *Sufism: An Account of the Mystics of Iszlam* (London: Mandal Books/Unwin Paperbacks, 1979), 109.

17 Ibid.

18 Ibid., 117.

19 Quoted from H. A. R. Gibb, *Muhammedanism* (Oxford: Oxford University Press, 1961), 150–1.

20 See Schimmel, *Mystical Dimensions of Islam*, 345–6.

21 Ibid., 24.

22 See Charles Upton, *Doorkeeper of the Heart: Versions of Rabi`a* (Putney, VT: Threshold Books, 1988), 23, 27, 43.

23 John Moyne and Coleman Barks, *Open Secret: Versions of Rumi* (Putney, VT: Threshold Books, 1984), 77, 82.

24 Mathnawi IV, 2683–96, in Coleman Barks et al., *The Essential Rumi* (San Francisco: HarperCollins, 1995).

25 <http://www.allamaiqbal.com/>.

Chapter 3

1 See his "Dialogues between a Christian and a Saracen," in *Migne Patrologiae Graecae*, vol. XCIV (Paris, 1860), col. 1585; vol. XCVI (Paris, 1864), cols. 1335–48.

2 Cited in Philip K. Hitti, *Islam and the West* (Princeton, NJ: D. Van Nostrand, 1962), 51.

3 See Guibert of Nogent, *RHC Historiens Occidentaux 1844–95*, IV: 137–10, cited in Terry Jones and Alan Ereira, *Crusades* (London: Penguin/BBC Worldwide, 1996), 13.

4 See Jones and Ereira, *Crusades*, 52.

5 Francesco Gabrieli, *Arab Historians of the Crusades* (Berkeley and Los Angeles: University of California Press, 1984), 11.

6 Cited ibid., 12.

7 Ibid., 93–145.

8 Ross E. Dunn. *The Adventures of Ibn Battuta: A Muslim Traveler of the 14th Century* (Berkeley and Los Angeles: University of California Press, 1989), 174–6.

9 Mohammad Khatami, *Islam, Liberty and Development* (Binghamton, NY: Institute of Global Cultural Studies, 1998), 73.

10 See Monisha Mukundan, *Akbar and Birbal: Tales of Humour* (New Delhi: Rupa & Co., 1994), 7–11.

11 Quoted in Marilyn Waldman and R. Waldman, "Islamic World," *The New Encyclopaedia Britannica* (Chicago, 1991), 22:127. Nasroddin had counterparts in other parts of the Muslim world as well. He is known as Juha in the Arabic-speaking world, Nasreddin Hoca in Turkey, and Musfiqi in Tajikistan, for example.

12 Gabrieli, *Arab Historians of the Crusades*, 11.

13 Ibn Khaldun, *The Muqaddimah*, trans. Rosenthal, 238–40.

14 He calls them "stupid" and "weak-minded." See *The Muqaddimah*, 258.

Chapter 4

1 For a discussion of the various agreements between the Arabs and the Europeans see Don Peretz, *The Middle East Today* (New York: Praeger, 1983), 101–59.

2   See George Antonius, *The Arab Awakening* (New York: Capricorn Books, 1965), 266–7.

3   See Janet Abu-Lughod, "The Demographic War for Palestine," *The Link*, 19/5 (Dec. 1986), 1–14.

4   Ruhollah Khomeini, *Islam and Revolution*, trans. Hamid Algar (Berkeley, CA: Mizan Press, 1981), 182.

5   See Alasdair Drysdale and Gerald H. Blake, *The Middle East and North Africa: A Political Georgraphy* (Oxford: Oxford University Press, 1985), 320ff., for a full description of how Middle Eastern countries lost control of their resources.

6   For the entire text of the Constitution of Medina, reportedly dictated by Muhammad, see W. Montgomery Watt, *Islamic Political Thought: The Basic Concepts* (Edinburgh: Edinburgh University Press, 1968), 130–4.

7   Joseph Schacht, *An Introduction to Islamic Law* (Oxford: Clarendon Press, 1982), 70–1.

8   Translated by Fazlur Rahman in *Islam* (Chicago: University of Chicago Press, 1979), 112, from Ibn Taymiyya, *Al-Ihtijaj bi'l-Qadar*, in his *Rasa'il* (Cairo, 1323 AH), II:96–7.

9   Muhammad Abduh, *The Theology of Unity*, trans. Ishaq Musa'ad and Kenneth Cragg (London: Allen & Unwin, 1966), 39–40.

10 Nikki R. Keddie, *An Islamic Response to Imperialism: Political and Religious Writings of Sayyid Jamal ad-Din "al-Afghani"* (Berkeley and Los Angeles: University of California Press, 1983), 103–7.

11 Abduh, *The Theology of Unity*, 39–40.

12 Muhammad Iqbal, *The Reconstruction of Religious Thought in Islam* (Lahore: Institute of Islamic Culture, 1986), 118–21, 141.

Chapter 5

1   Quoted in Keddie, *An Islamic Response to Imperialism*, 102.

2   See the discussion in Leila Ahmed, *Women and Gender in Islam: Historical Roots of a Modern Debate* (New Haven, CT: Yale University Press, 1992), 156–7.

3   See Rahman, *Islam and Modernity*, 64.

4   Quoted in Richard P. Mitchell, "The Society of the Muslim Brothers" (Ph.D. diss., Princeton, 1960), 524.

5   Ibid., 379.

6   Ibid., 373.

7   Ibid., 384.

8   Quoted in Y. Y. Haddad, "Sayyid Qutb: Ideologue of Islamic Revival," in J. L. Esposito, ed., *Voices of Resurgent Islam* (New York: Oxford University Press, 1983), 73.
9   Sayyid Qutb, *Milestones* (Indianapolis, IN: American Trust Publications, 1990), 137–8.
10 Haddad, "Sayyid Qutb," 70.
11 Syed Qutb Shaheed, *Islam, the True Religion*, trans. Rafi Ahmad Fidai (Karachi: International Islamic Publishers, 1981), 3.
12 Haddad, "Sayyid Qutb," 79.
13 See Rudolph Peters, *Jihad in Classical and Modern Islam* (Princeton, NJ: Markus Wiener, 1996), 107–8.
14 Abul A'la Mawdudi, *Islamic Law and Constitution*, ed. and trans. Khurshid Ahmad (Lahore: Islamic Publications, 1967), 53.
15 Quoted in Michael M. J. Fischer, "Imam Khomeini: Four Levels of Understanding" in Esposito, ed., *Voices of Resurgent Islam*, 154, from *Zendigi-Nameh Imam Khomeini* (Teheran: Fifteenth of Khordad Publishers, n.d.), II:38–43.
16 Imam Khomeini, *Islam and Revolution: Writings and Declarations of Imam Khomeini*, trans. and annotated H. Algar (London: KPI, 1985), 187.
17 Ibid., 210–11.
18 Haddad, "Sayyid Qutb," 71.
19 Sayyid Qutb Shaheed, *This Religion of Islam* (*hadha 'd-din*) (Kuwait: International Islamic Federation of Student Organizations, 1988), 49–64.
20 See S. M. Zafar, "Constitutional Development," in Hafeez Malik, ed., *Pakistan: Founders' Aspirations and Today's Realities* (Oxford: Oxford University Press, 2001), 30.
21 Cited in Malik, introduction to id., ed., *Pakistan: Founders' Aspirations*, 5–6.
22 Shibzada Masul-ul-Hassan Khan Sabri, *The Constitution of Pakistan, 1973 (with All Amendments up to 1994)* (Lahore: Publishers' Emporium, 1994), 24–5.
23 Rahman, *Islam and Modernity*, 37–8.
24 Vali Nasr describes this process in his book about the Jamaat-i Islami, *The Vanguard of the Islamic Revolution* (New York: Oxford University Press, 1994).
25 See Mawdudi, *Islamic Law and Constitution*, 172, 158.
26 Sabri, *The Constitution of Pakistan*, 423–9.
27 Statement by H. E. Seyyed Mohammad Khatami, President of the Islamic Republic of Iran and Chairman of the Eighth Session of the

Islamic Summit Conference, Tehran, Dec. 9, 1997; <http://www.undp.org/missions/iran/new.html>.

28 Mohammad Khatami, *Islam, Liberty and Development* (Binghamton, NY: Institute of Global Cultural Studies, Binghamton University, 1998), 3.

29 Ibid., 11.

30 Ibid., 54–5.

31 Mohammad Khatami, *Hope and Challenge: The Iranian President Speaks* (Binghamton, NY: Institute of Global Cultural Studies, Binghamton University, 1997), 77–8.

32 <www.gooya.com>. Quoted in *Washington Post*, Dec. 8, 2002.

33 Elaine Sciolino, "Daughter of Iran Revolution Struggles against the Veil," *New York Times*, Apr. 2, 2003, A6.

34 A collection of anti-terrorism statements may be found at <http://www.unc.edu/~kurzman/terror.htm>.

35 Sherman A. Jackson, "Domestic Terrorism in the Islamic Legal Tradition," *The Muslim World*, 91(Fall 2001), 293–310.

36 Sources on the *maqasid*: Subhi Mahmassani, *The Philosophy of Jurisprudence in Islam*, trans. Farhat J. Ziadeh (Leiden: Brill. 1961), 152–9; Mohammad Hashim Kamali, *Principles of Islamic Jurisprudence* (Cambridge: Islamic Texts Society, 1991), 267–81; Khaled Abou El Fadl, *Speaking in God's Name* (Oxford: Oneworld, 2001), 196–7.

37 This position is often based on the Quran's command to "enjoin good and forbid evil" (*amr bi'l-ma'ruf wa nahya 'an al-munkar*), and the *hadith* that says "religion is advice" (*al-din nasiha*).

38 "[T]hose who avoid serious sin and when they are angry forgive, and those who answer their Lord and perform prayer, their affairs being [settled in consultation] among them, and [who] spend [in charity] what We have provided them" are described as pleasing to God at 42:36–8.

39 Tariq Ramadan, "The Notion of Shura: Shura or Democracy?"; <http://www.tariq=ramadan.org/document.asp?id=10&fichier=Shura. 9/28/03>.

40 Ibid.

41 Fahmy Huwaidy, *Islam and Democracy* (Cairo: Al-Ahram Center for Publications and Translations, 1993), 121.

42 Kamal Abu'l Magd, *Dialogue, Not Confrontation* (Cairo: Dar al-Sharuq, 1988), 133.

43 Salim al-Awa, in al-Shaab, Nov. 21, 1995, quoted in Raymond William Baker, *Islam Without Fear: Egypt and the New Islamists* (Cambridge, MA: Harvard University Press, 2003), 31.

44 "Islam's Forgotten Heritage: A Conversation with Khaled Abou el Fadl"; <http://www.eppc.org/programs/islam/publicatons/pubID.1588, programID.36/pub_detail.asp. 10/2/03>.

45 Abou El Fadl, "Islam and the Challenge of Democracy"; <http://www.bostonreview,net/BR28.2/abou.html>, Oct. 2, 2003.

46 Ibid.

47 Ibid.

48 Amina Wadud, *Qur'an and Woman: Rereading the Sacred Text from a Woman's Perspective* (New York: Oxford University Press, 1999), 49.

49 Ibid., p. x.

50 Gisela Webb anthologizes a number of Muslim women reformers in *Windows of Faith: Muslim Women Scholar Activists in North America* (Syracuse, NY: Syracuse University Press, 2000). At one and the same time they argue against non-Muslims who claim that Islam is misogynist, and traditional Islamic interpretations that appear to violate the egalitarian spirit of the Quran. See also Asma Barlas, *Believing Women in Islam: Unreading Patriarchal Interpretations of the Qur'an* (Austin: University of Texas Press, 2002).

51 "Fatwa by Dr. Abou El Fadl: On Women Leading Prayer"; <http://www.scholarofthehouse.org/onwolepr.html>.

52 Ibid.

53 "Muslims Accept Falwell Apology," *Washington Post*, Oct. 15, 2002.

54 "Excerpts from Bin Laden's Alleged Statement," ibid.

55 *Washington Post*, Oct. 15, 2002, A16.

56 Kamran Khan, "Gunmen Kill 7 Christians at Karachi Charity," *Washington Post*, Sept. 26, 2002.

57 Michael Wolfe, ed., *Taking Back Islam: American Muslims Reclaim their Faith* (New York: Rodale, 2002).

58 Ibid., p. xi.

59 <http://www.ifyc.org>.

Further Reading

Art and Architecture

Blair, Sheila, and Bloom, Jonathan, *The Art and Architecture of Islam, 1250–1800.* New Haven, CT: Yale University Press, 1994.

Ettinghausen, Richard, Grabar, Oleg, and Jenkins-Madina, Marilyn, *Islamic Art and Architecture 650–1250,* 2nd edn. New Haven, CT: Yale University Press, 2003.

Fathy, Hassan, *Architecture for the Poor: An Experiment in Rural Egypt.* Chicago: University of Chicago Press, 1976.

Hoag, John D., *Islamic Architecture,* 3rd edn. London: Phaidon Press/ Electra. US edn. 2004.

Current Affairs

Cardini, Franco, *Europe and Islam,* trans. Caroline Beamish. Oxford: Blackwell, 1999.

Fuller, Graham F., *The Future of Political Islam.* New York: Palgrave Macmillan, 2004.

Mandaville, Peter, *Global Political Islam.* London: Routledge, 2007.

Rashid, Ahmed, *Taliban: Militant Islam, Oil and Fundamentalism in Central Asia.* Waterville, ME: Thorndike Press, 2002.

Rubin, Barry, *Political Islam: Critical Concepts in Islamic Studies.* London: Routledge, 2007.

Smith, Jane I., *Islam in America.* New York: Columbia University Press, 1999.

History

Armstrong, Karen, *Islam: A Short History*. New York: Modern Library, 2002.
Esposito, John L. (ed.), *The Oxford History of Islam*. New York: Oxford University Press, 1999.
Hitti, Philip K., *History of the Arabs: From the Earliest Times to the Present*. New York: Palgrave Macmillan, 2002.
Hourani, Albert H., *A History of the Arab Peoples*, Cambridge, MA: Belknap Press of Harvard University Press, 2002.
Jenkins, Everett, *The Muslim Diaspora: A Comprehensive Reference to the Spread of Islam in Asia, Africa, Europe and the Americas*. Jefferson, NC: McFarland, 1999.
Robinson, Francis, *Cambridge Illustrated History of the Islamic World*. New York: Cambridge University Press, 1996.

Literature

Burton, Richard Francis, *The Arabian Nights: Tales from a Thousand and One Nights*. New York: Modern Library, 2001.
Gibran, Khalil, *The Eye of the Prophet*. Berkeley, CA: Frog, 1995.
Khayyam, Omar, *Rubaiyat of Omar Khayyam*. Broomall, PA: Chelsea House, 2003.

Philosophy

Adamson, Peter, and Taylor, Richard (eds.), *The Cambridge Companion to Arabic Philosophy*. Cambridge: Cambridge University Press, 2005.
Campanini, M., *An Introduction to Islamic Philosophy*. Edinburgh: Edinburgh University Press, 2008.
Fakhry, Majid, *A History of Islamic Philosophy*. New York: Columbia University Press, 2004.

Reference

Belt, Don, *World of Islam*. Washington, DC: National Geographic, 2001.
Esposito, John L. (ed.), *The Oxford Dictionary of Islam*. New York: Oxford University Press, 2003.

Esposito, John L. (ed.), *The Oxford Encyclopedia of the Islamic World*. New York: Oxford University Press, 2009.

Glasse, Cyril, *The Concise Encyclopedia of Islam*. San Francisco: Harper & Row, 1989.

Leaman, Oliver (ed.), *The Qur'an: An Encyclopedia*. London: Routledge, 2006.

McAuliffe, Jane Dammen (ed.), *Cambridge Companion to the Qur'an*. Cambridge: Cambridge University Press, 2006.

McAuliffe, Jane Dammen (ed.), *Encyclopedia of the Qur'an*. Leiden: Brill, 2001–7.

Rippin, Andrew (ed.), *The Blackwell Companion to the Qur'an*, Oxford: Blackwell, 2006.

Religion

Ali, Ahmed, *Al-Quran. A Contemporary Translation*. Princeton, NJ: Princeton University Press, 2001.

Armstrong, Karen, *Muhammad: A Biography of the Prophet*. San Francisco: HarperSanFrancisco, 1992.

Mattson, Ingrid, *The Story of the Qur'an: Its History and Place in Muslim Life*. Oxford: Blackwell, 2008.

Nasr, Seyyed Hossein, *The Garden of Truth: The Vision and Promise of Sufism, Islam's Mystical Tradition*, San Francisco: HarperOne, 2007.

Nasr, Vali, *The Shia Revival: How Conflicts within Islam Will Shape the Future*. New York: Norton, 2006.

Neusner, Jacob, and Sonn, Tamara, *Comparing Religions through Law: Judaism and Islam*. London: Routledge, 1999.

Sachedina, Abdulaziz, and Montville, Joseph, *The Islamic Roots of Democratic Pluralism*. New York: Oxford University Press, 2001.

Rahman, Fazlur, *Major Themes of the Quran*. Minneapolis, MN: Bibliotheca Islamica, 1980.

Schimmel, Annemarie, *Mystical Dimensions of Islam*. Chapel Hill, NC: University of North Carolina Press, 1975.

Wolfe, Michael (ed.), *One Thousand Roads to Mecca: Ten Centuries of Travelers Writing about the Muslim Pilgrimage*. New York: Grove Press, 1997.

Science

Nasr, Seyyed Hossein, *Islamic Science: An Illustrated Study*. London: World of Islam Festival Publishing Company, 1976.

Saliba, George, *Islamic Science and the Making of the European Renaissance.* Cambridge, MA: MIT Press, 2007.

Women

Ahmed, Leila, *Women and Gender in Islam: Historical Roots of a Modern Debate.* New Haven, CT: Yale University Press, 1992.
Badran, Margot, *Feminism in Islam: Secular and Religious Convergence.* Oxford: Oneworld Publications, 2009.
Stowasser, Barbara Freyer, *Women in the Quran: Traditions and Interpretation.* New York: Oxford University Press, 1994.

Websites

IslamOnline Network: Islamic news, articles, *fatwas,* and business <www.islamonline.com>.
Oxford Islamic Studies Online: Reference works, Quranic studies resources, teaching resources <www.oxfordislamicstudies.com>.
Statements against Terrorism: Compendium of Islamic statements against terror <www.unc.edu/~kurzman/Terror.htm>.
University of Southern California Muslim Students Association: Quranic studies and other religious sources for Muslim students <www.usc.edu/dept/MSA/>.

Source Acknowledgments

The author and publisher are grateful for permission to reprint the following sources in Chapter 2:

Ibn Arabi, "My Beloved ..." from "Theophanies and Lights in the Thought of Ibn ʿArabi" by Osman Yahya, *Journal of the Muhyiddin Ibn ʿArabi Society*, vol. X (1991), pp. 35–44. Reprinted with permission.

Jami, "Neighbor ..." from Annemarie Schimmel, *Mystical Dimensions of Islam* (Chapel Hill: University of North Carolina Press, 1975), p. 283. Reprinted with permission.

Farid al-Din al-Attar, "Who in your Fraction of Myself ..." from A. J. Arberry, *Sufism: An Account of the Mystics of Islam* (London, Boston, and Sydney: Mandal Books–Unwin Paperbacks, 1979), p. 109. Reprinted with permission of Anna Arberry Evans.

Rumi, "Happy was I ..." from A. J. Arberry, *Sufism: An Account of the Mystics of Islam* (London, Boston, and Sydney: Mandal Books–Unwin Paperbacks, 1979), p. 117. Reprinted with permission of Anna Arberry Evans.

Rumi, "For years, copying other people ..." from John Moyne and Coleman Barks, *Open Secret: Version of Rumi* (Putney, VT: Threshold Books, 1984), p. 82. Reprinted with permission of the author.

Rumi, "God has given us a dark wine ..." Mathnawi IV, 2683–96, from *The Essential Rumi*, ed. Coleman Barks et al. (HarperCollins Publishers, 1995). Reprinted with kind permission of the author.

Al-Ghazali, from H. A. R. Gibb, *Muhammedanism* (Oxford University Press, 1961), pp 150–1. Reprinted with permission of Oxford University Press.

Rabia, "My peace, brothers ..." from Annemarie Schimmel, *Mystical Dimensions of Islam*. Copyright © 1975 by The University of North Carolina Press. Used by permission of the publisher <www.uncpress.unc.edu>.

I am also grateful to the William & Mary Alumni Magazine for permission to use the material on pages 189–91, first published in the magazine's Winter 2007/8 edition.

Index

Page numbers in bold refer to illustrations.

Akkadia 187
Albania 90
alchemy 58
Aleppo 115
Alexander the Great 84
Alexandria 34, 119, 121, 122
algebra 59, 144
Algeria 92, 116
  Islamic Salvation Front (Jabhat
    al-Inqadh al-Islami, FIS) 159
Algiers 116
Ali
  Bektashi and 74
  caliphate of 35–6, 39
  as successor to Muhammad 32,
    38, 42, 135, 137
Alpharabius (Al-Farabi;
    d. 950) 54
amal 62
America *see* United States of
    America
American Civil War 121
Amin, Qasim (reformer; 19th
    century) 149–50
  Tahrir al-Mar'a (The Liberation
    of Woman) 149
amputation 47, 167, 169
Amsaya 95
Anatolia 89, 93, 94
Andalusia 39
Ankara 90
anti-Americanism 158, 169, 175,
    187, 190
anti-Semitism 128, 185, 190–1
Anti-Terrorism Convention 176
Antichrist 110–11
Antioch 81
apostasy (*riddah*) 34, 136–7, 182
  death penalty for 38, 47
  wars of 33
Aquinas, Thomas, *Summa contra
    Gentiles* 56–7

Arab culture, religio-political
    identity 34–5
Arab independence, and
    European colonialism 125
Arabia, western (Hijaz) 87, 88
Arabic language 2, 5–6, 52,
    53, 134
architecture
  Mughal 101
  Ottoman 91–2
  Safavid 97
Aristotle 54, **55**, 56, 58, 60
Arjun (Sikh leader; d. 1606)
    105, 106
art 101, 108, 121
art deco 120
`asabiyyah (solidarity) 109
al-Ashari (scholar; d. 935) 138
Assassins (Nizaris) 87
association, freedom of 182
Assyria 187
astronomy 59–60
atheism 154
Aurangzeb (Mughal; r.
    1659–1707) 106
Austria 92
Averroes (Ibn Rushd; d. 1198)
    54, 55, **55**, 56–7
Avicenna (Ibn Sina; d. 1037)
    54, 58
al-Awa, Salim 180–1
ayatollahs 174
  see also Khomeini, Ayatollah
Ayub Khan, General
    Mohammad 164–5
Ayyubid dynasty (1171–1250)
    88
Azerbaijan 94, 95, 108

Babur (d. 1530), Mughal India
    100
Babylonia 187

Francis I, King of France 114
Franks 108
freedom 163, 171, 184
    religious 28, 34, 40, 41, 52, 99,
        100, 134, 136, 162; *see also*
        pluralism
    of thought and expression 154,
        171–3, 179, 182, 184
fundamentalism, as term 152, 174

Gabriel, angel 2
Galen 53, 60
Gallup World Poll, *Who Speaks for
    Islam?* 184
Gambia 72
gambling 26, 47
Gaul (France) 39
Genghis Khan 83, 85, 100
Germany 53, 124, 125
    Nazi regime 115, 127, 129
al-Ghazali, Abu Hamid (theolo-
        gian; d. 1111) 55–6, 57, 66,
        70–1, 177
    Ihya' 'Ulum al-Din 66
    al-Munquidh min al-Dalal 67
Ghazna (Ghazni) 98, 99
Ghaznavid empire 98–9
Ghurid empire 99
Gibraltar 39
al-Gilani, Abd al-Qadir (spiritual
        guide; d. 1166) 72–3
Golden Age 39–78
    cultural achievements 52–61
    institutions 40–1
    law *see* law, Islamic
    political structure 49–51
    spirituality 61–78
Gospels 7, 14, 141
governance 42–4, 49–51
Graham, Franklin 186, 187
Greece

and piracy 116
and science 147
Greek learning, influence of 52,
    53–4, 60, 143–4
Gulf (petroleum company) 125–6
Gulf War (2003) 187
Gundaishapur Hospital 57

Habsburgs 92–3
hadith reports, Islamic law 44,
    45, 84
Hagar (Hajar) 8
hajj (pilgrimage to Mecca) 6,
    29, 30
halaqat (circles) 64
al-Hallaj (d. 922) 65, 70
HAMAS (Islamic Resistance
    Movement) 175
Hamza Yusuf, Shaykh 191
Hanafi school of law 44, 46, 47
Hanbali school of law 46, 47, 50
haram (forbidden) actions 47
Hartford Seminary, Macdonald
    Center for Islamic Studies
    and Christian–Muslim
    Relations 184
Harun al-Rashid (d. 809) 52–3,
    57, 85
Hasan of Basra 64
Hashemites 124–5, 126
Hashishin 87
Hebrew Bible 21
Herman the Dalmatian 60
Hijra calendar 25, 29, 73
Himalayas 84
Hindu Kush 84
Hinduism 42, 98, 99, 101
    British colonialism 118, 119
    Mughal India 106
    Pakistan 164
    polytheism 104

mosques (cont'd)
  in Gulf War (2003) 187
  Ibn Tulun, Cairo 87
  in Isfahan 97
  segregation of sexes in 183–4
  of Selim 92
  of Shah Abbas 97
  of Shaykh Lutfallah **192**
  of Suleiman 92
  waqf funds 51
  women leading prayer in 184
Mosaddeq, Muhammad 132,
  156
Mosul 34
  European colonialism 123,
  125, 126
Mousavi Tabrizi, Ayatollah
  Hussein 186–7
Muawiyah 36, 42
Mughal India *see* India, Mughals
Muhammad
  Bektashi and 74
  cartoons ridiculing 187–8
  and Christian scriptures 10
  Christians' disrespect for 186,
  187–8
  death of 4, 5, 31, 35, 36, 39,
  80, 95, 142
  descendants 87, 95–6, 124
  and Islamic law 139
  on Jews 136
  as last prophet 13
  life and teachings 2, 4–5, 16,
  24–7, 42, 63, 141; *see also*
  Quran; Sunna
  and Mahdi 110
  and Quran 3–4, 7, 78, 170
  on scholarship 61
  successors to 32–8, 41–2, 95,
  157; *see also* Ali; caliphs
  (*khalifah*); Husayn

Muharram, period of mourning
  97
al-Muhasibi (Harith bin Asad of
  Basra, scholar; d. 857) 64
mujaddid (renewer) 146
Mujahideen (*mujahiddin*) 89–90,
  159, 161
Mulla Sadra (philosopher;
  d. 1636) 67
Mumtaz Mahal 101
al-Muntazar, Muhammad 96
Muridis 72
Murji'is ("Postponers") 137
Musharraf, General Pervez 168
Muslim Brotherhood 153–5, 156,
  175–6, 180
Muslim, Imam, *hadith* collection 45–6
Muslim League 162
muslim (one who submits to
  God) 8, 19
al-Mutawakkil III, Caliph 86
Mutazilis 138
mysticism 95, 103, 104, 106, 111,
  138, 173

Nahdatul Ulama 170
Nanak (Sikh founder; d. 1539)
  104–5
Napoleon I, Emperor of France, in
  Egypt 119–20
al-Naqshband, Baha al-Din (d. ca.
  1390) 74
Naqshbandi order (Sufism)
  74, 105
naskh (abrogation) 26
Nasroddin (legendary figure)
  102–3
National Iranian Oil Company
  132
Nawaz Sharif 167–8

Roncesvalles 80
Rosetta Stone 120
Royal Dutch Shell 124
Rumi, Jalal al-Din (Mevlevi
    founder; d. 1273) 69–70, 75,
    76–7
Rushdie, Salman, *The Satanic Verses*
    186
Russia 53, 124
    communism 154
    and Iran 131
    see also Soviet Union

sacrifice 8–9, 18, 30
sadaqa 62
Saddam Hussein 148, 170–1
Safavid empire (1502–1722)
    94–8, 100, 108
    cultural achievements 97–8
    as Shii Muslims 95–7
saints 72, 74, 75, 134, 138,
    142
Salah al-Din (Saladin; d. 1193)
    57, 81, 82–3, 87–8
Salih 11
Samanids 89, 98
Samarkand 85, 86, 89, 98
al-Sarraj, Abu Nasr (scholar;
    d. 987) 65–6, 76
Sasanian empire 33, 39, 40, 41
Saudi Arabia 24, 47, 126, 159,
    161, 185
    US embassy 176
Saudi family 121, 126
    and the Hashemites 126
    and the Wahhabis 121,
    160
SAVAK (secret police, Iran) 132
Schacht, Joseph 140
scholarship 44–5, 49, 61
    Christian 52

in Mughal India 102
see also legal scholars; religious
    scholars
science 58–9, 108, 149, 150–1
    Afghani on 147–8
    Ibn Khaldun on 111
    and Islamic reform 144–5
    in Mughal India 102
    Qasim Amin on 149
Scotland 60
    see also Britain
Sebuktegin (d. 997) 98
"Seceders" *see* Kharijis
secularism 170
self-criticism 169–70, 173
"self-hating Muslims" 150
self-reliance, and Islamic
    reform 152
Selim I, Sultan 95
Selim II, Sultan 90–1
Seljuks (Seljuqs) 82, 89, 90,
    94, 98
Senegal 72
September 11 attacks 148, 161,
    175–6, 188, 189
Serbia 90
sexual crimes 47, 48
al-Shadhili, Abu'l Hasan Ali
    (d. 1258) 73
Shadhili order (Sufism) 73
al-Shafii, Muhammad ibn Idris
    (d. 820) 45–6
Shafii school of legal
    thought 45–6, 67
Shah, Kamal 188
shahadah (pledge of
    commitment) 29
Shariah *see* law, Islamic
Shariati, Ali (d. 1977) 157
Sharif, Nawaz 167
al-Shaybani 44

Suleiman (r. 1520–66) 91, 94,
112
civil law 140–1
and European colonialism
114–15
sultans, Mamluk 88
Sumeria 187
Sunna 27, 36, 45, 176
and Islamic law 44, 141
Sunni Muslims 32, 38, 73, 87, 94,
108, 123, 174
Iraq 126
and Islamic law 139
Lebanon 128
Ottomans as 95
scholarship 151
see also Muhammad, successors to
Sweden 53
Sykes–Picot Agreement (1916)
125
Syria 33, 60, 81, 84, 87, 88, 91,
94, 121, 127
colonialism 113, 115, 118, 125,
127

tafsir (Quranic interpretation) 26
Tahmasp I, Shah 94
Taj Mahal 101–2
Taking Back Islam 190
Taliban 84, 99, 148, 159–61, 169,
173, 176
Talibanization, Pakistan 168
Tamerlane *see* Timur Lang
Tantawi, Shaykh 186
taqlid (following precedent),
Islamic law 140, 142, 147
taqwa, virtue of 19–20, 62
see also Sufism
Tariq 39
tariqas (orders) *see* Sufism
tawhid (monotheism) 14

see also monotheistic
tradition
taxation 35, 40, 41, 86, 91, 100,
106, 120
and trade 115
technical developments 58–9
Tegh Bahadur 106
Tehran, University 173
Templars 83
terrorism 47–8, 148, 161, 170,
175, 188–9
condemned by Islamic scholars 188
theft 47
theo-democracy 167
theology (*kalam*) 43, 54–6, 66–7,
166, 181
Third World 112
Thousand and One Nights 52, 85
Tigris, river 85
Timur Lang (Timur the Lame;
Tamerlane; d. 1405)
86, 89, 90, 94, 99,
100, 187
Toledo 60
Torah, the 7, 9–10, 14, 141
Toynbee, Arnold 61
trade, European
colonialism 83–4, 88,
114, 118, 120
see also Silk Road
traditionalism 151–2, 165–6,
169, 172
Transjordan 125, 127
translation 6, 52, 53–4,
57, 60
tribes 49
early Muslim community
34–5, 37
trigonometry 59
Trinity, belief in 10, 14